AGENCY AND DEONTIC LOGIC

AGENCY AND DEONTIC LOGIC

John F. Horty

OXFORD
UNIVERSITY PRESS

2001

OXFORD

UNIVERSITY PRESS

Oxford   New York
Athens   Auckland   Bangkok   Bogotá   Buenos Aires   Calcutta
Cape Town   Chennai   Dar es Salaam   Delhi   Florence   Hong Kong   Istanbul
Karachi   Kuala Lumpur   Madrid   Melbourne   Mexico City   Mumbai
Nairobi   Paris   São Paulo   Shanghai   Singapore   Taipei   Tokyo   Toronto   Warsaw

and associated companies in
Berlin   Ibadan

Library of Congress Cataloging-in-Publication Data
Horty, John P.
Agency and deontic logic / by John F. Horty.
p.   cm.
Includes bibliographical references and index.
ISBN 0-19-513461-3
1. Deontic logic.   2. Agent (philosophy)   I. Title.
BC145.H67   2000
160—dc21   00-020964

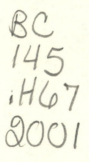
1 3 5 7 9 8 6 4 2

Printed in the United States of America
on acid-free paper

For my parents—
John Horty and
Bebe Rosenberry Black

Acknowledgements

I am especially grateful to Nuel Belnap and Richmond Thomason for encouragement, criticism, and for the use I make of their ideas. In addition, I have received valuable suggestions from a number of friends and colleagues, particularly Brian Chellas, Risto Hilpinen, Tamara Horowitz, Krister Segerberg, Leon van der Torre, and Heinrich Wansing.

I owe a different kind of debt to the National Endowment for Humanities for a fellowship that supported much of my work on this project.

Contents

AGENCY AND DEONTIC LOGIC

Chapter 1

Overview

The purpose of this study is to explore a new deontic logic for representing and reasoning about what agents ought to do, a notion that must be distinguished from that of what ought to be the case. The interplay between these two ideas, and the question of which should form the central focus for deontic logic, has long been a delicate problem in the area.

In his seminal article on the subject, Georg Henrik von Wright [1951] first introduced the deontic operators as syntactic expressions applying, not to sentence letters standing for states of affairs, but instead to special symbols representing kinds of actions. The resulting formalism provided the resources for expressing the idea that certain actions are obligatory or permissible—that closing the window, for example, is obligatory. For a variety of reasons, several other early researchers in the area—Alan Anderson [1956], Stig Kanger [1957], Arthur Prior [1955]—felt that it was better to conform to the more usual style of modal syntax by allowing deontic operators to apply to arbitrary sentences. This perspective, which has shaped most subsequent work in the field, initiated a line of research that has led to the development of a number of formal systems capable of distinguishing among various aspects of the general idea that certain states of affairs ought or ought not to be—that it ought to be that the window is closed, for example.

Part of the reason for the popularity in deontic logic of the perspective that takes what ought to be as fundamental is sheer technical convenience, the ease of working with formalisms so closely analogous to ordinary modal systems. There is also, however, a philosophical thesis at work—sometimes defended, but often just taken for granted—according to which this perspective is supposed to be more general. The study of what agents ought to do, it is thought, can naturally be subsumed under the broader study of what ought to be, for the simple reason that among the various things that ought or ought not to be are the things that agents do, the actions they perform or refrain from. According to this thesis, saying that an agent ought to close the window, for example, is equivalent to saying that it ought to be that the agent closes the window.

It has occasionally been argued, most notably by Peter Geach [1982], that the emphasis in deontic logic on the notion of what ought to be leads to severe distortions when the resulting theories are applied to the task of analyzing what agents ought to do. And von Wright himself has always maintained that a deontic logic adequate for such a task must be built upon the foundation of a more general theory of action; in his own work, he has endeavored both to supply such a foundation [1963] and to integrate it with deontic logic [1968].

This book attempts a similar integration, relying, however, not on von Wright's theory of action, but instead on a more recent treatment developed by Nuel Belnap, Michael Perloff, and Ming Xu in an important series of papers beginning with Belnap and Perloff's [1988] and culminating in Belnap, Perloff, and Xu's [2001]. This treatment of action, which is itself cast against the background of an indeterministic tense logic due to Prior [1967], is known as *stit semantics*, because it concentrates on constructions of the form "α (an agent) sees to it that A," usually abbreviated simply as [α *stit*: A]. The goal is to provide a precise semantic account of various stit operators within the overall setting of indeterministic time.

As it happens, Prior's indeterministic temporal framework allows for the introduction of a standard deontic operator ○, meaning "It ought to be that." It is therefore natural to explore the interactions between this deontic operator and the stit operators representing agency; and it may seem reasonable to propose a logical complex of the form ○[α *stit*: A]— meaning "It ought to be that α sees to it that A"—as an analysis of the idea that seeing to it that A is something α ought to do. The motive for this analysis, of course, is the philosophical thesis mentioned above, according to which the notion of what an agent ought to do can be identified with the notion of what it ought to be that the agent does.

In this book, I set out what seems to be an incontestable objection to this philosophical thesis, at least as it might be developed using a standard deontic logic; and driven by this objection, I propose a new analysis of the notion of what an agent ought to do. The new analysis is based on a loose parallel between action in indeterministic time and choice under uncertainty, as it is studied in decision theory. Very broadly, a particular preference ordering—a kind of dominance ordering—is adapted from the study of choice under uncertainty to the present account of action, and then used to define both the optimal actions that an agent should perform and the propositions whose truth the agent should guarantee.

The overall structure of the book is as follows. Chapter 2 reviews the theory of indeterministic time that forms the general background and provides a self-contained introduction to the underlying treatment of action, focusing on a particularly simple stit operator. Chapter 3 then introduces a standard deontic operator into this framework, allowing for a precise formulation of the idea that what an agent ought to do can be identified with what it ought to be that the agent does; this idea is defended against certain objections found in the literature, and the new objection is set out. Chapter 4 is the heart of the work, introducing a dominance relation among actions and then using this relation to define a deontic operator that captures a new analysis of what agents ought to do. The remaining three chapters extend and develop this core analysis. Chapter 5 generalizes the account so that it applies to conditional as well as absolute oughts, and then explores certain forms of act utilitarianism. Chapter 6 generalizes the account so that it applies to the oughts governing groups of agents as well as individuals, and then explores a form of rule utilitarianism. Finally, Chapter 7 generalizes the account of oughts so that it applies over extended periods of time as well as to single moments, and then explores the debate between actualism and possibilism in the evaluation of actions.

For the sake of clarity, I have stated definitions and results precisely, but no real mathematical sophistication is involved; any reader with an understanding of elementary modal logic should be able to follow the entire discussion. To preserve readability, all formal proofs are collected into the Appendix.

Although this work is primarily concerned with deontic logic, the emphasis is conceptual rather than technical. I have attempted throughout to relate the various formal options considered to issues from the philosophical literature, showing how the framework developed here allows for a number of positions from recent moral theory to be set out clearly and discussed from a uniform point of view. In doing so, I am aware that I have followed a rather narrow path through some difficult terrain, leaving much of the surrounding territory unexplored. That is not always the right way to work, but in this case I thought it best simply to push ahead.

Chapter 2

Indeterminism and agency

2.1 Branching time

2.1.1 Frames and models

The indeterministic framework that forms the background for our study is the theory of branching time, originally presented in Prior's [1967], and developed in more detail by Richmond Thomason in [1970] and [1984]. This theory is based on a picture of moments as ordered into a treelike structure, with forward branching representing the openness or indeterminacy of the future, and the absence of backward branching representing the determinacy of the past. The picture can be captured formally through the postulation of a nonempty set *Tree* of moments together with a transitive and irreflexive ordering $<$ on these moments that satisfies also the treelike property according to which, for any moments m_1, m_2, and m_3 from *Tree*, if $m_1 < m_3$ and $m_2 < m_3$, then either $m_1 = m_2$ or $m_1 < m_2$ or $m_2 < m_1$.

A set h of moments from *Tree* is said to be linearly ordered whenever, for any moments m_1 and m_2 belonging to h, either $m_1 = m_2$ or $m_1 < m_2$ or $m_2 < m_1$; the set h is a maximal linearly ordered set of moments whenever it is linearly ordered and can be no larger while still remaining linearly ordered (that is, whenever there is no linearly ordered set g that properly includes h). Such a maximal set of linearly ordered moments from *Tree* is known as a *history*. Intuitively, each history represents some complete temporal evolution of the world, one possible way in which things might work out. If m is a moment and h is a history, the fact that $m \in h$ can be taken to mean that m occurs at some point in the course of the history h, or that h passes through the moment m. Of course, because of indeterminism, a single moment might be contained in several different histories: we let $H_m = \{h : m \in h\}$ represent the set of histories passing through m, those histories in which m occurs.

These ideas can be illustrated as in Figure 2.1, where the upward direction represents the forward direction of time. This diagram depicts a tree

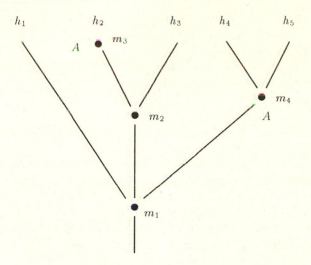

Figure 2.1: Branching time: moments and histories

containing five histories, h_1 through h_5. The moments m_1 through m_4 are highlighted; and we have, for example, $m_2 \in h_3$ and $H_{m_4} = \{h_4, h_5\}$.

We turn now to the matter of developing a tense logic against the background of branching time. The language of our tense logic results from supplementing the ordinary truth functional connectives with two additional temporal operators. The first is an operator P that represents simple past tense and can be read "It was the case that." The second is an operator F representing simple future tense, and so read "It will be the case that."

As usual with intensional logics, a formula of tense logic is evaluated as true or false only with respect to an index; and it is tempting, at first, to think that the appropriate indices at which to evaluate these formulas in the context of branching time might be moments. This idea leads to a sensible evaluation rule for formulas constructed through ordinary truth functional connectives. A formula of the form $A \wedge B$, for example, could be defined as true at the moment m just in case both A and B are true at m; and a formula of the form $\neg A$ could be defined as true at m just in case A is not true at m. The idea of using moments as indices of evaluation seems to work also for formulas constructed through an application of the simple past tense operator. A formula of the form PA might reasonably be defined as true at a moment m just in case there is another moment m' such that $m' < m$ and A is true at m'; that is, PA could be defined as true at m just in case A is true at some earlier moment.

But now, consider those formulas constructed through an application of the future tense operator. Since the indeterministic framework allows for alternative possible futures passing through a given moment, it is not so easy to see how these formulas might be evaluated at a moment alone. Returning again to Figure 2.1, suppose that, as depicted, the formula A is true at m_3 and at m_4, but nowhere else. In that case, what truth value should be assigned to the formula FA at the moment m_1?

On the approach advocated by Prior and Thomason, there is just no way to answer this question. Evidently, FA is true at m_1—A really does lie in the future—if one of the histories h_2, h_4, or h_5 is realized; but it is false on the histories h_1 and h_3. And since, at m_1, each of these histories is still open as a possibility, that is simply all we can say about the situation. In general, in the context of branching time, a moment alone does not seem to provide enough information for evaluating a statement about the future; and what Prior and Thomason suggest instead is that a future tensed statement must be evaluated with respect to a more complicated index consisting of a moment together with a history through that moment. We let m/h represent such an index: a pair consisting of a moment m and a history h from H_m. operator.

Using these more complicated indices, it is now possible to present a natural evaluation rule for the future tense. A formula FA can be defined as true at a moment/history pair m/h just in case there is another moment $m' \in h$ such that $m < m'$ and A is true at m'/h; that is, FA can be defined as true at a moment m along the history h just in case there is some later moment in that history at which A is true.

Let us now solidify some of these basic ideas into formal definitions, beginning with the notion of a branching time frame.

Definition 2.1 (Branching time frames) A *branching time frame* is a structure $\mathcal{F}$ of the form $\langle Tree, < \rangle$, with *Tree* a nonempty set of moments, and $<$ a transitive, irreflexive, and treelike ordering on *Tree*.

Since future tensed statements are to be evaluated at pairs consisting of moments and histories together, semantic uniformity suggests that other formulas should be evaluated at these more complicated indices as well. We therefore define propositional models based on these temporal frames by associating with each sentence letter a set of m/h pairs at which, intuitively, it is thought of as true.

Definition 2.2 (Branching time models) A *branching time model* is a structure $\mathcal{M}$ of the form $\langle \mathcal{F}, v \rangle$, with $\mathcal{F} = \langle Tree, < \rangle$ a branching time frame and v an evaluation function mapping each sentence letter from the background language into a set of m/h pairs from *Tree*.

This definition illustrates the general schema to be adopted throughout this book for extending frames to models: whenever $\mathcal{F}$ is a frame containing *Tree* as one of its components, a model $\mathcal{M}$ based on $\mathcal{F}$ will be defined as a structure of the form $\langle \mathcal{F}, v \rangle$ with v a function mapping sentence letters into sets of m/h pairs from *Tree*.

The satisfaction relation $\models$ between an index m/h belonging to some branching time model $\mathcal{M}$ and the formulas true at that index can then be defined as follows.

Definition 2.3 (Evaluation rules: basic operators) Where m/h is an index and v the evaluation function from a branching time model $\mathcal{M}$,

- $\mathcal{M}, m/h \models A$ if and only if $m/h \in v(A)$, for A an atomic formula,

- $\mathcal{M}, m/h \models A \wedge B$ if and only if $\mathcal{M}, m/h \models A$ and $\mathcal{M}, m/h \models B$,

- $\mathcal{M}, m/h \models \neg A$ if and only if $\mathcal{M}, m/h \not\models A$,

- $\mathcal{M}, m/h \models \mathsf{P}A$ if and only if there is an $m' \in h$ such that $m' < m$ and $\mathcal{M}, m'/h \models A$,

- $\mathcal{M}, m/h \models \mathsf{F}A$ if and only if there is an $m' \in h$ such that $m < m'$ and $\mathcal{M}, m'/h \models A$.

We will suppose that the operators $\vee$, $\supset$, and $\equiv$, representing truth functional disjunction, implication, and equivalence, are defined in the usual way, that the universally true sentence $\top$ is defined as $A \vee \neg A$, and that the universally false sentence $\bot$ is defined as $\neg \top$. Where the context allows, we omit explicit reference to the background model $\mathcal{M}$ in our informal discussion, speaking of a statement A as true or false simply at an index m/h (in the model to which this index belongs). And as usual, we define a formula as *valid* in some class of models if it is true at each index—in this case, each m/h pair—of each model belonging to that class.

It is easy to see that, as long as we confine ourselves to P, F, and truth functional connectives, the validities generated by this definition in branching temporal models coincide with those of ordinary linear tense logic, for the evaluation rules associated with these operators never look outside a single, linear history of evaluation. However, the framework of branching time allows us to supplement the usual temporal operators with an additional concept of settledness, or *historical necessity*, along with its dual concept of *historical possibility*: the formula $\Box A$ is taken to mean that A is settled, or historically necessary; $\Diamond A$, that A is still open as a possibility. The intuitive idea is that $\Box A$ should be true at some moment if A is true at that moment no matter how the future turns out, and that $\Diamond A$ should be true if there is still some way in which the future might evolve that would lead to the truth of A. The evaluation rule for historical necessity is straightforward.

Definition 2.4 (Evaluation rule: $\Box A$) Where m/h is an index from a branching time model $\mathcal{M}$,

- $\mathcal{M}, m/h \models \Box A$ if and only if $\mathcal{M}, m/h' \models A$ for each history $h' \in H_m$.

And historical possibility can then be characterized in the usual way, with $\Diamond A$ defined as $\neg\Box\neg A$.

It is convenient to incorporate the concept of settledness represented by historical necessity also into the metalanguage: we can say that a formula A is *settled true* at a moment m just in case $m/h \models A$ for each h in H_m, and that A is *settled false* at m just in case $m/h \not\models A$ for each h in H_m. A formula is *moment determinate* if it is always, at any moment, either settled true or settled false; evidently, any formula of the form $\Box A$ or $\Diamond A$ is moment determinate.

Once the standard temporal operators are augmented with the additional concepts of historical necessity and possibility, the framework of branching time poses some technical challenges not associated with standard tense logics, but it is also directly applicable to a number of the philosophical problems presented by indeterminism. Details concerning both the technical issues surrounding branching time and its philosophical applications can be found in Thomason [1984].

2.1.2 Propositions

We will frequently want to speak of the proposition expressed by a sentence; and here, our treatment is based on the familiar idea, going back at least to Carnap, that such a proposition can be represented by the set of possible worlds in which that sentence is true. Of course, the most straightforward way of developing this familiar idea in the present setting would be to allow our indices of evaluation to play the role of the traditional possible worlds, so that the proposition expressed by a sentence would then be identified with the set of moment/history pairs at which it is true. Rather than follow this straightforward method of development, however, it will be more convenient to adopt a refinement of the familiar idea—similar to that found in David Kaplan's work on indexicals [1989]—according to which the particular proposition expressed by a sentence is allowed to vary from moment to moment.

On the present approach, then, the set of possible worlds accessible at a moment m is identified with the set H_m of histories passing through that moment; those histories lying outside of H_m are taken to represent worlds that are no longer accessible. The propositions at m are then identified with sets of accessible histories, subsets of H_m. And the particular proposition expressed by a sentence A at a moment m in a model $\mathcal{M}$—here represented as $|A|_m^{\mathcal{M}}$—is identified with the set of histories from H_m in which that sentence is true.

Definition 2.5 (Proposition expressed by a sentence; $|A|_m^{\mathcal{M}}$) Where m is a moment from a branching time model $\mathcal{M}$, the proposition expressed by the sentence A at the moment m from $\mathcal{M}$ is the set

$$|A|_m^{\mathcal{M}} = \{h \in H_m : \mathcal{M}, m/h \models A\}.$$

Again, we often omit explicit reference to the background model $\mathcal{M}$, referring to the proposition expressed by A at m (in the model to which this moment belongs) simply as $|A|_m$.

Although not bearing directly on the issues involved in this book, it is worth noting that the treatment of propositions adopted here allows for a distinction in the intuitive concept of meaning much like Kaplan's distinction between content and character—where the *content* expressed by a tokening of a sentence is what determines its truth or falsity in the different circumstances in which it might be evaluated, and the *character* of a sentence is what controls the content it expresses in the different contexts in which that sentence might be tokened. In the setting of branching time, it is most natural to identify a *context* in which a sentence might be tokened as a particular moment m, and the various *circumstances* in which such a tokening might be evaluated as the set $\{m/h : h \in H_m\}$ of indices determined by the histories passing through that moment.

The content expressed by a tokening of a sentence A in the context m, a particular moment, can then be identified with the proposition $|A|_m$ expressed by A at m, the set of circumstances in which that tokening is true; and the character of a sentence A can be defined as the function $|A|$ mapping each context m into the content $|A|_m$ expressed by A at m. As in Kaplan's theory of indexicals, these different aspects of meaning can then vary independently. Two sentences A and B might happen to express an identical content in the context m even though they do not carry the same character more generally: we might have $|A|_m = |B|_m$ even though $|A| \neq |B|$. And the single sentence A, with its selfsame character, might express a different content at the two moments m and m': even though, of course, $|A| = |A|$, we might have $|A|_m \neq |A|_{m'}$.

2.2 Individual agency

We now turn to the treatment of individual agency within the setting of branching time.[1] Although we work within the general framework set out by Belnap and Perloff in [1988], the particular approach followed here differs in detail, resulting in a modal account of agency that is simpler and for certain purposes more natural. The current treatment is derived most immediately from that presented in Horty and Belnap [1995], which contains a detailed

---

[1] A survey of a number of formal approaches to the topic of agency is provided by Segerberg [1992]; an attempt to demonstrate a degree of uniformity among some of the resulting theories can be found in Hilpinen [1997].

comparison of the approach followed here with the earlier work of Belnap and Perloff.

2.2.1   Agents and choices

The idea that an agent α sees to it that A is taken to mean that the truth of the proposition A is guaranteed by an action, or choice, of α. In order to capture this idea, then, we must be able to speak of individual agents, and also of their actions, or choices; the basic framework of branching time is therefore supplemented with two additional primitives.

The first is simply a set *Agent* of agents, individuals thought of as acting in time.

Now what is it for one of these agents to act? Throughout this book, we idealize in three ways: by ignoring any intentional components that might be involved in the concept of action, by ignoring vagueness and probability, and by treating actions as momentary in duration. In this rarefied environment, the idea of acting at a moment can be thought of simply as constraining the future course of events so as to lie within some definite subset of the possible histories still available at that moment. When Jones butters the toast, for example, the nature of his action, according to this picture, is simply to guarantee that the history to be realized will lie among those in which the toast is buttered. Of course, such an action still leaves room for a good deal of variation in the course of events, and so cannot determine a unique history: there may be one history in which Jones butters the toast and Smith scratches his left ear, one history in which Jones butters the toast and Smith scratches his right ear, and so on. Still, the action does impose a significant constraint: it rules out all those histories in which the toast is not buttered.

Our second additional primitive, then, is a device for representing the possible constraints that an agent is able to exercise upon the course of events at a given moment, the actions or choices open to the agent at that moment. These constraints are encoded formally through a function *Choice*, mapping each agent α and moment m into a partition $Choice_\alpha^m$ of the set of histories H_m through m. The idea behind this formalism is that, by acting at m, the agent α selects a particular one of the equivalence classes—or *choice cells*—from $Choice_\alpha^m$ within which the history to be realized must then lie, but that this is the extent of his influence.

Apart from specifying, for each agent, a partition of the histories through each moment, the *Choice* function is subject to two further requirements. The first is a condition of *independence of agents*, which says, roughly, that at any given moment, the particular choice cell that is selected by one agent cannot affect the choices available to another; this requirement will be formulated precisely in Section 2.4, dealing with multiple agents. The second requirement stipulates that the choices available to an agent at a given mo-

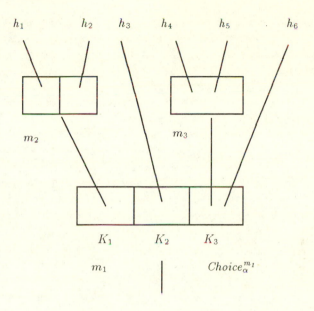

Figure 2.2: An agent's choices

ment should not allow a distinction between histories that do not divide until some later moment. Let us say that two histories are undivided at m whenever they share a moment that is properly later than m. The requirement of *no choice between undivided histories* can then be expressed as the condition that, for each agent α, any two histories that are undivided at m must belong to the same choice cell of the partition $Choice_\alpha^m$.

If K is a choice cell belonging to $Choice_\alpha^m$, one of the equivalence classes specified by this partition, we speak of K as an *action* available to the agent α at the moment m, and we say that α *performs* the action K at the index m/h just in case h is a history belonging to K. It is important to notice that, just as in the evaluation of the future tense, all of the information provided by a full index is required in determining whether an agent performs an action: it makes no sense to say that an agent performs an action at a moment, but only at a moment/history pair. We let $Choice_\alpha^m(h)$ (defined only when $h \in H_m$) stand for the particular action from $Choice_\alpha^m$ that contains the history h—$Choice_\alpha^m(h)$ thus represents the particular action performed by the agent α at the index m/h. And we speak of the histories belonging to an action K as the *possible outcomes* that might result from performing this action. The idea behind this phrase, of course, is that by performing the action K at the moment m, the agent can guarantee that the history to be realized will lie among those belonging to K, but that he cannot determine which one it will be.

These various concepts relating to choice partitions are illustrated in Figure 2.2, which depicts a frame containing six histories, and in which the actions available to the agent α at the three moments m_1, m_2, and m_3 are highlighted. Evidently, there are three actions available to α at the moment m_1—$Choice_\alpha^{m_1} = \{K_1, K_2, K_3\}$, with $K_1 = \{h_1, h_2\}$, $K_2 = \{h_3\}$, and $K_3 = \{h_4, h_5, h_6\}$. Due to the requirement of no choice between undivided histories, the two histories h_1 and h_2, which are still undivided at m_1, must fall within the same choice cell there, and likewise for h_4 and h_5. The agent α faces two choices at m_2, but at m_3 he effectively has no choice: histories divide, but there is nothing that α can do to constrain the outcome. At such a moment, it would be possible to treat the choice function as undefined for α; but it is easier to treat it as defined but vacuous, placing the entire set of histories through the moment in a single equivalence class.

Returning to the moment m_1, we can say, for example, that α performs the action K_1 at the index m_1/h_2, that he performs the action K_2 at the index m_1/h_3, and the action K_3 at the index m_1/h_6. Again: since the agent performs different actions along different histories through the moment m_1, it makes no sense to ask what action he performs at that moment alone, but only at a full index. The particular choice cell containing the history h_5, for instance, is K_3; so we have $Choice_\alpha^{m_1}(h_5) = K_3$, representing the action performed by α at the index m/h_5. And we can speak of h_4, h_5, and h_6 as the possible outcomes that might result from the performance of the action K_3.

Having supplemented the basic framework of branching time with the additional primitives *Agent* and *Choice*, we can now formally introduce stit frames and models.

Definition 2.6 (Stit frames/models) A *stit frame* is a structure of the form

$$\langle \mathit{Tree}, <, \mathit{Agent}, \mathit{Choice} \rangle,$$

with *Tree* and $<$ as in branching time frames, *Agent* a nonempty set of agents, and *Choice* a function mapping each agent α and moment m into a partition of H_m subject to the requirements of independence of agents and no choice between undivided histories. A *stit model* is a model based on a stit frame.

It is these structures that provide the backdrop for the current treatment of agency; the claim is that the structures are not just mathematical curiosities, but that they describe—up to a legitimate idealization—the world in which agents act.

2.2.2   Stit operators

The stit operator playing the central role in this book is known as the "Chellas stit"—and represented as *cstit*—because it is an analogue of the

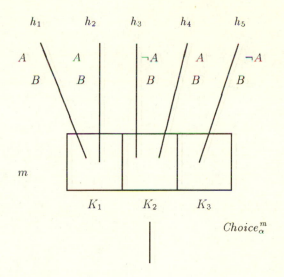

Figure 2.3: [α *cstit*: A] true at m/h_1

operator introduced over thirty years ago in Brian Chellas's [1969], the first sustained treatment of agency within the framework of modern intensional semantics.[2]

In the present setting, the semantic analysis of this *cstit* operator is straightforward. A statement of the form [α *cstit*: A], expressing the idea that the agent α sees to it that A, is defined as true at an index m/h just in case the action performed by α at that index guarantees the truth of A; the action might result in a variety of possible outcomes, but the statement A must be true in each of them. Formally, we can say that some action K available to α at the moment m guarantees the truth of A just in case $K \subseteq |A|_m$—just in case, that is, each possible outcome of K is one in which the statement A is true. And since the particular action K that is performed by α at the index m/h is simply $Choice_\alpha^m(h)$, our semantic analysis can be captured through the following evaluation rule.

Definition 2.7 (Evaluation rule: [α *cstit*: A]**)** Where α is an agent and m/h an index from a stit model $\mathcal{M}$,

- $\mathcal{M}, m/h \models [\alpha$ *cstit*: $A]$ if and only if $Choice_\alpha^m(h) \subseteq |A|_m^{\mathcal{M}}$.

The result is illustrated in Figure 2.3, where $Choice_\alpha^m = \{K_1, K_2, K_3\}$, with $K_1 = \{h_1, h_2\}$, $K_2 = \{h_3, h_4\}$, and $K_3 = \{h_5\}$.[3] In this sit-

---

[2]Although the Chellas stit defined here is analogous to Chellas's original agency operator, the two are not identical; a comparison is found in Horty and Belnap [1995].

[3]A convention for interpreting figures: when a formula is written next to some history

uation, the statement $[\alpha \ cstit : A]$ is true at the index m/h_1, for example, since $Choice_\alpha^m(h_1) = K_1$ and $|A|_m = \{h_1, h_2, h_4\}$, so that, of course, $Choice_\alpha^m(h_1) \subseteq |A|_m$. But $[\alpha \ cstit: A]$ is not true at m/h_4, since $Choice_\alpha^m(h_4) = K_2$, so that we do not have $Choice_\alpha^m(h_4) \subseteq |A|_m$. Even though the statement A itself happens to hold at m/h_4, the action K_2 that is performed by α at this index does not guarantee the truth of A.

An operator closely related to the Chellas stit is the "deliberative stit," first introduced, prior to the work of Belnap and Perloff, in Franz von Kutschera's [1986], suggested independently in Horty [1989] as an alternative to the account of Belnap and Perloff, and then explored extensively in Horty and Belnap [1995]. This operator, represented as $dstit$, can be defined as follows.

Definition 2.8 (Evaluation rule: $[\alpha \ dstit: A]$**)** Where α is an agent and m/h an index from a stit model $\mathcal{M}$,

- $\mathcal{M}, m/h \models [\alpha \ dstit: A]$ if and only if $Choice_\alpha^m(h) \subseteq |A|_m^{\mathcal{M}}$ and $|A|_m^{\mathcal{M}} \neq H_m$.

Evidently, the $dstit$ operator differs from the previous $cstit$ only in the requirement that $|A|_m^{\mathcal{M}} \neq H_m$—known as the *negative condition*—which enforces the idea that an agent cannot be said to see to it that A if he really has no choice in the matter, if the truth of A is guaranteed no matter which action he performs. Because of this negative condition, the complement of a true deliberative stit statement, which is most naturally thought of as future tensed, cannot be settled true; the formula $[\alpha \ dstit: A] \supset \neg \Box A$ is valid. And it is because of this also that the operator is characterized as "deliberative." The terminology echoes most immediately the notion of deliberative obligation from Thomason [1981b], but it goes back to Aristotle's observation in the *Nicomachean Ethics* that we can properly be said to deliberate only about "what is future and capable of being otherwise" [1139b7; see also 1112a19-b10].

The $dstit$ operator can be illustrated again through Figure 2.3. Again, we have $[\alpha \ dstit: A]$ true at m/h_1, since $Choice_\alpha^m(h_1) \subseteq |A|_m$ and $|A|_m \neq H_m$. But the statement $[\alpha \ dstit: B]$ is false at m/h_1 even though $Choice_\alpha^m(h_1) \subseteq |B|_m$, since $|B|_m = H_m$. Here, the agent has no choice in the matter; the statement B is true regardless of the action performed, and so the negative condition fails.

2.2.3   Some logical considerations

Although this book does not treat the proof theory of the various operators defined here, it is useful to illustrate the behavior of these operators by

---

emanating from a moment, the formula should be taken as true at that moment/history pair. Thus, A should be taken as true at m/h_1 in Figure 2.3, for example, and $\neg A$ as true at m/h_3.

considering the validity of a number of central principles.[4]

Because of its simple evaluation rule, the logic of the *cstit* operator is especially transparent. It is clear at once from the structure of the evaluation rule that this operator supports the principles

$RE.$ $A \equiv B$ / $[\alpha\ cstit:\ A] \equiv [\alpha\ cstit:\ B]$,

$N.$ $[\alpha\ cstit:\ \top]$,

$M.$ $[\alpha\ cstit:\ A \wedge B] \supset ([\alpha\ cstit:\ A] \wedge [\alpha\ cstit:\ B])$,

$C.$ $[\alpha\ cstit:\ A] \wedge [\alpha\ cstit:\ B] \supset [\alpha\ cstit:\ A \wedge B]$,

and is thus a normal modal operator.[5] Moreover, because the semantic $Choice_\alpha^m$ primitive partitions the histories through a moment m into equivalence classes, it is easy to see that *cstit* is, in fact, an *S5* operator, since it supports the additional principles

$T.$ $[\alpha\ cstit:\ A] \supset A$,

$4.$ $[\alpha\ cstit:\ A] \supset [\alpha\ cstit:\ [\alpha\ cstit:\ A]]$,

$B.$ $A \supset [\alpha\ cstit:\ \neg[\alpha\ cstit:\ \neg A]]$.

Among these principles, the rule RE and the theses C and T seem to be unobjectionable, at least within the current framework for reasoning about agency, or any of its close relatives. RE says that an agent who is responsible for guaranteeing the truth of one proposition is responsible likewise for guaranteeing the truth of any logically equivalent proposition; this rule makes intuitive sense in the present environment, where the intentional components in the concept of action have been set aside. Because of the absence of intentional considerations, the thesis C seems likewise to be justified: one could imagine that an agent might see to it that A holds and that B holds as well without intentionally seeing to it that they hold jointly, but it is hard to deny simply that the agent does see to it that they hold jointly. And T is again unexceptionable: if an agent sees to it that a certain proposition holds, then that proposition holds.[6]

The principle 4, on the other hand, does seem to express a substantive claim about agency—that an agent who sees to it that A also sees to it that

---

[4] A thorough proof theoretic discussion of the Chellas and deliberative stit operators can be found in Xu [1998]; related work appears in Xu [1994a].

[5] The labels for these principles, as well as those for several others appearing throughout this book, are patterned after the scheme employed in Chellas [1980]; this text can be consulted also for an explanation of various background concepts from modal logic, such as the notions of normal or *S5* modal operators. Note also that, throughout this book, we adopt the common convention that syntactic ambiguities are to be resolved by association to the left, so that, for example, the principle C above could be written more explicitly as $([\alpha\ cstit:\ A] \wedge [\alpha\ cstit:\ B]) \supset [\alpha\ cstit:\ A \wedge B]$.

[6] A principle of agency analogous to T has been denied by von Wright [1983, pp. 195–196], but from the perspective of an analytical setting differing substantially from that adopted here.

he sees to it that A—which it is not incoherent to deny; and the principle has indeed been denied in closely related treatments of agency, such as that of Chellas's own [1969], which does not incorporate the present assumption that the actions available to an agent at a moment partition the histories through that moment into equivalence classes. The theses N, M, and B are even more locally problematic. Although supported by the *cstit* operator, the analogues of these theses all fail for *dstit*; and in fact, each of these *dstit* analogues is falsified at the index m/h_1 from Figure 2.3. This is most evident in the case of N, since the validity of $[\alpha \ dstit: A] \supset \neg\Box A$ mentioned earlier tells us that the truth of $[\alpha \ dstit: \top]$ would entail the conclusion that $\neg\Box\top$; indeed, we can now note the validity of the formula

$$\overline{N}. \quad \neg[\alpha \ dstit: \top].$$

In the case of M, it is clear that $[\alpha \ dstit: A \wedge B]$ holds at m/h_1, since $Choice_\alpha^m(h_1) \subseteq |A \wedge B|_m$ and $|A \wedge B|_m \neq H_m$; but as we have seen, $[\alpha \ dstit: B]$ fails. And in the case of the principle B, it is easy to see that, although the statement B is itself true at m/h_1, the statement $[\alpha \ dstit: \neg[\alpha \ dstit: \neg B]]$ is not—for if it were, we could then conclude that $\neg\Box\neg[\alpha \ dstit: \neg B]$, or $\Diamond[\alpha \ dstit: \neg B]$; but since B is settled true at m, it is impossible for α to perform an action that guarantees its falsity.

Because the *dstit* operator fails to validate the analogues to M and N, and validates $\overline{N}$ instead, it follows at once that this operator is not closed under logical consequence. In a recent study of a variety of agency operators, Chellas finds these results—each an upshot of the negative condition—to be objectionable. Concerning M and closure under consequence, he writes:

> One feels that seeing to a conjunction does imply seeing to the conjuncts and, more generally, that *sees to it that* is closed under consequence. If I see to it that (both) Alphonse is in Alabama and Betty buys a brick, then it follows that I see to it that Alphonse is in Alabama and I see to it that Betty buys a brick. Readers may fashion their own examples and see if they do not concur. [Chellas, 1992, Section 11]

And concerning $\overline{N}$ and logical truth:

> Can it ever be the case that someone sees to it that something logically true is so? I believe the answer is yes. When one sees to something, one sees to anything that logically follows, including the easiest such things, such as those represented by $\top$. One should think of seeing to it that (e.g.) $0 = 0$ as a sort of trivial pursuit, attendant upon seeing to anything at all. [Chellas, 1992, Section 12]

We will see in the following section that, although the negative condition may seem to yield awkward results in simple constructions of the kind

Chellas considers, it also has certain advantages in the treatment of nested agency constructions, where it enables an attractive analysis of the notion of refraining from an action. Still, it is worth noting that, even if we restrict our focus to simple, nonnested constructions, intuitions concerning the negative condition are not uniform: although Chellas feels that closure of the agency operator under logical consequence is intuitively appealing, this view runs against a certain tradition in philosophy, at least. Anthony Kenny, for example, writes that "the President of the United States has the power to destroy Moscow, i.e., to bring it about that Moscow is destroyed; but he does not have the power to bring it about that either Moscow is destroyed or Moscow is not destroyed," noting that "the power to bring it about that either p or not p is one which philosophers, with the exception of Descartes, have denied even to God" [1976, p. 214]. And in any case, it is clear that the *cstit* and *dstit* operators are interdefinable in the presence of historical necessity:

$$[\alpha \; dstit: A] \equiv ([\alpha \; cstit: A] \land \neg\Box A),$$
$$[\alpha \; cstit: A] \equiv ([\alpha \; dstit: A] \lor \Box A).$$

Given these straightforward interdefinability relations, the question as to which of these two operators more accurately represents our everyday notion of "seeing to it that" may not be such an important issue; it is perhaps best to embrace both operators, appealing to each for different analytic purposes.

2.3   Individual ability

One advantage of the current framework for studying agency is that it allows also for a natural treatment of the related concept of personal ability—what an agent is able to do. This concept of personal ability must be distinguished from that of mere impersonal possibility: even though it is possible for it to rain tomorrow, no agent has the ability to see to it that it will rain tomorrow. Nevertheless, it seems that the concept of personal ability can be analyzed in the current framework through a combination of ordinary impersonal possibility together with an agency operator, for it seems reasonable to identify the notion of what an agent is able to do with the notion of what it is possible that the agent does. Representing agency through the *cstit* operator, for example, the result is a proposal according to which a formula of the form

$$\Diamond[\alpha \; cstit: A],$$

which carries the literal meaning that it is possible for the agent α to see to it that A, can be taken also to express the claim that α has the ability to see to it that A. Let us now explore this proposal.

2.3.1 Kenny's objections

We first note that this style of analysis runs contrary to a well-known thesis of Kenny's, who argues in [1975] and [1976] that the notion of ability cannot be formalized using the techniques of modal logic. Kenny follows von Wright in describing the "can" of ability as a dynamic modality, and puts the point as follows: "ability is not any kind of possibility; ... dynamic modality is not a modality" [1976, p. 226].

The core of Kenny's argument is directed against attempts to represent the notion of ability as a possibility operator in a modal system with the usual style of possible worlds semantics. Although possibility operators developed along these lines generally satisfy the two theses

$$T\Diamond. \quad A \supset \Diamond A,$$
$$C\Diamond. \quad \Diamond(A \vee B) \supset (\Diamond A \vee \Diamond B),$$

Kenny argues persuasively that the notion of ability does not satisfy either. As a counterexample to the first thesis, he considers the case in which a poor darts player throws a dart and actually happens, by chance, to hit the bull's-eye. Although this shows that it is possible in the impersonal sense for the darts player to hit the bull's-eye, it does not seem to establish that he has the ability to do so. As a counterexample to the second thesis, Kenny imagines another darts player whose skill is sufficient to guarantee only that he can hit the dartboard, but who has no further control of placement beyond that. Any dart that hits the dartboard at all must land either in the top half or in the bottom half, and so it seems that this player must have the ability to hit either the top half or to hit the bottom half of the dartboard; but as long as the player has no further control over placement, it seems clear that he does not have the ability to hit the top half of the dartboard, and also that he does not have the ability to hit the bottom half.

The analysis of personal ability suggested here is developed within a general modal framework, and can be said to represent ability as a kind of modality; but even so, this analysis escapes from Kenny's objections. Of course, the notion of historical possibility involved in our analysis, as an $S5$ modality, does validate both the theses $T\Diamond$ and $C\Diamond$ that Kenny finds objectionable. However, it is not historical possibility alone that is taken to represent ability, but rather a combination of historical possibility together with the *cstit* operator, which fails, as it turns out, to validate the analogous formulas: both

$$A \supset \Diamond[\alpha \; cstit\colon A],$$
$$\Diamond[\alpha \; cstit\colon A \vee B] \supset (\Diamond[\alpha \; cstit\colon A] \vee \Diamond[\alpha \; cstit\colon B])$$

can be falsified.[7]

---

[7]It is interesting to note that Kenny himself briefly explores [1976, pp. 226–229] the

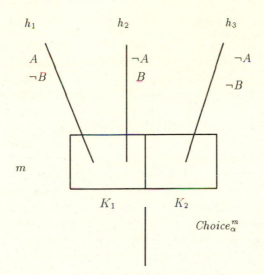

Figure 2.4: The darts examples

A joint countermodel to these two theses, based on Kenny's two darts stories, is provided in Figure 2.4, where we can imagine that m is some moment at which the agent α must choose between the action K_1 of throwing the dart and the action K_2 of refraining. To interpret Kenny's first story, we take the sentence A to mean that the dart will hit the bull's-eye (and we ignore the sentence B). Evidently, then, if α chooses to perform the action of throwing the dart and things evolve along the history h_1, then the dart will hit the bull's-eye. But this is not a proposition whose truth the agent has the ability to guarantee: although A is true at m/h_1, the formula $\Diamond[\alpha \; cstit: A]$ is not. For the second story, we take A to mean that the dart will hit the top half of the dartboard, and B to mean that the dart will hit the bottom half. Since, by performing the action K_1, the agent α is able to see to it either that the dart will hit the top half or that the dart will hit the bottom half, the formula $\Diamond[\alpha \; cstit: A \vee B]$ is settled true at m. But both $\Diamond[\alpha \; cstit: A]$ and $\Diamond[\alpha \; cstit: B]$ are settled false, since no action available to α can guarantee that the dart will hit the top half of the dartboard, and no action available to α can guarantee that the dart will hit the bottom half.

---

strategy developed here of representing the notion of personal ability by combining ordinary impersonal possibility with a special operator representing action. However, the action operator he employs in his analysis is that set out in von Wright [1963]; and Kenny then abandons this strategy for representing ability because of certain problems that he runs into in attempting to develop the idea with this particular operator. The present proposal can thus be seen as developing this idea of Kenny's with a different representation of action, the *cstit* operator.

2.3.2   Brown's theory

Perhaps the best known response to Kenny's objections against the modal analysis of ability is that set out by Mark Brown in [1988]. Kenny himself observes that, because the modal schema $T\Diamond$ can be falsified in standard models of modal logics (those based on a binary accessibility relation among possible worlds), the fact that counterexamples to this schema can be constructed using the "can" of ability does not count as a conclusive argument against the possibility of a modal analysis of this concept. But since $C\Diamond$ is valid in standard models, he judges that the counterexamples to this schema do show that the techniques of possible worlds semantics cannot be used in analyzing the logic of ability.

Brown points out, however, that even this conclusion is too strong, since Kenny limits his attention only to standard models for modal logics, and does not consider more general, nonstandard models in which even $C\Diamond$ can be falsified. He then goes on himself to develop an account of ability as a modal operator definable using minimal models—those nonstandard models in which accessibility is thought of as relating each individual world not simply to a set of worlds, a proposition, but to a set of sets of worlds, a set of propositions.[8]

More exactly, Brown's analysis is based on models of the form $\mathcal{M} = \langle W, N, v \rangle$, in which W is a set of worlds, v is an ordinary valuation, and N is a function mapping each individual world w into some subset $N(w)$ of $\mathcal{P}(W)$, the power set of worlds. Intuitively, the various members of $N(w)$, each a proposition or collection of worlds, represent the results of performing the various actions open to some agent in the world w; and of course, the reason actions are supposed to lead to sets of worlds, rather than individual worlds, is to avoid the assumption that an agent can determine through his actions every detail of the resulting situation. The basic idea underlying Brown's analysis is that the agent can be thought of as having the ability, in some world, to bring it about that a proposition A holds just in case there is an action open to him in that world whose performance would guarantee the truth of A. If we take $\oplus$ as a special modal operator representing the "can" of ability, this idea is represented by defining $\oplus A$ as true at a world w just in case there is some action K in $N(w)$ such that A is true at w' for each w' from K.

This operator of Brown's escapes Kenny's objections, allowing the analogues of both $T\Diamond$ and $C\Diamond$ to be falsified; and Brown advances other arguments as well for regarding it as an appropriate formalization for the "can" of ability. Rather than considering the proposal more closely, however, we simply show that, in spite of some differences in detail, it is actually quite close in conception to the analysis suggested here.

---

[8]An introduction to minimal models for modal logic can be found in Chapter 7 of Chellas [1980].

In order to see this, let us introduce the new, temporary operator *bstit*—for "Brown stit." This operator is supposed to function in the present environment as an analogue to Brown's representation of the "can" of ability, so that $[\alpha \; bstit: A]$ means that α has the ability to see to it that A; and in interpreting the operator formally, we will show how Brown's ideas might be adapted from their original minimal model environment to the context of stit semantics.

One difference between the two contexts is that both agents and temporal information are treated more explicitly in the present framework than in minimal models. However, Brown himself says that the idea of ability analyzed in his logic is to be construed "neither timelessly nor impersonally," but simply that these matters are left tacit in his approach [1988, p. 6]. A second difference is that, although Brown represents the actions available to an agent at a world as propositions, or sets of worlds, it is more natural in the context of stit semantics—and more in keeping with our current treatment of propositions—to represent the actions available to an agent at a moment, not as sets of moments, but as sets of histories through that moment; and in fact, it is reasonable to use the choice primitive already present in stit models for that purpose, thinking of the possible actions available to the agent α at the moment m as the members of the partition $Choice_{\alpha}^{m}$.

We can then mirror Brown's analysis in the present framework by defining $[\alpha \; bstit: A]$ as true at an index m/h just in case there is some action K in $Choice_{\alpha}^{m}$ such that A is true at m/h' for each h' from K—just in case, that is, $K \subseteq |A|_m$. It should be clear that this definition is simply a transposition of Brown's ideas into the current setting. And the introduction of this *bstit* operator, with its connections to Brown's analysis, allows us also to see the links between Brown's proposal and the current suggestion of treating ability through a combination of historical possibility together with a stit operator; for it is now easy to verify the validity of the formula $[\alpha \; bstit: A] \equiv \Diamond[\alpha \; cstit: A]$. The ideas underlying the *bstit* operator, with their roots in Brown's work, thus coincide with those underlying our current suggestion.

Still, it would be a mistake to overemphasize the similarities between Brown's minimal model analysis of ability and the current suggestion, developed in the framework of stit models. Even apart from the more explicit treatment of temporal matters in stit models, there are other important differences between the logics of ability resulting from Brown's analysis and that proposed here. The reason for this is that Brown's minimal models are much less constrained than stit models. Apart from nonemptyness, Brown imposes no conditions at all on the actions open to an agent at a world w, the propositions belonging to $N(w)$. These propositions are not required to exhaust the space of possibilities, with each world belonging to some member of $N(w)$; and they are permitted to overlap, so that the same world might actually belong to two different members of $N(w)$. In stit models, however, the possible actions open to an agent α at a moment m—the members of $Choice_\alpha^m$—are required to partition the relevant set of possibilities.

Because it places more restriction on the structure of actions, our current suggestion results in a logic of ability that is stronger than Brown's, validating statements whose analogues in Brown's framework are invalid. As an example, Brown's theory allows countermodels to the formula $\diamondsuit\diamondsuit A \supset \diamondsuit A$, while the analogous statement,

$$\diamondsuit[\alpha \ cstit: \ \diamondsuit[\alpha \ cstit: \ A]] \supset \diamondsuit[\alpha \ cstit: \ A],$$

is valid in stit models.

In fact, Brown sees it as an advantage of his account that it does not validate this principle; he views it as an incorrect principle for reasoning about ability, illustrated by the following example:

> Suppose I am a skillful enough golfer that on the short par 3 hole I can hit the green in one stroke, and that, no matter where on the green the ball lands, I can then putt out in one additional stroke. Nonetheless, until I know where the ball lands on the green I don't know which further action to take to get the ball into the hole. It may not be true that I am able to get a hole in one, nor even that there is some pair of strokes I can choose in advance that will assure the ball's going into the hole. [Brown, 1988, p. 20]

Apparently, the point of this example is that, at the tee, the golfer is able to get himself into a position from which he will then be able to put the ball into the hole, but that it is incorrect to say of him at the tee simply that he is able to put the ball into the hole. Although there is a sense—investigated later, in Section 7.2—in which it can be said that an agent is able to bring about an outcome whenever there is a sequence of actions he can perform that will guarantee its occurrence, Brown seems to be right in claiming that, at least on the momentary reading of ability, it is incorrect to think of the golfer at the tee as having the ability then to put the ball into the hole. Still, this need not cast doubt on the principle in question; for it is not clear that, in the same momentary sense of ability, the golfer at the tee is able to be able to put the ball in the hole: instead, it seems that what the golfer at the tee is able to do in the momentary sense is bring it about that in the future he will be able to put the ball in the hole. If this is right, then Brown's example does not undermine the principle stated above, but only the principle

$$\diamondsuit[\alpha \ cstit: \ F\diamondsuit[\alpha \ cstit: \ A]] \supset \diamondsuit[\alpha \ cstit: \ A],$$

which is indeed invalid in stit models.

2.3.3 Refraining and ability

Let us now turn to the treatment of ability that results when the deliberative rather than the Chellas stit is used in our schematic analysis, so that the formula

$$\Diamond[\alpha \; dstit\colon A]$$

is now taken to represent the idea that the agent α has the ability to see to it that A. Relying on this analysis, we show that the deliberative stit operator can be used to provide a robust treatment, not only of action, but also of the concept of refraining from an action—a concept characterized by von Wright [1963, p. 45] as the "correlative" of action.[9]

Even among philosophers explicitly concerned with action, this correlative concept is seldom treated in any detail, perhaps because it is so difficult to understand. When an agent refrains from smoking, for example, he does not smoke; but there seems to be more to it than that. An agent is not naturally thought to refrain from doing whatever it is he does not do—particularly, as von Wright notes, when those actions lie beyond his capacity. Even if it is true that some agent does not alter the course of a tornado, for example, it still does not seem correct to say that he refrained from doing so.

Because refraining involves more than simple not doing, some writers have pursued a strategy of conjunctive definition, attempting to characterize refraining as not doing plus "something else." One example is von Wright himself, who feels that the concept of refraining cannot be defined in terms of action and truth functional connectives alone, at least if action is to be analyzed as he proposes. Instead, he suggests that refraining should be defined as not acting conjoined with the ability to act: an agent refrains from doing a certain thing whenever "he *can do* this thing, but *does* in fact *not do* it" [1963, p. 45]. Adapting von Wright's style of analysis to the present setting, the idea that an agent α refrains from seeing to it that A can be taken to mean that α does not see to it that A but that he has the ability to do so—an idea it is then natural to represent through a statement of the form

$$\neg[\alpha \; dstit\colon A] \wedge \Diamond[\alpha \; dstit\colon A].^{10}$$

---

[9]The mode of action described here as refraining is characterized by von Wright in [1963] as "forbearing" and in [1981] as "omitting." Von Wright notes that refraining (forbearing, omitting), as analyzed in his work, is the logically weakest member in a series of progressively stronger notions. Refraining from an action involves the ability to perform that action, but not necessarily any awareness of that ability; stronger notions can be obtained if one requires an awareness of the ability, an actual decision to refrain, or a decision to refrain in the face of inclination (which he describes as "abstaining").

[10]This is not necessarily a representation that von Wright would accept, since—perhaps for reasons applying only to his own theory of action—he rejects the general idea that "the notion of 'can do' involves a superposition of operators, one for 'can' and another for 'do'," and prefers instead to take the notion of ability as primitive [1976, p. 391].

Working from the perspective of their own analysis of agency, Belnap and Perloff [1988] rejected von Wright's suggestion that refraining is definable as not acting together with the ability to act. Instead, they chose to develop another theme also present in von Wright—that refraining, although it involves not acting, is itself a kind of acting, a "mode of action or conduct" [1981, p. 12]. When an agent refrains from smoking, he does not smoke; but not smoking itself seems to be something he does. In the present setting, not smoking is represented as not seeing to it that one smokes; and so it seems that refraining from smoking—performing the action of not smoking—can be represented as seeing to it that one does not see to it that one smokes. More generally, it is suggested by Belnap and Perloff that the idea that α refrains from seeing to it that A can be captured as the claim that α sees to it that he does not see to it that A, and then represented through a statement of the form

$$[\alpha \ dstit: \neg[\alpha \ dstit: A]].$$

Evidently, this analysis casts refraining as a concept definable in terms of an agency operator and truth functions alone, contrary to von Wright's view that additional linguistic resources are necessary; and the source of this difference is easy to see. Unlike von Wright's representation of action, which forbids nesting, stit operators do allow the nesting of one action expression within another.

Both von Wright's treatment of refraining and that of Belnap and Perloff are attractive; both seem to capture something essential to the concept. And, fortunately, we do not have to choose between them, for it turns out in the present setting that these two approaches actually coincide, as we can see from the validity of the formula

$$[\alpha \ dstit: \neg[\alpha \ dstit: A]] \equiv (\neg[\alpha \ dstit: A] \wedge \Diamond[\alpha \ dstit: A]).$$

The implication from left to right follows at once from the validity of the *dstit* analogue to the principle T, together with the fact that $[\alpha \ dstit: A]$ implies $\neg\Box A$ for any statement A. To see the implication from right to left, suppose that $\neg[\alpha \ dstit: A] \wedge \Diamond[\alpha \ dstit: A]$ is true at some index m/h. Since $\neg[\alpha \ dstit: A]$ holds at m/h, we must have $\neg[\alpha \ dstit: A]$ true also at m/h' for each h' in $Choice_\alpha^m(h)$; hence, $Choice_\alpha^m(h) \subseteq |\neg[\alpha \ dstit: A]|_m$, and so the positive condition is satisfied for $[\alpha \ dstit: \neg[\alpha \ dstit: A]]$ to hold at m/h. But since $\Diamond[\alpha \ dstit: A]$ holds also at m/h, there must be some h' in H_m such that $[\alpha \ dstit: A]$ holds at m/h'. Therefore, $|\neg[\alpha \ dstit: A]|_m \neq H_m$, and so the negative condition is satisfied as well.

Having defined refraining through the nesting of stit operators, it is now natural to consider also more complicated, deeply nested concepts, such as refraining from refraining. Working with our analogue to Belnap and Perloff's definition, the idea that α refrains from seeing to it that he refrains from seeing to it that A translates into the formula

$$[\alpha \; dstit: \neg[\alpha \; dstit: [\alpha \; dstit: \neg[\alpha \; dstit: A]]]],$$

which says, of course, that α sees to it that he does not see to it that he sees to it that he does not see to it that A; this is equivalent by the principles T, 4, and RE to the marginally less confusing

$$[\alpha \; stit: \neg[\alpha \; stit: \neg[\alpha \; stit: A]]],$$

telling us that α sees to it that he does not see to it that he does not see to it that A. We can now turn to a question considered by Meinong in the manuscript of his *Ethische Bausteine*:

> One may ask whether the essential features of the law of omission are to be found in the law of double negation or in some analogues thereof. In such a case omission of omission would yield commission, just as the negation of a negation yields an affirmation.[11]

In the present context, this question—whether refraining from refraining is equivalent to doing—can be cast as a question concerning the validity of the formula

$$RR. \quad [\alpha \; dstit: A] \equiv [\alpha \; dstit: \neg[\alpha \; dstit: \neg[\alpha \; dstit: A]]].$$

And it is then a simple matter to establish the validity of this formula, showing that the present analysis of agency supports the identification of refraining from refraining with doing—contrary, as it turns out, to Meinong's view.[12]

It is interesting that the question whether refraining from refraining is equivalent to doing can be formulated so clearly in the framework set out here; but the question itself is perhaps not terribly important: it is hard to think of any fundamental philosophical views that would be shattered either by a positive or a negative answer. A more important issue concerns the proper sense, if any, in which performing an action can be said to imply the ability to do otherwise. That acting does imply the ability to do otherwise is a view going back at least to Aristotle, who writes in the *Nicomachean Ethics* that "where it is in our power to do something, it is also in our power

---

[11] This passage is cited in footnote 15 of Chisholm [1963].

[12] The formula RR is dubbed the "Refref" equivalence in Belnap [1991b]. That paper as well as Belnap [1991a] discuss the matter in detail from the perspective of the agency operator defined in Belnap and Perloff [1988]; more technical studies of RR in the context of this logic can be found in Xu [1994b], Xu [1994c], and Xu [1995]. It is worth noting that the *cstit* analogue to RR is valid also, since *cstit* is an $S5$ modality.

not to do it, and when the 'no' is in our power, the 'yes' is also" [1113b7-8]; and the topic has been much debated in the contemporary literature as well.[13]

Taking the notion of "doing otherwise" as refraining, the idea that acting implies the ability to do otherwise—to refrain—can now be expressed through the principle

ACR. $[\alpha \; dstit: A] \supset \Diamond[\alpha \; dstit: \neg[\alpha \; dstit: A]]$;

and it is a simple matter to see that this principle is valid. Suppose $[\alpha \; dstit: A]$ holds at some index m/h. By the negative condition, we know that there must be some h' from H_m such that A is false at m/h', from which it follows that $Choice_\alpha^m(h') \subseteq |\neg[\alpha \; dstit: A]|_m$. The positive condition is thus satisfied for $[\alpha \; dstit: \neg[\alpha \; dstit: A]]$ to hold at m/h', and the negative condition is satisfied also, since $[\alpha \; dstit: A]$ is true at m/h by assumption, so that $|\neg[\alpha \; dstit: A]|_m \neq H_m$. Therefore, $[\alpha \; dstit: \neg[\alpha \; dstit: A]]$ is true at m/h'; and so $\Diamond[\alpha \; dstit: \neg[\alpha \; dstit: A]]$ must be true at the original index m/h. Not only does acting imply the ability to refrain, according to this analysis, but it turns out also, as it should, that refraining from acting entails the ability to act; the principle

RCA. $[\alpha \; dstit: \neg[\alpha \; dstit: A]] \supset \Diamond[\alpha \; dstit: A]$

is likewise valid, as we can see from the previous equivalence between von Wright's analysis of refraining and that of Belnap and Perloff.

Because both ACR and RCA are valid, and since historical necessity is an S5 modality, ordinary modal reasoning leads us to the conclusion

CACR. $\Diamond[\alpha \; dstit: A] \equiv \Diamond[\alpha \; dstit: \neg[\alpha \; dstit: A]]$,

a formula that can be taken as expressing the Aristotelian principle, cited above, that the ability to act coincides with the ability to refrain from acting. Such a principle of two-way ability is advanced by Kenny, for example, who argues that it can be used to distinguish "full-blooded" abilities, for whose exercise we can be held responsible, from mere "natural powers," such as the power to grow old [1976, pp. 226–228].[14] And the principle has been endorsed also by von Wright as a "fundamental law of ability logic," according to which the "ability to do and to omit [refrain] are reciprocal" [1976, p. 391].

The validity of ACR, RCA, and the Aristotelian principle CACR, along with the equivalence between our present analogues of von Wright's definition of refraining and that of Belnap and Perloff, all argue for the usefulness

---

[13] See, for example, Chisholm [1967], Frankfurt [1969], and van Inwagen [1978].

[14] See Kenny [1979, pp. 7–9] for a discussion of this distinction in Aristotle.

of the deliberative stit in the analysis of the concepts of action and refraining. Each of these results depends on the negative condition in the semantics of the deliberative stit; if the deliberative stit were replaced with the Chellas stit, where the negative condition is absent, all would fail. The reason for this is easy to see: each of these validities relies upon the distinction between true refraining and simple not doing, a distinction for which the negative condition is crucial. Because it lacks the negative condition, the Chellas stit collapses these two ideas—refraining and simple not doing—into one, due to the validity of the statement

$$\neg[\alpha \ cstit\colon A] \equiv [\alpha \ cstit\colon \neg[\alpha \ cstit\colon A]].$$

We noted earlier that intuitions concerning the intuitive desirability of the negative condition in the semantics for the deliberative stit operator are divided when one focuses only on simple, nonnested agency constructions; but we now see that this condition allows for the definition of a rich notion of refraining, with illuminating connections to action and ability.

Nevertheless, in spite of these advantages of the deliberative stit, we will find it convenient to continue working with the Chellas stit throughout the remainder of the book, for we will soon begin to explore an area in which the benefits of richness are outweighed by those of simplicity.

2.4   Group agency and ability

So far we have concentrated on the actions and abilities only of individual agents. We now show that the techniques employed to explicate these notions can be applied also to group agency and ability.

It is best to begin with an example; so consider the multiple agent situation depicted in Figure 2.5. Here, the actions open to the agent α at the moment m are depicted by the vertical partitions of H_m; that is, $Choice_\alpha^m = \{K_1, K_2\}$, with $K_1 = \{h_1, h_2, h_3\}$ and $K_2 = \{h_4, h_5, h_6\}$. The actions open to the agent β are depicted by the horizontal partitions; $Choice_\beta^m = \{K_3, K_4\}$, with $K_3 = \{h_2, h_3, h_4\}$ and $K_4 = \{h_1, h_5, h_6\}$. As indicated, the sentence A is true at the indices m/h_2, m/h_3, and m/h_6, and false everywhere else.

It should be clear that, in this situation, neither the agent α nor the agent β acting alone has the ability to see to it that A; both $\Diamond[\alpha \ cstit\colon A]$ and $\Diamond[\beta \ cstit\colon A]$ are settled false at m. Neither of the actions available to α or β individually guarantees the truth of A; each action available to each of these agents allows for a possible outcome in which A is false. Still, it seems that the group of agents $\{\alpha, \beta\}$ acting together does have the ability to see to it that A. If α performs the action K_1 and β performs the action K_3, the group $\{\alpha, \beta\}$ can then be said to perform the action $K_1 \cap K_3$, and the truth of A is guaranteed: A holds at m/h for each history h contained in $K_1 \cap K_3$.

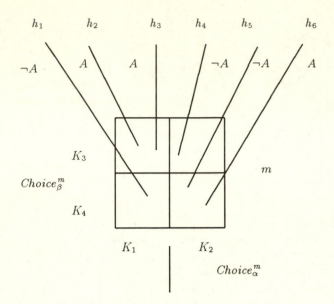

Figure 2.5: Group actions

2.4.1   Group actions

In order to develop the intuition conveyed by this example into a firm proposal, it is necessary, first, to characterize the actions or choices available to a group of agents at a moment. Fortunately, there is no need for a new primitive notion of group action. As our example suggests, group actions can be defined as patterns of individual actions: an action available to a group of agents can be defined as an intersection of the actions available to the individual agents belonging to that group, one action for each agent.

Before carrying through this definition, however, we must first set out a more precise formulation of the requirement governing the *Choice* partition that was described earlier, in Section 2.2, as the condition of *independence of agents*. The force of this requirement, we recall, is that simultaneous actions by distinct agents must be independent in the sense that the choices of one agent cannot affect the choices available to another; at each moment, each agent must be able to perform any of his available actions, no matter which actions are performed at that moment by the other agents. In the setting of branching time, this idea—that each agent must be able to perform any available action no matter which actions are performed by others—can be taken to mean that there is always, for each action available to the agent, some history belonging to that action which is consistent with any possible pattern of action selected by the others. The independence requirement thus reduces to the following condition: at each moment, for any way of selecting one of the actions available to each agent, the intersection of all the selected actions must be nonempty.

In order to formalize this requirement, it is convenient to reify the patterns of action that might be selected by the various agents. We therefore define an *action selection* function at a moment m as a function assigning to each agent some action available to that agent at m—that is, a function s from *Agent* into subsets of H_m satisfying the condition that $s(\alpha) \in Choice_\alpha^m$. Evidently, each of these action selection functions represents a possible pattern of action, a selection for each agent of some action available to that agent at the moment m. And these possible patterns of action can then be collected together into the set $Select_m$ containing each of the action selection functions at m, each pattern of action available to the various agents at m.

Definition 2.9 (*$Select_m$*) Where m is a moment and *Agent* is the set of agents from a stit frame, $Select_m$ is the set of functions s from *Agent* into H_m satisfying the condition that $s(\alpha) \in Choice_\alpha^m$.

The condition of independence of agents—that the intersection of any pattern of selected actions must always be nonempty—can now be stated quite simply as the requirement that, for any moment m, we must have

$$\bigcap_{\alpha \in Agent} s(\alpha) \neq \emptyset$$

for each function s in $Select_m$.

Given these definitions, it is now straightforward also, where Γ is some particular group of agents, to define the set $Choice_\Gamma^m$ of actions available to this group at the moment m, as follows.

Definition 2.10 (*$Choice_\Gamma^m$*) Where m is a moment and *Agent* is the set of agents from a stit frame, and where $\Gamma \subseteq Agent$,

$$Choice_\Gamma^m = \{\bigcap_{\alpha \in \Gamma} s(\alpha) : s \in Select_m\}.$$

And it is clear that this definition says what it should: the set of actions available to the group Γ is identified with the set of intersections of actions available to the agents belonging to that group, one action for each agent.

It follows from the independence requirement, of course, that each action belonging to $Choice_\Gamma^m$ must be nonempty; and indeed, it is easy to see that, like the set $Choice_\alpha^m$ of actions available to the individual α at the moment m, the set $Choice_\Gamma^m$ of actions available to the group Γ will partition H_m. Where K is some group action belonging to $Choice_\Gamma^m$, we say, as with individual actions, that the group Γ *performs* the action K at the index m/h just in case h is a history belonging to K. We again speak of the histories contained in K as *possible outcomes* of the group action K. And we again let $Choice_{\Gamma}^{m}(h)$ (again, defined only when $h \in H_m$) represent the particular action from $Choice_{\Gamma}^{m}$ that contains the history h, the particular action that the group Γ performs at the index m/h.

These various definitions can be illustrated by returning to Figure 2.5. For simplicity, let us suppose that the only agents belonging to $Agent$ are those depicted, α and β. Since each of these two agents has two available actions at m, there are then four patterns of action available to the entire set of agents, and so $Select_m$ will contain the four functions s_1, s_2, s_3, and s_4, as follows:

$$s_1(\alpha) = K_1 \quad \text{and} \quad s_1(\beta) = K_3,$$
$$s_2(\alpha) = K_1 \quad \text{and} \quad s_2(\beta) = K_4,$$
$$s_3(\alpha) = K_2 \quad \text{and} \quad s_3(\beta) = K_3,$$
$$s_4(\alpha) = K_2 \quad \text{and} \quad s_4(\beta) = K_4.$$

Now, where Γ is the group $\{\alpha, \beta\}$, we have

$$
\begin{aligned}
Choice_{\Gamma}^{m} &= \{\bigcap_{\alpha \in \Gamma} s(\alpha) : s \in Select_m\} \\
&= \{s(\alpha) \cap s(\beta) : s \in Select_m\} \\
&= \{s_1(\alpha) \cap s_1(\beta), s_2(\alpha) \cap s_2(\beta), s_3(\alpha) \cap s_3(\beta), s_4(\alpha) \cap s_4(\beta)\} \\
&= \{K_1 \cap K_3, K_1 \cap K_4, K_2 \cap K_3, K_2 \cap K_4\}.
\end{aligned}
$$

We can say that, at the index m/h_2, for example, the group Γ performs the action $K_1 \cap K_3$; the possible outcomes that might result from this group action are h_2 and h_3. And since $K_1 \cap K_3$ is the particular action available to Γ at m that contains the history h_2, we have $Choice_{\Gamma}^{m}(h_2) = K_1 \cap K_3$.

2.4.2   A group agency operator

Using the concept $Choice_{\Gamma}^{m}$ to represent the set of actions available to a group Γ at a moment m, the evaluation rule for a $cstit$ operator representing group agency can now be defined as follows.

Definition 2.11 (Evaluation rule: $[\Gamma \ cstit: A]$) Where Γ is a group of agents and m/h an index from a stit model,

- $\mathcal{M}, m/h \models [\Gamma \ cstit: A]$ if and only if $Choice_{\Gamma}^{m}(h) \subseteq |A|_{m}^{\mathcal{M}}$.

And the idea, of course, runs parallel to that underlying individual agency: the statement $[\Gamma \ cstit: A]$ is to hold at an index m/h whenever the group Γ performs an action at that index guaranteeing the truth of A. In the case of Figure 2.5, for example, it is now easy to see, where $\Gamma = \{\alpha, \beta\}$, that the statement $[\Gamma \ cstit: A]$ holds at both m/h_2 and m/h_3, and nowhere else.

Since the set $Choice_{\Gamma}^{m}$ of group actions, like the set $Choice_{\alpha}^{m}$ of individual actions, partitions the histories belonging to H_m, and since the evaluation rules for the individual and group *cstit* operators are otherwise identical, it is clear that the group *cstit* mirrors the individual operator in its logical properties; it is likewise an *S5* modal operator. Indeed, individual agency can be identified with a special case of group agency. It is easy to see that $Choice_\alpha^m = Choice_{\{\alpha\}}^m$, so that the actions available to the individual α and the group $\{\alpha\}$ are identical. And from this, the validity of the formula

$$[\alpha \; cstit: A] \equiv [\{\alpha\} \; cstit: A]$$

follows at once: the individual α sees to it that A just in case the group $\{\alpha\}$ does so as well.

Of course, a particular group of agents might guarantee the truth of some proposition through the performance of a group action, even though no action performed by any subset of that group is sufficient to do so; in the case of Figure 2.5, for instance, again taking $\Gamma = \{\alpha, \beta\}$, the statement $[\Gamma \; cstit: A]$ is true at the index m/h_2, even though both $[\alpha \; cstit: A]$ and $[\beta \; cstit: A]$ are false. But according to the theory developed here, whenever a particular group guarantees the truth of some proposition, each superset of that group does so as well. To see this, we need only note that, whenever $\Gamma \subseteq \Delta$ for two groups of agents Γ and Δ, the set $Choice_\Delta^m$ contains a partitioning of H_m at least as fine as that contained in $Choice_\Gamma^m$, so that $Choice_\Delta^m(h) \subseteq Choice_\Gamma^m(h)$ must hold for each h in H_m; the validity of $[\Gamma \; cstit: A] \supset [\Delta \; cstit: A]$ then follows immediately from the group *cstit* evaluation rule.[15]

Finally, let us note that, just as with individual ability, a useful notion of group ability can be introduced through a combination of ordinary historical possibility together with the concept of group action. Just as before, the notion of what a group of agents is able to do can be identified with the notion of what it is possible for that group of agents to do, so that the statement $\Diamond[\Gamma \; cstit: A]$ can be taken to represent the idea that the group Γ is able to see to it that A. Turning once more to Figure 2.5 for illustration, and again taking $\Gamma = \{\alpha, \beta\}$, we can see, for example, that the statement $\Diamond[\Gamma \; cstit: A]$ is settled true at m.

---

[15]Because of this feature in the current analysis of group agency—that, whenever a group guarantees the truth of some proposition, each of its supersets does so as well—the analysis is said to allow for *free riders* in group action. A notion of group agency that does not permit free riders is explored in Belnap and Perloff [1993]; the basic idea there is that a group *properly* sees to it that A only if it is a minimal group that sees to it that A in the sense described here, so that the contribution of each member of the group can be regarded as essential.

Chapter 3

Ought to be

3.1 The standard theory

We begin our treatment of deontic logic by considering a way of incorporating the standard deontic operator $\bigcirc$—meaning "It ought to be that"— into the framework of branching time. Typically in deontic logic, this standard ought operator is interpreted against a background set of possibilities, usually possible worlds. A number of these possibilities are classified as ideal, those in which things turn out as they ought to; and a sentence of the form $\bigcirc A$ is then defined as true just in case A holds in each of these ideal possibilities. The idea behind this definition is that $\bigcirc A$ should hold just in case A is a necessary condition for things turning out as they ought to.

It is a straightforward matter to transpose this standard deontic picture into the context of branching time.[1] Here, the set of possibilities at a moment m is identified with H_m, the set of histories still available at m; and a nonempty subset of these is taken to represent the ideal histories. A sentence of the form $\bigcirc A$ is then defined as true at an index m/h just in case A is true at m/h' for each history h' from H_m that is classified as ideal.

This picture can be captured formally by supplementing the stit frames and models described earlier with a function $Ought$ mapping each moment m into a nonempty subset $Ought_m$ of H_m.

Definition 3.1 (Standard deontic stit frames/models) A *standard deontic stit frame* is a structure of the form

$$\langle Tree, <, Agent, Choice, Ought \rangle,$$

[1] A discussion of standard deontic logic from a historical perspective can be found in Føllesdal and Hilpinen [1971]; a more analytical treatment, situating this system within the family of modal logics, is found in Chapter 6 of Chellas [1980]. The present adaptation of this standard theory to branching time follows that of Thomason [1981b]; a related approach, cast against the background of a discrete temporal framework, is presented in Åqvist and Hoepelman [1981]. The matter of incorporating deontic operators into a tense logic had previously been explored in Chellas [1969], Montague [1968], and Scott [1967]; historical details can be found in Thomason [1984].

34

with *Tree*, $<$, *Agent*, and *Choice* as in stit frames, and with *Ought* a function mapping each moment m from *Tree* into a nonempty subset $Ought_m$ of H_m. A *standard deontic stit model* is a model based on a standard deontic stit frame.

The set $Ought_m$ is to be thought of intuitively as containing the ideal histories through m; the standard ought operator can thus be defined through the following evaluation rule.

Definition 3.2 (Standard evaluation rule: $\bigcirc A$) Where m/h is an index from a standard deontic stit model $\mathcal{M}$,

- $\mathcal{M}, m/h \models \bigcirc A$ if and only if $\mathcal{M}, m/h' \models A$ for each history $h' \in Ought_m$.

Several logical features of the ought operator developed in this standard way should be noted. First, it is clear from the structure of the evaluation rule that statements of the form $\bigcirc A$ are moment determinate; like statements of the form $\Box A$, they are always either settled true or settled false. Second, it is easy to verify that this standard ought operator is a normal modal operator, satisfying the principles

$$RE\bigcirc. \quad A \equiv B \ / \ \bigcirc A \equiv \bigcirc B,$$
$$N\bigcirc. \quad \bigcirc\top,$$
$$M\bigcirc. \quad \bigcirc(A \wedge B) \supset (\bigcirc A \wedge \bigcirc B),$$
$$C\bigcirc. \quad \bigcirc A \wedge \bigcirc B \supset \bigcirc(A \wedge B).$$

Third, because the set $Ought_m$ is always required to be nonempty, it can be seen also that the formula

$$D\bigcirc. \quad \bigcirc A \supset \Diamond A$$

must be validated as well. This formula expresses one version of the characteristic deontic idea that ought implies can—in this case: if it ought to be that A, then it is possible that A. A familiar argument shows that, taken together with $C\bigcirc$, the characteristic deontic formula $D\bigcirc$ leads to the validity of the statement

$$D^*\bigcirc. \quad \neg(\bigcirc A \wedge \bigcirc \neg A).$$

For suppose $\bigcirc A \wedge \bigcirc \neg A$ were true at some index. By $C\bigcirc$, we could conclude also that $\bigcirc(A \wedge \neg A)$ must be true at that index, and then by $D\bigcirc$, that $\Diamond(A \wedge \neg A)$ must be true as well; but this is impossible. The formula $D^*\bigcirc$ expresses the idea, also characteristic of standard deontic logic, that normative conflicts are ruled out.

Finally, it is worth mentioning that, even though the present treatment involves only a straightforward transposition of the standard deontic picture into the context of branching time, the resulting account of the ought operator is somewhat stronger than what is usually known as "standard deontic logic"—the smallest normal system containing the axiom $D\bigcirc$. In particular, because the set $Ought_m$ of ideal histories relevant to an index m/h depends only on the moment m, and not on the history h as well, the present account validates the additional formulas

$$4\bigcirc. \quad \bigcirc A \supset \bigcirc \bigcirc A,$$
$$5\bigcirc. \quad \neg \bigcirc A \supset \bigcirc \neg \bigcirc A,$$

characteristic of the modal system known as deontic $S5$. These formulas have sometimes been criticized in the literature as too strong to capture a legitimate sense of the moral ought, but as Thomason points out in [1981b], many of the criticisms arose in a setting in which it was easy to confuse temporal and deontic relations, and often relied on such a confusion. Indeed, the validity of these formulas follows from the simple fact that ought statements are moment determinate—so that $\bigcirc A$ implies $\square \bigcirc A$, and $\neg \bigcirc A$ implies $\square \neg \bigcirc A$—together with the observation that whatever is necessary ought to be the case: $\square A$ implies $\bigcirc A$ for any formula A.

3.2   A utilitarian theory

3.2.1   General models

Although the study of deontic logics has led to the clarification of a number of problems involved in normative reasoning, the topic is sometimes viewed with indifference by researchers interested in ethics more generally. Part of the reason for this, I believe, lies in the impression that these logics are able to model only very crude normative theories—theories that can do no more than classify situations, simply, as either ideal or nonideal. However, while it is true that standard deontic logics have concentrated on this simple classification of situations, the underlying semantic framework can be generalized to accommodate a broader range of normative theories. In the context of branching time, one such generalization results when we imagine that each history through a moment, rather than being classified simply as ideal or nonideal, is instead assigned a particular value at that moment. These values, chosen from some general space of values, are to represent the worth or desirability of the histories.

This change in perspective can be effected formally by replacing the primitive $Ought$ in the standard deontic frames described above with a function $Value$ that associates each moment m with a mapping $Value_m$ of the histories from H_m into some set of values. Depending on the nature of the particular normative theory that is being modeled, the background set of values can be conceived of in different ways, and subject to different ordering relations. But we can assume that the set of values is always at least partially ordered by a relation $\leq$, so that $Value_m(h) \leq Value_m(h')$ means that the value assigned to the history h' at m is at least as great as that assigned to the history h.

Definition 3.3 (General deontic stit frames/models) A *general deontic stit frame* is a structure of the form

$$\langle Tree, <, Agent, Choice, Value \rangle,$$

with *Tree*, $<$, *Agent*, and *Choice* as in stit frames, and where *Value* is a function associating each moment m belonging to *Tree* with a mapping $Value_m$ from H_m into a set of values partially ordered by $\leq$. A *general deontic stit model* is a model based on a general deontic stit frame.

In this new, more general environment, the standard evaluation rule for ought statements must be abandoned, of course; we can no longer think of a statement of the form $\bigcirc A$ as true whenever A is true in each ideal history, since we are no longer presented with a set of histories classified as ideal. Still, it is possible to define a coherent ought operator by requiring that $\bigcirc A$ should be true at an index m/h whenever A is true along some history h' through m, and then true also at every history h'' through m whose value is at least as great as that of h', as follows.

Definition 3.4 (General evaluation rule: $\bigcirc A$) Where m/h is an index from a general deontic stit model $\mathcal{M}$,

- $\mathcal{M}, m/h \models \bigcirc A$ if and only if there is some history $h' \in H_m$ such that (1) $\mathcal{M}, m/h' \models A$, and (2) $\mathcal{M}, m/h'' \models A$ for each history $h'' \in H_m$ such that $Value_m(h') \leq Value_m(h'')$.

This general evaluation rule for the deontic operator is similar in spirit to the standard version. In the case in which the set of values of the histories through a given moment contains a "greatest" value (an upper bound, a value at least as great as any belonging to that set), the general rule entails that $\bigcirc A$ is true if A holds along each history with that greatest value. In this case, then, rather than defining $\bigcirc A$ as true whenever A is a necessary condition for achieving an ideal history, the new rule simply stipulates that $\bigcirc A$ is true whenever A is a necessary condition for achieving a history of greatest value—a straightforward generalization of the standard idea. But the general framework allows also for the possibility that the set of values of histories through a given moment might contain no greatest value (no upper bound, no value at least as great as any other in the set), and in this case, the general rule defines $\bigcirc A$ as true whenever there is some history such that the truth of A is a necessary condition for achieving a history at least as great in value as that one.

In fact, not only is the general evaluation rule similar in spirit to the standard version, but it can be seen also that the standard deontic framework can actually be subsumed within the general framework as a special case: any standard deontic model can be encoded as a general model in such a way that the same set of statements, including ought statements, is supported by each. In defining the general models that can be taken to encode standard models, we need only the two values 0 and 1, ordered so that $0 \leq 1$ (and it is not the case that $1 \leq 0$). We can then map each standard deontic model into a general model identical to that standard model except that it assigns the value 1 to those histories that are classified as ideal in the standard model and the value 0 to all the others. More exactly, where $\mathcal{M}$ is a standard deontic stit model, we can let $g[\mathcal{M}]$—the general model analogue to $\mathcal{M}$—be a general deontic stit model just like the standard model $\mathcal{M}$ except that the function $Ought$ from $\mathcal{M}$ is replaced in $g[\mathcal{M}]$ with a function $Value$, defined as follows: for each moment m and each history h through m, $Value_m(h) = 1$ if $h \in Ought_m$, and $Value_m(h) = 0$ if $h \notin Ought_m$. It is then a simple matter to verify that a statement is true at an index of the standard model $\mathcal{M}$ just in case it is true also at the corresponding index of the general model $g[\mathcal{M}]$.

3.2.2   Utilitarian models

The general deontic framework, then, subsumes the standard framework as a special case, but it enables us also to represent more sophisticated normative theories, allowing for more than two values, and in which the ordering among values may be more complex. Although there are a number of theories of this kind, we concentrate in this book on utilitarian theories, which take as their space of values a set of utilities usually thought of as isomorphic to the real numbers. These utilitarian theories can be modeled within the general deontic framework by taking the $Value$ function to be governed by two additional constraints.

The first constraint is simple. We require that, at each moment m, the function $Value_m$ should assign to each history passing through m, as its value, some real number representing the utility of that history, where the space of values, the real numbers, is subject to its usual ordering. This characterization of values, or utilities, as real numbers is abstract, and intended to accommodate a variety of different approaches. It says nothing about what is ultimately taken as a measure of an individual agent's utility— pleasure, mental states of intrinsic worth, happiness, money, an index of basic goods. And it says nothing about the way in which the utility of a world, or history, is determined from the utilities of individual agents; the overall utility assigned to a history might be taken to reflect, for example, the total utility of the set of agents in that history, their average utility, or perhaps some distribution-sensitive aggregation of the utilities of these individual agents. The only assumption is that the set of utilities assigned to histories is isomorphic with a subset of the real numbers, so that the utilities themselves can be represented as real numbers.

The second constraint is that the assignment of utilities to histories should be *uniform along histories*, in the sense that the value assigned to a single history cannot vary from moment to moment. Formally, this constraint is enforced as the requirement that $Value_m(h) = Value_{m'}(h)$ for any two moments m and m' belonging to the history h. The point of this second constraint calls for some discussion.

We note to begin with that the analogous constraint is omitted in the standard deontic framework. Here, histories are not classified as ideal or nonideal absolutely, once and for all, but only relative to moments: the same history might be classified as ideal at one moment but as nonideal at another. In fact, this variability of classification is essential in the standard framework. As Thomason has emphasized, it is necessary for the proper treatment of "reparational" oughts—those oughts that arise due to the violation of previous oughts.

This point can be illustrated through Figure 3.1, which is based on an example considered by Thomason [1984]. We are to suppose that, for one reason or another, it ought to be the case at the moment m_1 that an agent will soon board a plane to visit his aunt. The statement letter A, which holds at m_1/h_1, stands for the proposition that the agent will board the plane; the statement letter B, which holds at m_1/h_2 and m_2/h_2, stands for the proposition that the agent will call his aunt to say that he is not coming. We imagine that, at the moment m_1, three histories unfold before the agent. In the history h_1, he boards the plane, and of course does not call his aunt to tell her otherwise. The histories h_2 and h_3 both represent scenarios in which the agent does not board the plane; but in h_2 he calls his aunt to tell her that he will not be visiting, while he neglects this nicety in h_3.

Since, as we have assumed, it ought to be the case at m_1 that the agent boards the plane, the unique ideal history available there must be that in which he does so. In the standard deontic framework, this is represented by taking $Ought_{m_1} = \{h_1\}$, which results, according to the standard evaluation rule, in the settled truth at m_1 of $\bigcirc A$ and the settled falsity of $\bigcirc B$. But now, suppose that—perhaps through some fault of his own, perhaps not— the agent winds up at the moment m_2, where is it settled true that he will not board the plane. An ought that was operative at the moment m_1 is thus violated. Still, it is natural to suppose that new oughts now come into play; it is natural to suppose, for example, that the agent ought now to call his aunt. To capture this idea within the standard deontic framework, it is then necessary to take $Ought_{m_2} = \{h_2\}$, which results, according to the standard evaluation rule, in the settled truth at m_2 of $\bigcirc B$.

In the standard framework, then, we are forced to allow the classification of histories as ideal or nonideal to vary from moment to moment in order

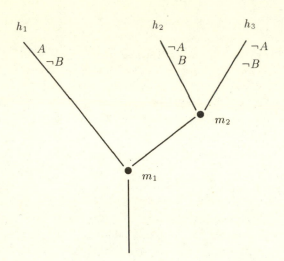

Figure 3.1: A case of reparational oughts

to provide a proper treatment of these reparational cases: whenever it is no longer possible to proceed along a history previously classified as ideal, certain histories that were previously classified as nonideal, but which represent the best scenarios still available, must then be reclassified as ideal. In our particular example, the history h_2, which was classified as nonideal at m_1, represents the best scenario still available at m_2, and so must be classified as ideal there.

Now, let us return to the utilitarian framework, which takes real numbers representing utilities as values. How should we treat reparational oughts within this setting? Well, it is possible to adopt a strategy similar to that followed in the standard framework, relying on a nonuniform assignment of values to histories. In the situation depicted in Figure 3.1, for example, we might hope to generate the appropriate oughts by defining

$$Value_{m_1}(h_1) = 1,$$
$$Value_{m_1}(h_2) = 0,$$
$$Value_{m_1}(h_3) = 0,$$

and then

$$Value_{m_2}(h_2) = 1,$$
$$Value_{m_2}(h_3) = 0.$$

(This is the assignment of values to histories that would result from the g-function described earlier, which maps standard models into general models by assigning to each history the value 1 wherever it was originally classified as ideal, and the value 0 elsewhere. The assignment is nonuniform, of course, since it assigns different values to the history h_2 at the moments m_1 and m_2: $Value_{m_1}(h_2) \neq Value_{m_2}(h_2)$.) The general evaluation rule would then yield the intuitively desirable result that $\bigcirc A$ is settled true at m_1 and $\bigcirc B$ is settled false there, but that $\bigcirc B$ is settled true at m_2.

However, with the entire space of real numbers available as values, we are no longer forced to adopt a nonuniform assignment of values to histories in order to allow for a proper treatment of reparational oughts. The situation depicted in our example can now be characterized by a uniform assignment of values, such as the following:

$$Value_{m_1}(h_1) = 10,$$
$$Value_{m_1}(h_2) = Value_{m_2}(h_2) = 4,$$
$$Value_{m_1}(h_3) = Value_{m_2}(h_3) = 0.$$

Again, with this value assignment, the general deontic evaluation rule yields the correct results: $\bigcirc A$ is settled true at m_1 while $\bigcirc B$ is settled false, but $\bigcirc B$ is settled true at m_2.

Even though both the uniform and nonuniform assignments of utilities to histories generate the correct set of ought statements, the uniform assignment seems to be more natural as a characterization of the situation. It avoids the unfortunate suggestion that the history h_2 is somehow just as valuable at m_2 as the history h_1 was at m_1; it carries the additional information that h_1 is a better history than h_2, that h_2 is a second best scenario. And it allows us to regard histories themselves as the ultimate bearers of utility, without worrying about how a history carrying a certain utility at one moment might carry a different utility at another.[2]

For these reasons—because the utilitarian setting allows us to handle reparational oughts while maintaining a uniform assignment of values to histories, and because such an assignment seems more natural—we build this uniformity constraint into our definition of the utilitarian framework.

Definition 3.5 (Utilitarian stit frames/models) A *utilitarian stit frame* is a general deontic stit frame satisfying two constraints: (1) the underlying space of values is a set of real numbers representing utilities, with $\leq$ the usual ordering on the real numbers; (2) the assignment of values to histories is uniform along histories. A *utilitarian stit model* is a model based on a utilitarian stit frame.

We will concentrate on this particular case of the general deontic framework—the utilitarian framework—throughout the remainder of this book. Because of the uniformity constraint, according to which $Value_m(h) = Value_{m'}(h)$

---

[2]Another reason for adopting a uniform assignment of utilities to histories is that it avoids the need for complicated conditions governing "ought kinematics," such as Condition (3) in the definition of temporal deontic frames found in Thomason [1984, p. 155].

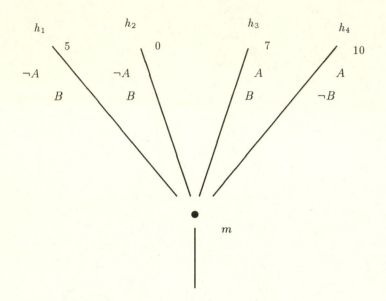

Figure 3.2: $\bigcirc A$ and $\neg \bigcirc B$

for any moments m and m' belonging to a history h, we can now safely omit the subscript on the value function, speaking of the value assigned to a history h at any moment along that history simply as $Value(h)$.

In depicting utilitarian stit models, we adopt the convention of marking each history through a moment with a number corresponding to its utility at that moment. Thus, Figure 3.2, for instance, represents a situation in which, at the moment m, the histories h_1, h_2, h_3, and h_4 are taken to possess the utilities 5, 0, 7, and 10, respectively. As a result, we can see from the general evaluation rule that the formula $\bigcirc A$ is settled true at m in this situation, since A holds in h_3 and at each history at least as valuable as h_3. The formula $\bigcirc B$, however, is settled false, since for each history in which B is true, there is a history of equal or greater value in which it is false. A more complicated situation is depicted in Figure 3.3. Here, we are faced with an infinite number of histories $(h_1, h_2, h_3, \ldots)$ of ever increasing value $(1, 2, 3, \ldots)$; the formula A is true at the history h_i when i is odd, and false when i is even; and the formula B is true at h_i when i is greater than 3, and otherwise false. As a result, we can see that $\bigcirc A$ is settled false at m, since for each history in which A is true there is a history of equal or greater value in which it is false; but $\bigcirc B$ is settled true, since B is true at all histories at least as valuable as h_4.

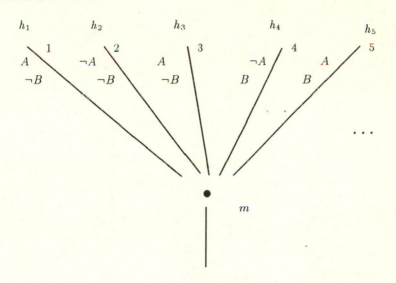

Figure 3.3: $\neg \bigcirc A$ and $\bigcirc B$

3.2.3 Logic of the utilitarian ought

The general ought operator introduced here shares many of the properties of the ought defined in the standard deontic framework. It is apparent from the structure of the general evaluation rule, for example, that the characteristic deontic formula $D\bigcirc$ is valid in the class of general deontic models, and also that any statement of the form $\bigcirc A$ is always either settled true or settled false. In addition, it is easy to verify that the principles $RE\bigcirc$, $N\bigcirc$, and $M\bigcirc$, as well as $4\bigcirc$ and $5\bigcirc$, are valid in general deontic models. But if we consider the entire class of general deontic models, there are cases in which the underlying space of values might be ordered in such a way that instances of $C\bigcirc$ are falsified.

A simple example can be constructed on the basis of the situation depicted in Figure 3.4. Let us suppose that our background setting allows only for two values—say, v_1 and v_2—and that these two values are incomparable with each other: we have neither $v_1 \leq v_2$ nor $v_2 \leq v_1$. Let us suppose further that, at the moment m, the history h_1 carries the first of these values while the history h_2 carries the second: $Value_m(h_1) = v_1$ and $Value_m(h_2) = v_2$. In that case, according to the general evaluation rule, the statement $\bigcirc A$ is then settled true at m—for A holds along the history h_1, and also along each history through m at least as great in value as h_1. The statement $\bigcirc \neg A$ is likewise settled true at m. But of course, the statement $\bigcirc(A \wedge \neg A)$ is settled false, since there is no history along which $A \wedge \neg A$ is true. The situation

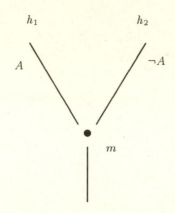

Figure 3.4: A countermodel to $C\bigcirc$

described here thus serves to falsify the formula

$$\bigcirc A \wedge \bigcirc \neg A \supset \bigcirc (A \wedge \neg A),$$

an instance of the thesis $C\bigcirc$.[3]

Things are different, however, once we confine our attention to utilitarian models. In these models, since the underlying space of values is the set of real numbers representing utilities, the partial order governing the values is, of course, a linear order: for any histories h and h', we have either $Value(h) \leq Value(h')$ or $Value(h') \leq Value(h)$. And it is easy to see that the schema $C\bigcirc$ is valid in any general deontic model in which the underlying space of values is linearly ordered, a fact established formally as Validity A.1 (see Appendix). As long as our attention is restricted to the class of utilitarian stit models, then, the ought operator defined by our new evaluation rule is a normal modal operator, satisfying $C\bigcirc$ as well as $RE\bigcirc$, $N\bigcirc$, and $M\bigcirc$.

3.3   The Meinong/Chisholm analysis

3.3.1   The analysis

The two deontic logics sketched so far—the standard theory and the utilitarian theory—are both impersonal, offering accounts only of what ought to be. According to these theories, it makes perfect sense to say, for example, that it ought not to rain tomorrow. In the standard theory, this means,

---

[3]This kind of situation does not simply register a meaningless formal possibility—achievable only through the introduction of artificial values, such as our v_1 and v_2—but is actually realized in certain deontic logics, such as that of van Fraassen [1973], that do attempt to provide a realistic representation of the phenomena involved in normative conflict.

simply, that it does not rain tomorrow in any of the ideal histories; in the utilitarian theory, it means that there is some history in which it does not rain tomorrow, and that it fails to rain also in any history at least as valuable as that one. In neither case is there any implication that anyone ought to see to it that it does not rain tomorrow, or that anyone can do this.

Still, even though these logics offer only an impersonal account of what ought to be, there is some reason to hope that, against the background of the current theory of agency, this account might be sufficient to allow also for the definition of a personal notion of what an agent ought to do. Earlier, in Section 2.3, we saw that a useful notion of personal ability— what an agent is able to do—could be constructed through a combination of ordinary, impersonal possibility together with an agency operator; the resulting analysis identified what an agent is able to do with what it is possible that the agent does. And we might now hope to explicate the notion of what an agent ought to do in a similar way, by combining an agency operator with our impersonal account of what ought to be, leading to an analysis that identifies the notion of what an agent ought to do with the notion of what it ought to be that the agent does.

The idea of analyzing what an agent ought to do as what it ought to be that the agent does was advanced by a number of Austrian and German writers toward the beginning of the twentieth century, notably Meinong and Nicolai Hartmann. And the strategy has been explicitly endorsed by at least one contemporary: Roderick Chisholm suggests in [1964, p. 150] that "S ought to bring it about that p" can be defined as "It ought to be that S brings it about that p."[4] Chisholm develops this idea by appealing to his own treatment of what ought to be (a treatment based on the notion of defeasible requirement), and to a simple modal analysis of agency drawn from the writings of St. Anselm. In this book, we instead employ the *cstit* operator as a representation of agency and the utilitarian account of what ought to be, resulting in a proposal according to which the idea that an agent α ought to see to it that A is to be analyzed through a formula of the form

$$\bigcirc[\alpha \ cstit: A].$$

Since this analysis conforms to the overall strategy suggested by Meinong and Chisholm for analyzing what an agent ought to do, differing only in implementational details, we refer to the proposal as the *Meinong/Chisholm analysis.*[5]

---

[4]Chisholm's paper contains a reference to Hartmann's work; a recent discussion of Meinong's proposal can be found in García [1986].

[5]Although Meinong and Chisholm are perhaps the clearest proponents, the idea that what an agent ought to do can be represented through the combination of an impersonal deontic operator with a *seeing to it that* operator has been suggested or hinted at also by a number of modern logicians; see Anderson [1962], Kanger [1957], Kanger [1972], and Kanger and Kanger [1966] for the use of this construction in the analysis of Hohfeldian

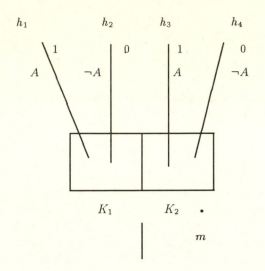

Figure 3.5: $\bigcirc A$ without $\bigcirc[\alpha\ cstit\colon A]$

This present version of the Meinong/Chisholm analysis leads to a picture in which what an agent α ought to do at a particular moment m is determined by the way in which the histories of various value filter through the $Choice_\alpha^m$ partition. Consider, for example, the situation depicted in Figure 3.5. Here, although $\bigcirc A$ is settled true at m, the formula $\bigcirc[\alpha\ cstit\colon A]$ is settled false. One way to see this is to note that $\Diamond[\alpha\ cstit\colon A]$ is itself settled false: the agent α does not even have the ability to see to it that A. Since, as we have seen, each instance of the principle $D\bigcirc$ is valid in the utilitarian setting, we have as a special case the validity of the formula

$$D_\alpha\bigcirc.\quad \bigcirc[\alpha\ cstit\colon A] \supset \Diamond[\alpha\ cstit\colon A],$$

which can be taken to express a personal version of the characteristic deontic idea that ought implies can: whenever an agent α ought to see to it that A, the agent must have also the ability to see to it that A. Because α is unable at m to see to it that A, we can thus conclude at once that $\bigcirc[\alpha\ cstit\colon A]$ must be settled false as well.

By contrast, Figure 3.6 depicts a situation in which $\bigcirc[\alpha\ cstit\colon A]$ is settled true: the statement $[\alpha\ cstit\colon A]$ holds along the history h_1, and also along each history through m whose utility is at least as great as that of h_1.

---

propositions, and Hilpinen [1974] more generally.

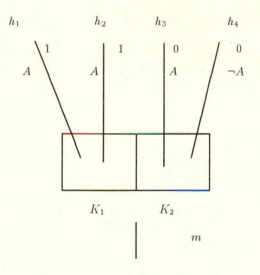

Figure 3.6: $\bigcirc[\alpha\ cstit\colon A]$

3.3.2 Some logical features

Although a statement of the form $\bigcirc[\alpha\ cstit\colon A]$ is, in fact, constructed grammatically through an application of the deontic operator $\bigcirc$ to the formula $[\alpha\ cstit\colon A]$, it is nevertheless possible to consider the amalgam $\bigcirc[\ldots\ cstit\colon\ldots]$ itself as a logically complex connective representing what an agent ought to do, and to investigate its properties. As we have already seen, this complex connective satisfies the principle $D_\alpha\bigcirc$, expressing a personal form of the idea that ought implies can. And it is easy to verify also that this complex connective is a normal modal operator, satisfying the principles

$RE_\alpha\bigcirc$. $A \equiv B\ \ /\ \ \bigcirc[\alpha\ cstit\colon A] \equiv \bigcirc[\alpha\ cstit\colon B]$,

$N_\alpha\bigcirc$. $\bigcirc[\alpha\ cstit\colon \top]$,

$M_\alpha\bigcirc$. $\bigcirc[\alpha\ cstit\colon A \wedge B] \supset (\bigcirc[\alpha\ cstit\colon A] \wedge \bigcirc[\alpha\ cstit\colon B])$,

$C_\alpha\bigcirc$. $\bigcirc[\alpha\ cstit\colon A] \wedge \bigcirc[\alpha\ cstit\colon B] \supset \bigcirc[\alpha\ cstit\colon A \wedge B]$.

We noted earlier that, since it validates both the theses $C\bigcirc$ and $D\bigcirc$, the class of standard deontic models—and so, the class of utilitarian models as well—must validate the principle $D^*\bigcirc$, which rules out conflicting impersonal oughts, the joint truth of statements of the form $\bigcirc A$ and $\bigcirc\neg A$. In exactly the same way, since it validates both $C_\alpha\bigcirc$ and $D_\alpha\bigcirc$, the utilitarian framework will also support the validity of

$D^*_\alpha\bigcirc$. $\neg(\bigcirc[\alpha\ cstit\colon A] \wedge \bigcirc[\alpha\ cstit\colon \neg A])$,

which rules out the possibility of conflicts among the personal oughts of a

single agent, a situation in which the agent ought to guarantee the truth
of incompatible propositions. For again, suppose that both $\bigcirc[\alpha$ $cstit$: $A]$
and $\bigcirc[\alpha$ $cstit$: $\neg A]$ were true. By $C_\alpha\bigcirc$, we would be led to the truth of
$\bigcirc[\alpha$ $cstit$: $A \wedge \neg A]$, and then by $D_\alpha\bigcirc$, to the truth of $\Diamond[\alpha$ $cstit$: $A \wedge \neg A]$,
which is impossible.

Where the two agents α and β are distinct, it is easier still to establish
the validity of

$$D^*_{\alpha,\beta}\bigcirc . \quad \neg(\bigcirc[\alpha \ cstit: A] \wedge \bigcirc[\beta \ cstit: \neg A]),$$

which rules out the possibility of conflicts among the personal oughts of
different agents. For again, suppose that both $\bigcirc[\alpha$ $cstit$: $A]$ and $\bigcirc[\beta$ $cstit$:
$\neg A]$ were true. By $D_\alpha\bigcirc$, then, we could conclude that both $\Diamond[\alpha$ $cstit$: $A]$
and $\Diamond[\beta$ $cstit$: $\neg A]$ must be true as well. But as long as the agents α and
β are distinct, it is impossible for these two statements to hold jointly: the
first will hold at a moment only if there is an action available to α that
guarantees the truth of A, regardless of what β does, while the second will
hold only if there is an action available to β guaranteeing the truth of $\neg A$,
regardless of what α does. And of course, if α is in a position to guarantee
the truth of A regardless of what β does, then β cannot also be in a position
to guarantee the truth of $\neg A$ regardless of what α does.

In addition to considering internal relations among formulas of the form
$\bigcirc[\alpha$ $cstit$: $A]$, it is also useful to consider the relations between these formulas and those of the form $\bigcirc A$—representing, according to the present
analysis, the relations between what an agent ought to do and what ought
to be the case. It is easy to verify, for example, that the statement

$$\bigcirc[\alpha \ cstit: A] \supset \bigcirc A$$

is valid in the present context: if α ought see to it that A, then it ought to be
that A. This can seem like a cheering result, since it means that the agent
is never obliged to waste his time bringing about a state of affairs that, in
itself, need not hold.

We noted earlier the failure of the converse implication,

$$\bigcirc A \supset \bigcirc[\alpha \ cstit: A];$$

even if it ought to be that A, the agent may not be required to bring about
such a state of affairs. But let us look more closely at the countermodel set
out in Figure 3.5 to illustrate the invalidity of this formula. As mentioned,
the example involves a situation in which the agent α does not even have the
ability to see to it that A—the statement $\Diamond[\alpha$ $cstit$: $A]$ fails—and so, since
obligation implies ability, we are able to conclude at once that $\bigcirc[\alpha$ $cstit$: $A]$
should fail as well. Now, it might appear that this kind of countermodel

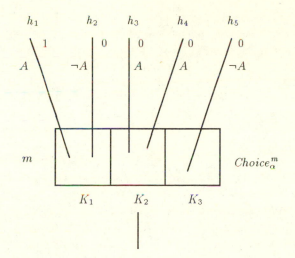

Figure 3.7: $\bigcirc A$ and $\Diamond[\alpha\ cstit:\ A]$ without $\bigcirc[\alpha\ cstit:\ A]$

depends essentially on the agent's lack of ability, so that a weaker statement of the form

$$\bigcirc A \wedge \Diamond[\alpha\ cstit:\ A] \supset \bigcirc[\alpha\ cstit:\ A]$$

might hold: if it ought to be that A, and the agent is actually able to see to it that A, then the agent ought to do so. It turns out, however, that even this weaker implication is invalid, as we can see from Figure 3.7. Here, both $\bigcirc A$ and $\Diamond[\alpha\ cstit:\ A]$ are settled true at m: it ought to be that A, and the agent α is able to see to it that A. But $\bigcirc[\alpha\ cstit:\ A]$ is settled false, and indeed we have $\bigcirc[\alpha\ cstit:\ \neg[\alpha\ cstit:\ A]]$: there is no ought compelling α to see to it that A, and in fact he ought to see to it that he does not do so.

Although formally transparent, the situation depicted in Figure 3.7 is complicated enough conceptually that it is worth fleshing out the abstract model with a story. So suppose that the agent, Karen, wishes to buy a horse, but that she has only \$10,000 to spend and the horse she wants is selling for \$15,000. We imagine that Karen offers \$10,000 for the horse at the moment m, choosing to perform the action K_1, and that the matter is then out of her hands; it is up to the owner of the horse to decide whether to accept the offer. The history h_1 represents a scenario in which the owner accepts Karen's offer, h_2 a scenario in which the offer is rejected, and A the statement that Karen will become less wealthy by the amount of \$10,000. As the diagram shows, the unique best history is h_1, in which the offer is accepted, and, as a consequence, Karen buys the horse and becomes less wealthy by \$10,000. Since Karen is less wealthy by \$10,000 in the unique best history, we must conclude that it ought to be that she is less wealthy by \$10,000. Of course, Karen also has the ability to see to it that she is less wealthy by \$10,000—perhaps by throwing the cash down a storm drain, represented here by the action K_2. But we would not wish to conclude that Karen ought to see to it that she is less wealthy by \$10,000.

As a further example of the relation between what ought to be and what, on the present analysis, an agent ought to do, we just mention the validity of $\bigcirc(\bigcirc[\alpha\ cstit: A] \supset [\alpha\ cstit: A])$, which says that it ought to be that an agent does what the agent ought to do. The verification of this statement does not depend on any features of our agency operator at all, but only on the observation that the statement is a particular instance of the general schema $\bigcirc(\bigcirc A \supset A)$, which is itself valid in our background deontic logic.

Finally, it should be apparent that the strategy underlying the Meinong/Chisholm analysis of what an individual agent ought to do can be applied also to yield an account of what a group of agents ought to do. By combining our utilitarian theory of what ought to be with the treatment of group agency from Section 2.4, we arrive at the formula $\bigcirc[\Gamma\ cstit: A]$ as a representation of the idea that the group of agents Γ ought to see to it that A. Results analogous to those for statements of the form $\bigcirc[\alpha\ cstit: A]$ can be established also for statements of the form $\bigcirc[\Gamma\ cstit: A]$.

3.4   Evaluating the analysis

3.4.1   Agency in the complement

The general idea underlying the Meinong/Chisholm analysis—the idea that what an agent ought to do can be identified with what it ought to be that the agent does—has been subject to logical objections by Geach in [1982], and by Gilbert Harman in an appendix to [1986]. The arguments by Geach and Harman are similar: both turn on the claim that the analysis leads to judgments about what agents ought to do that are inappropriately insensitive to considerations concerning agency in the complement of the ought. As we see in the present section, however, this kind of criticism does not apply to our current version of the Meinong/Chisholm analysis, developed within a framework that allows for an explicit treatment of agency.

Geach's argument, which he traces to St. Anselm, is motivated by the following chain of reasoning, which relies crucially on the Meinong/Chisholm analysis. Suppose, for example, that Fred ought to dance with Ginger, that this is something Fred ought to do. According to the Meinong/Chisholm analysis, this is taken to mean that it ought to be that Fred dances with Ginger. Now as it happens, the relation of dancing with is symmetric. In any possible world in which Fred dances with Ginger, it must be the case also that Ginger dances with Fred, and vice versa; and so it seems that the two statements "Fred dances with Ginger" and "Ginger dances with Fred" are necessarily equivalent. It follows from the general deontic validity

RE$\bigcirc$ that if two statements A and B are necessarily equivalent, then the statement $\bigcirc A$ is likewise equivalent to $\bigcirc B$. We can thus conclude, since it ought to be that Fred dances with Ginger, that it ought to be also that Ginger dances with Fred; and then by the Meinong/Chisholm analysis again, this would force us to the conclusion that Ginger ought to dance with Fred.

Of course, this chain of reasoning is incorrect; the conclusion does not follow from the premise. It could easily happen that, because of the customs governing some social occasion, Fred ought to dance with Ginger—this is something that Fred ought to do—even though there is no reason why Ginger ought to dance with Fred. Since the chain of reasoning is incorrect, it must be broken at some point; and Geach locates the error in its appeal to the Meinong/Chisholm analysis. This analysis must be rejected, he suggests, because the argument is otherwise adequate, so that if we were to adopt the Meinong/Chisholm analysis, we would have to accept the entire chain of reasoning.[6]

Within the present framework, however, it is possible to break this incorrect chain of reasoning without questioning the Meinong/Chisholm analysis, by focusing instead on considerations of agency. Suppose A represents the statement that Fred and Ginger dance together, and that α and β represent the agents Fred and Ginger, respectively. The statement that Fred ought to dance with Ginger would then be represented, according·to the Meinong/Chisholm analysis, through the formula $\bigcirc[\alpha \; cstit: A]$, in which Fred's agency is explicit: it ought to be that Fred sees to it that he and Ginger dance together. Now it is easy to see that, within the setting of stit semantics, the formulas $[\alpha \; cstit: A]$ and $[\beta \; cstit: A]$—that Fred sees to it that he and Ginger dance, and that Ginger sees to it that she and Fred dance—are not equivalent. And so even given the validity of the principle *RE*$\bigcirc$, there is no way to argue from the premise $\bigcirc[\alpha \; cstit: A]$ to the conclusion $\bigcirc[\beta \; cstit: A]$, representing the idea that it ought to be that Ginger sees to it that she and Fred dance, or according to the Meinong/Chisholm analysis, that Ginger ought to dance with Fred.

The situation can be illustrated as in Figure 3.8. Here, the choices available to α at m are represented by the vertical partition of H_m, and the choices open to β by the horizontal partition; the sentence letter A, true everywhere but m/h_3, represents the statement that the two agents will dance together; and the history h_2 is assigned a utility of 1, while all other histories receive a utility of 0. Evidently, the statement $\bigcirc[\alpha \; cstit: A]$—representing

---

[6]This dancing example is not Geach's own. Geach himself develops the objection by arguing that the statement "Tom ought to be beaten up by John" might be true even though "John ought to beat up Tom" is false, and even though "Tom is beaten up by John" seems to be necessarily equivalent to "John beats up Tom." I change the example here not just for the sake of delicacy, but also because I agree with García [1986] that Geach's own example appeals to considerations concerning the logic of just desert that are irrelevant to the matter at hand.

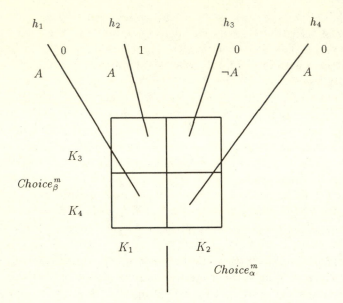

Figure 3.8: $\bigcirc[\alpha\ cstit\colon A]$ without $\bigcirc[\beta\ cstit\colon A]$

the idea that α ought to see to it that the two agents dance together—is settled true at m; for $[\alpha\ cstit\colon A]$ is true along the history h_2, and also, trivially, along each history whose value is at least as great as that of h_2. Of course, the agent β also has the ability to see to it that the two agents dance together; $\Diamond[\beta\ cstit\colon A]$ is settled true at m, since $[\beta\ cstit\colon A]$ is true in the history h_4. But $\bigcirc[\beta\ cstit\colon A]$ is settled false: for each history along which $[\beta\ cstit\colon A]$ holds, there is another history at least as great in value along which $[\beta\ cstit\colon A]$ fails. Even though A represents a proposition that ought to be the case, and that α ought to see to, and that β has the ability to see to, it is not something that β ought to see to.

We turn next to Harman's objection to the Meinong/Chisholm analysis, which is based on a distinction, pointed out originally by I. L. Humberstone [1971], between two kinds of ought statements—which he describes as "situational" and "agent-implicating" oughts.

To illustrate the distinction, let us first imagine a case in which Albert has competed in a gymnastics event. Suppose Albert's performance is clearly superior, but that the judge is biased, and it is likely that he will award the medal to someone else. If one then said, "Albert ought to win the medal," this is the kind of statement that Humberstone would classify as a situational ought. It reflects a judgment about the situation, not about Albert, and can legitimately be paraphrased as "It ought to be that Albert wins the medal." There is no implication that Albert will be at fault if he fails to win the medal, or that winning the medal is now within his power. By contrast, suppose Albert has not kept up with his training schedule. One might then say, "Albert ought to practice harder," and this would be the kind of ought statement that Humberstone classifies as agent-implicating. It implies that Albert is able to practice harder, and places the blame on him if he fails to do so.

Now Harman's objection to the Meinong/Chisholm suggestion for analyzing personal oughts in terms of impersonal oughts is simply that it obscures the distinction between the two kinds of ought statements that Humberstone has identified. According to the suggestion, the statement "Albert ought to practice harder" is itself to be analyzed as "It ought to be that Albert practices harder." This statement is thus similar in form to "It ought to be that Albert wins the medal," and so it is hard to see why one of these ought statements should be classified as agent-implicating and the other as situational.

Again, however, the objection can by met without abandoning the Meinong/Chisholm analysis, by focusing, not on the relation between the ought operator and its complement, but instead on the treatment of agency within its complement. In those ought statements that Humberstone regards as agent-implicating, the complement should be represented as a stit sentence. For example, the statement that Albert ought to practice harder should be represented through the formula $\bigcirc[\alpha\ cstit: A]$, where α is Albert, and A is the statement that he practices harder. As we have seen, this implies $\Diamond[\alpha\ cstit: A]$, that Albert is able to practice harder. On the other hand, in a situational ought, the complement should not be represented as a stit sentence. The idea that Albert ought to win the medal, for example, might be represented as $\bigcirc B$, where B is the statement simply that he wins the medal, that it is awarded to him, and not the statement that he sees to it that he wins the medal. Of course, $\bigcirc B$ alone does not imply $\Diamond[\alpha\ cstit: B]$, that Albert is able to see to it that he wins the medal.

3.4.2 The gambling problem

The particular version of the Meinong/Chisholm analysis set out here seems to be especially robust. As we have seen, it leads to a standard logical account of what an agent ought to do, and supports some plausible relations between what an agent ought to do and what ought to be the case. Moreover, because it is based upon an explicit treatment of agency, the present version of the Meinong/Chisholm analysis is able to withstand at least some of the objections—those having to do with agency in the complement—that were advanced by Geach and Harman against the general strategy of identifying what an agent ought to do with what it ought to be that the agent does. Is it reasonable to think, then, that this analysis might actually be correct? Could the formula $\bigcirc[\alpha\ cstit: A]$ really be taken as an accurate representation of the notion that an agent α ought to see to it that A?

Well, there are some very general reasons to doubt this approach. Out of the entire normative realm, the only factor that is represented within the present semantic framework is the value, or utility, assigned to histories. The underlying framework is thus purely utilitarian, but many of us are not pure utilitarians at heart: our conception of what we ought to do is often influenced, not only by the utility of the outcomes that might result from our actions, but also by considerations involving a number of additional normative concepts, such as rights or personal integrity. If Smith makes a promise to Jones, for example, Jones has a right, a claim against Smith, that Smith should keep the promise, even if the outcome that would result from Smith's keeping the promise carries less utility than the outcome that would result if the promise were broken. Many people feel that this claim of Jones's must be given some weight in determining what Smith ought to do, and that in some cases it should be allowed to override considerations based on utility alone. Or suppose it could be shown that things would go better—the overall utility would be greater—if Smith were to abandon all of his current interests and devote himself instead entirely to charitable work. Still, even if this course of action were guaranteed to result in the greatest utility, many people would be reluctant to conclude from this simply that Smith ought to abandon all of his current interests.

For these very general reasons, then, it seems unlikely that a formula of the form $\bigcirc[\alpha \ cstit: A]$ could be taken as an accurate representation of our intuitive idea that an agent α ought to see to it that A. The semantic framework presented here, within which this formula is given its meaning, is entirely utilitarian; but our intuitive judgment that α ought to see to it that A often seems to be sensitive also to nonutilitarian considerations.

This kind of objection to the idea of analyzing what an agent ought to do through a formula of the form $\bigcirc[\alpha \ cstit: A]$ is, however, although persuasive, perhaps too broad to be illuminating: the objection is directed not so much against the analysis itself as against the utilitarian framework within which the analysis is developed. Let us, therefore, sharpen the issue. Rather than attempting to model our ordinary, common sense notion of what an agent ought to do, governed as it is by a variety of normative considerations, we will instead restrict our attention only to those oughts generated by considerations of utility. Our goal, then, is to model only a more limited, utilitarian notion of what an agent ought to do, a notion of what the agent ought to do on the basis of utilitarian considerations alone.

Once our attention is explicitly restricted in this way, the general limitations of the underlying utilitarian framework can be set aside, and we can concentrate on the accuracy of our analysis, within this framework, of the utilitarian notion of what an agent ought to do. Even though the formula $\bigcirc[\alpha \ cstit: A]$ may be, for very general reasons, inadequate as an analysis of our intuitive idea that an agent α ought to see to it that A, we are now in a position to ask a sharper, more interesting question: can this formula be taken as an accurate analysis at least of the utilitarian notion that α ought to see to it that A?

Some writers suggest as much. Although, as we have seen, Harman criticizes the Meinong/Chisholm analysis as a general account of what an agent ought to do, he does seem to allow that this analysis might provide a correct account at least of the more limited, utilitarian notion; at one point he accuses utilitarianism of "simply identifying or confusing what a person ought morally to do with what it ought to be that he does"[1983, p. 318].[7] And it was it was likewise suggested by Horty and Belnap that an analysis identifying the notion of what an agent ought to do with what it ought to be that the agent does, although not generally applicable, "does seem to capture the notion of personal obligation at work in certain ethical theories— particularly, pure consequentialist theories, such as act utilitarianism" [1995, p. 627].

It now seems plain, however, that the particular version of the Meinong/ Chisholm analysis under consideration here must be rejected, even in a purely utilitarian setting: the formula $\bigcirc[\alpha \ cstit: A]$ cannot be taken as an adequate representation even of the purely utilitarian notion that α ought to see to it that A. The proposed analysis is vulnerable to a very simple objection, described here as the *gambling problem*.

Imagine that an agent α is faced with two options at the moment m: to gamble the sum of five dollars, or to refrain from gambling. If α gambles, we suppose that there is a history in which he wins ten dollars, and another in which he loses his stake; but of course, α cannot determine whether he wins or loses. If α does not gamble, we suppose that he preserves his original stake of five dollars no matter how things turn out. Finally, we suppose that the utility associated with each history at m is entirely determined by the sum of money that α possesses in that history. The situation can thus be depicted as in Figure 3.9. Here, K_1 represents the option of engaging in the gamble, and K_2 the option of refraining; the statement letter A represents the proposition that α gambles, and h_1 is the history along which α gambles and wins.

In this situation, as it turns out, the formula $\bigcirc[\alpha \ cstit: A]$ is settled true at the moment m—for $[\alpha \ cstit: A]$ is true along the history h_1, and also, trivially, along each history at least a valuable as h_1. The Meinong/Chisholm

---

[7]Elsewhere, Harman writes that utilitarianism "conflates" the idea that "What one ought to do is bring about X" with the idea that "What ought to be the case is that one bring about X" [1986, p. 132]. What Harman seems to mean in these passages from [1983] and [1986] is that utilitarianism actually does identify the notion of what an agent ought to do with what it ought to be that the agent does, but that, from a broader perspective, involving additional normative considerations, this simple utilitarian identification can be seen as incorrect—confused or conflated.

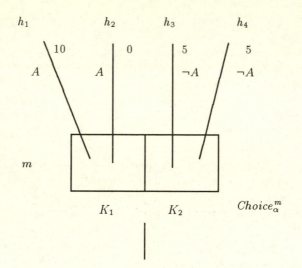

Figure 3.9: $\bigcirc[\alpha\ cstit\colon A]$ settled true

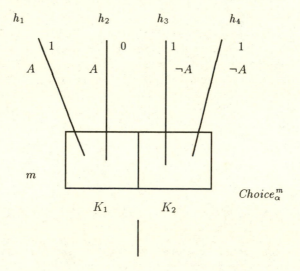

Figure 3.10: $\bigcirc[\alpha\ cstit\colon \neg A]$ settled false

analysis of what an agent ought to do thus tells us unambiguously that, in this situation, the agent ought to gamble: the most valuable history, with a utility of 10, is that in which he gambles and wins, and it is a necessary condition for achieving this outcome that he should gamble. But this is a strange conclusion; for by gambling, the agent risks achieving an outcome with a utility of 0, while he is able to guarantee a utility of 5 by refraining from the gamble. From an intuitive point of view, it appears to be impossible to say in this case whether or not the agent ought to gamble, at least without knowing the odds of winning; and we should be suspicious of any theory that makes a definite recommendation one way or the other.

The problem presented by this situation seems to reflect a real difficulty with the strategy of identifying even a purely utilitarian notion of what an agent ought to do with the notion of what it ought to be that the agent does—at least on the basis of any theory conforming to the standard deontic idea that whatever holds in all the best outcomes is what ought to be. Any such theory would have to yield the result that, in this situation, it ought to be that the agent gambles; after all, gambling is a necessary condition for achieving the unique best outcome, the outcome with the greatest utility. But it does not seem to follow from this that gambling is something the agent ought to do, since by doing so the agent risks attaining an outcome of less utility than he could otherwise guarantee.

It might appear that this kind of problem could arise only in a general utilitarian setting, with at least three different values, since it seems to rely upon the possibility that one choice might lead to outcomes both higher and lower in value than the intermediate outcome resulting from another choice. Perhaps, then, the kind of example necessary to establish an intuitive distinction between the notion of what an agent ought to do and the notion of what it ought to be that the agent does can be constructed only after we have moved from the standard deontic setting to the utilitarian setting—and perhaps the two ideas can safely be identified in the standard deontic setting. Not so. A similar example can be found in a standard deontic setting, with outcomes classified only as ideal or nonideal through the assignment of only two values, 1 and 0.

Consider the situation depicted in Figure 3.10, in which α again has two choices, and in which the histories carry the values indicated. Again, this situation can be thought of as one in which the agent is faced with the choice between gambling or refraining. Again, K_1 represents the option of engaging in the gamble, K_2 the option of refraining, and A represents the proposition that α gambles. As the assignment of values to histories shows, however, the gamble presented to the agent in this case is peculiar. If the agent accepts the gamble, we suppose that he attains an ideal outcome if he wins, as in the history h_1, and a nonideal outcome if he loses, as in h_2. What makes the situation peculiar, however, is that the agent can guarantee an ideal outcome (either h_3 or h_4) simply by declining the gamble.

It should be obvious that the gamble in this situation is not wise: why should the agent accept the risk of a nonideal outcome simply for the chance of achieving an outcome no greater in value than one that he could guarantee by not gambling at all? Since the gamble is not wise, a correct account of what the agent ought to do should tell us that the agent ought not to gamble. But this is not the result generated by the Meinong/Chisholm analysis. Here, the statement $\bigcirc[\alpha \; cstit: \neg A]$ is settled false at m, since for each history in which the agent refrains from gambling, there is a history of equal value in which he gambles.

Although it carries some initial plausibility, then, the present version of the Meinong/Chisholm analysis yields incorrect results in these two gambling examples, and must be rejected as a representation even of the purely utilitarian notion of what an agent ought to do.

Chapter 4

Ought to do

4.1 Dominance

One way of reacting to the two gambling situations depicted in Figures 3.9 and 3.10 is to ask for additional information—in particular, probabilistic information concerning the various outcomes that might result from the available actions. Suppose, for example, that, for each action open to an agent at a moment, we were provided with a probability distribution over the histories belonging to that action, where the probability assigned to a history represents its chance of occurring should the agent choose to perform the action. We could then define the expected value of an action in the usual way, as the sum of the values of the various histories belonging to that action, with each value weighted by the probability assigned to its associated history. This introduction of expected value would provide us with a preference ordering, not only of the histories through a moment, but of the actions themselves that are available to an agent at that moment. And once such a preference ordering on actions is defined, it is then natural to appeal to this ordering in characterizing an agent's oughts: we could suppose, very roughly, that the agent ought to see to it that some proposition holds whenever doing so is a necessary condition for performing any action whose expected value is among the greatest available.

The general approach just sketched—specifying what an agent ought to do by reference to a preference ordering on actions—does seem like a promising way to proceed. The particular ordering that results from a comparison of expected value relies, however, on a kind of probabilistic information concerning outcomes of actions that is often either unavailable or meaningless; and this is true especially in situations in which the outcome resulting from an agent's action may depend, not simply on a roll of the dice, but on the independent choice of another free agent. In the literature on decision theory, a situation in which the actions available to an agent might lead to their various possible outcomes with known probability is described as a case of *risk*, while a situation in which the probability with which the available actions might lead to their various possible outcomes is either unknown or meaningless is described as a case of *uncertainty*.[1] Our concern in this book is with uncertainty, rather than risk, and so a notion of expected value is not available. In order to carry out an approach along the lines sketched above, then, it is first necessary to define a preference ordering over the actions available to the agent in a way that does not rely on probabilistic information regarding their possible outcomes.

4.1.1   Ordering the propositions

We begin with the preliminary task of introducing preference orderings on propositions, arbitrary sets of histories through a moment.

Suppose, then, that X and Y are propositions at m, subsets of the set H_m of histories through m, and that each history belonging to Y is at least as valuable as each history belonging to X. In that case, the proposition Y can itself be described as at least weakly preferred to the proposition X, since, in any history at which Y is realized, we are sure to do at least as well as we would in a history at which X is realized. And if we suppose, further, that the proposition X is not weakly preferred to Y, the proposition Y can then be described as strongly preferred to X. These ideas are captured in the following definition.

Definition 4.1 (Preferences over propositions; $\leq, <$) Let X and Y be propositions at some moment from a utilitarian stit frame. Then $X \leq Y$ (Y is *weakly preferred* to X) if and only if $Value(h) \leq Value(h')$ for each $h \in X$ and each $h' \in Y$; and $X < Y$ (Y is *strongly preferred* to X) if and only if $X \leq Y$ and it is not the case that $Y \leq X$.

And it is easy to arrive at a useful reformulation of the strong preference relation, according to which the proposition Y is strongly preferred to the proposition X just in case we are sure to do at least as well if Y were realized as we would if X were realized, and we might do better.

Proposition 4.2 Let X and Y be propositions at some moment from a utilitarian stit frame. Then $X < Y$ if and only if (1) $Value(h) \leq Value(h')$

---

[1] A discussion of this terminology can be found, for example, in Sections 2.1 and 13.1 of Luce and Raiffa [1957]. Of course, the legitimacy of the distinction between uncertainty and risk is itself an issue: following Ramsey [1931] and Savage [1954], many writers in the Bayesian tradition assume that an agent's assessment of the possible outcomes in a given situation can always be represented through a probability measure, so that uncertainty always reduces to risk. However, there is an important tradition of resistance to the assimilation of uncertainty and risk in a single numerical measure. A classic paper in this tradition is Ellsberg [1961]; for more recent work on decision theory in situations that mix elements of risk and uncertainty, see the papers contained in Parts II and IV of Gärdenfors and Sahlin [1988].

for each $h \in X$ and each $h' \in Y$, and (2) *Value*$(h) < $ *Value*(h') for some $h \in X$ and some $h' \in Y$.

The weak and strong preference ordering defined over propositions can be shown to satisfy a number of desirable properties, recorded here for future reference.

Proposition 4.3 Let X and Y be propositions at some moment from a utilitarian stit frame. Then:

1. If $X < Y$, then $X \leq Y$.

2. If $X \leq Y$ and $Y \leq Z$, then $X \leq Z$.

3. If $X \leq Y$ and $Y < Z$, then $X < Z$.

4. If $X < Y$ and $Y \leq Z$, then $X < Z$.

5. If $X < Y$ and $Y < Z$, then $X < Z$.

6. If $X < Y$, then it is not the case that $Y < X$.

7. It is not the case that $X < X$.

The first of these clauses tells us simply that strong preference is at least as strong as weak preference. The second tells us that weak preference is transitive; the third and fourth, that transitivities in which one of the preference relations is strong preserve strength; and the fifth, that strong preference is itself transitive. The sixth and seventh clauses record the fact that the relation of strong preference among propositions is asymmetric and irreflexive. It is important to note that even the weak preference relation is not linear: as long as each of the propositions X and Y contains a history more valuable than some history belonging to the other, we will have neither $X \leq Y$ nor $Y \leq X$.

4.1.2 A sure-thing argument

In the present semantic framework, the actions available to an agent at a moment are reified as sets of histories through that moment. Each action is therefore a proposition, and so it is tempting to imagine that the actions might simply inherit their preference orderings from those defined on propositions more generally. According to this idea, where K and K' are actions available to some agent at a given moment, we would then say, for example, that K' is a better action than K for the agent to perform at that moment just in case $K < K'$.

This idea is plausible, and there are a number of cases in which it yields the correct results, including the two gambling situations set out earlier: in

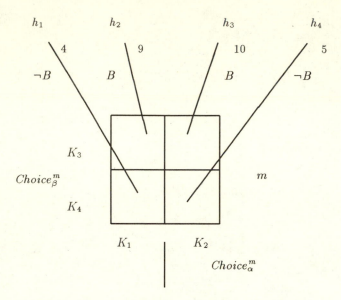

Figure 4.1: The first coin example

Figure 3.10, where the action K_2 is clearly preferable to K_1, we do have $K_1 < K_2$; and in Figure 3.9, where neither action seems to be intuitively preferable to the other, we have neither $K_1 < K_2$ nor $K_2 < K_1$. However, the suggestion of simply identifying the preference orderings over an agent's actions with the orderings already defined for propositions seems to fail in more complicated cases.

To see this, consider Figure 4.1, depicting a situation of simultaneous choice by two agents, and interpreted as follows. We suppose that the agent α is holding a nickel in his hand, and that at the moment m, he is faced with a choice between two actions: placing this nickel on a table before him either heads up, performing the action K_1, or tails up, performing the action K_2. At the same moment, the agent β must likewise choose between placing a dime onto the table either heads up or tails up, performing either the action K_3 or the action K_4. If α places the nickel on the table heads up, then the resulting utility is 9 if β places the dime heads up and 4 if β places the dime tails up; but if α places the nickel on the table tails up, the resulting utility is 10 if β places the dime heads up and 5 if β places the dime tails up. (The statement B—true at m/h_2 and m/h_3, and so expressing the proposition that the dime is placed heads up—does not figure into our present discussion, but is included for later reference.)

In this situation, it should be clear that neither of the two actions open to the agent α is even weakly preferred to the other in the sense of the propositional ordering, since each contains an outcome more valuable than some outcome belonging to the other: we do not have $K_1 \leq K_2$, since the history h_2 belonging to K_1 is more valuable than the history h_4 belonging to K_2, and we do not have $K_2 \leq K_1$, since the history h_3 belonging to K_2 is more valuable than either history belonging to K_1. Nevertheless, in spite of the fact that the actions K_1 and K_2 are incomparable according to the propositional ordering, there seems to be a persuasive argument in favor of the conclusion that K_2 is a better action than K_1 for α to perform. In the situation depicted, the agent β must place the dime on the table either heads up or tails up, performing either the action K_3 or the action K_4. Now suppose, first, that β places the dime heads up, performing the action K_3. In that case, it is clearly better for α to place the nickel on the table tails up, performing K_2 rather than K_1, since the unique history h_3 belonging to $K_2 \cap K_3$ is more valuable than the unique history h_2 belonging to $K_1 \cap K_3$. Next, suppose that β places the dime tails up, performing the action K_4. Then it is again better for α to place the nickel on the table tails up, again performing K_2 rather than K_1, since the unique history h_4 belonging to $K_2 \cap K_4$ is more valuable than the unique history h_1 belonging to $K_1 \cap K_4$. In each of these two cases, then, no matter whether β performs the action K_3 or K_4, it is better for α to perform K_2 rather than K_1; and since these two cases exhaust the possibilities, a pattern of reasoning sometimes described as the *sure-thing principle* suggests that K_2 is simply a better action than K_1 for α to perform.[2]

This application of sure-thing reasoning to the situation at hand seems sufficiently compelling to undermine the idea that the appropriate preference ordering on the actions available to an agent might be identified with the propositional ordering defined earlier: here, although K_2 is not even weakly preferable to K_1 in the sense of the propositional ordering, it seems clear that K_2 is a better action than K_1 for α to perform. The matter of arriving at a general formulation of the sure-thing principle guiding our analysis of this particular case, however, requires some care.

The key to applying sure-thing reasoning in a given situation lies in identifying an appropriate partition of the possible outcomes into a set of states (sometimes called "states of nature" or "conditioning events"), against the background of which the actions available to an agent can then be evaluated through a state-by-state comparison of their results. In the case of Figure 4.1, for example, our evaluation of the actions K_1 and K_2 available to α relied on a partitioning of the possible outcomes into those falling within

---

[2]This pattern of reasoning is first explicitly characterized as the "sure-thing principle" in Savage [1954], but the principle appears already in some of Savage's earlier work, such as [1951, p. 58], where he writes concerning situations of uncertainty that "there is one unquestionably appropriate criterion for preferring some act to some others: If for every possible state, the expected income of one act is never less and is in some cases greater than the corresponding income of another, then the former act is preferable to the latter."

K_3 and those falling within K_4, the two actions available to β. Taking K_3 and K_4 as our background states, we were then able to recognize K_2 as a better action than K_1 for α to perform because a state-by-state comparison revealed K_2 as leading to better results than K_1 in each case.

Once an appropriate partition of outcomes into states has been provided, it is comparatively straightforward to evaluate the various actions available to an agent through a state-by-state comparison of their results; but of course, not every partition forms an appropriate background for sure-thing reasoning. Suppose, for example, that a student considering whether to study for an exam were to partition the set of possible outcomes into those in which he passes the exam and those in which he fails, taking these as his set of background states. The student might then conclude, through a kind of parody of sure-thing reasoning, that he is better off not studying, because a state-by-state comparison reveals this as the better choice in each case. Given that he passes the exam, the student might reason, he is better off not studying because the outcomes in which he passes without studying are uniformly preferable to those in which he passes only after laborious study; but he is also better off not studying given that he fails the exam, because the outcomes in which he fails without the bother of studying are uniformly preferable to those in which he studies but fails anyway.

This argument is fallacious, of course, for in this situation, the student's decision whether or not to study can reasonably be taken to influence whether or not he passes the exam, but it is generally thought that sure-thing reasoning must be restricted to cases in which the background states against which actions are evaluated are, in some sense, independent of those actions. The literature is divided, however, over the precise sense in which these background states are required to be independent of an agent's actions for the purpose of sure-thing reasoning; two different strategies have been suggested for explicating this idea. The first of these strategies, as developed, for example, by Richard Jeffrey [1965], identifies the kind of independence relevant to sure-thing reasoning with ordinary probabilistic independence: the background states are required to be independent of the agent's actions in the sense that the conditional probability that a state holds should not vary depending on the action chosen by the agent. The second strategy, first described in detail by Allan Gibbard and William Harper [1978], identifies the kind of independence relevant to sure-thing reasoning, not with probabilistic independence, but instead with causal independence: the background states are required to be independent of the agent's actions in the sense that the action selected by the agent should not exert any causal influence over the occurrence of any given state. (Both these forms of the independence requirement succeed in blocking the student's fallacy, of course, since his decision whether or not to study would normally be thought both to affect the conditional probability of his passing the exam and to have some causal impact on his performance.)

The notion of independence advanced in this book is based on the second of these two strategies, the causal strategy, not only because the kind of probabilistic information necessary for carrying out the first strategy is unavailable, but also because—though this issue is not completely resolved—there are good reasons for believing that the causal strategy is correct.[3] Unfortunately, while it is not difficult to implement the probabilistic strategy using the tools of ordinary probability calculus, the most suitable machinery for encoding the information necessary to carry out the causal strategy has not yet been settled upon. In their seminal presentation of the topic, Gibbard and Harper rely on the resources of a conditional logic to express the necessary causal dependencies; but Brian Skyrms [1980] and David Lewis [1981] prefer to develop the theory against the background of an agent's maximally specific hypotheses concerning causal dependence, which need not be conveniently expressible in a conditional language. More recently, it was suggested in Thomason and Horty [1996] that the models underlying a decision problem in a branching temporal framework might be supplemented with explicit causal relations, allowing the notion of causal independence to be defined through the absence of these relations. The present study is based on a similar idea, but reversed: here, the notion of causal independence itself, rather than causal connection, is taken as fundamental.

This idea of taking causally independent states as fundamental could be implemented, of course, in a purely stipulative way. Our stit models could be supplemented with a primitive function $State$ mapping each agent α and moment m into a partition $State_\alpha^m$ of H_m, the collection of possible outcomes, with the various sets belonging to $State_\alpha^m$ taken to represent the narrowest, or most specific, propositions causally independent of the actions available to α; and the states confronting α at m could then be identified with these propositions. Apart from the condition that $State_\alpha^m$ partition the collection H_m, the only technical condition necessary for carrying out this approach is the requirement that the intersection of each state with each action available to the agent should be nonempty—but of course, the state partition could also be subject to whatever other constraints might seem

---

[3] In most realistic cases, of course, causal and conditional independence go hand in hand; but in examples such as Newcomb's problem, where the states confronting the agent are causally, though not probabilistically, independent of the available actions, many people feel that sure-thing reasoning is nevertheless justified. Gibbard and Harper present a kind of converse to Newcomb's problem in their Reoboam example [1978, Section 7], where the agent is faced with a set of states that are probabilistically, though not causally, independent of his actions, and where it now seems that sure-thing reasoning is incorrect—so that in both cases, Newcomb and Reoboam, the acceptability of sure-thing reasoning seems to stand or fall with causal independence. It is not entirely clear, however, that the intuitions suggested by these examples actually conflict with the probabilistic strategy; an attempt at reconciliation, as well as references to the extensive literature on Newcomb's problem, can be found in Eells [1982].

appropriate for modeling the notion of causal independence.

It may actually prove best, in the long run, to proceed through this kind of stipulative approach, simply postulating a causally independent state partition confronting each agent at each moment; but this is not the approach adopted here. In order to have a more concrete proposal to work with, we will rely instead on a preliminary analysis of the notion of causal independence. In the motivating example of Figure 4.1, it seemed reasonable to view the actions available to the agent β at the moment m as causally independent of the actions simultaneously available to α. And our preliminary analysis results simply from generalizing the idea underlying this example to the case of multiple agents: we will identify the states confronting an agent at any given moment with the possible patterns of action that might be performed at that moment by all other agents. The intuition guiding this analysis can be summarized as follows: a proposition is viewed as causally independent of the actions available to some agent whenever its truth or falsity is guaranteed by a source of causality other than that agent. Since the only sources of causality represented in the present framework are the actions of the various agents, we therefore take a proposition to be independent of the actions available to a particular agent whenever its truth or falsity is guaranteed by some pattern of action available to all the others; and we takes these patterns of action themselves—the narrowest causally independent propositions—as the states confronting the agent in question.

Although this preliminary analysis of the states confronting an agent is useful in the present setting, it is nevertheless only preliminary, and calls for further discussion. However, in order to avoid being sidetracked at this point into an extensive consideration of causal independence, we proceed as follows. First, in the remainder of the present section, we define a preference ordering over the actions available to an agent that relies on the preliminary analysis of causal independence sketched here; and then in the following two sections, we carry out our central project of defining what an agent ought to do by reference to this preference ordering over actions. With that project complete, we return in the final section of the present chapter to consider some of the issues involved in refining and generalizing this preliminary analysis of causal independence, and also to draw some comparisons between the present treatment and the conditional approach taken by Gibbard and Harper.

4.1.3   Ordering the actions

To begin with, then, it is necessary to arrive at a precise formulation of our preliminary analysis of the states confronting an agent at a moment as the patterns of action simultaneously available to all other agents. Let us first recall from Section 2.4 the definition of $Choice_F^m$ as the set of patterns of action available at a moment m to the agents belonging to an arbitrary group Γ. Of course, the group including all agents other than some particular individual α is $Agent - \{\alpha\}$, and so the set of patterns of action available at the moment m to the group of agents other than α is simply $Choice^m_{Agent-\{\alpha\}}$. Our preliminary analysis is therefore captured by treating the function $State$—which maps each agent α and moment m into the set $State^m_\alpha$ of states facing α at m—not as a fresh primitive, but instead as a defined concept, as follows.

Definition 4.4 ($State^m_\alpha$) Where α is an agent and m a moment from a stit frame,

$$State^m_\alpha = Choice^m_{Agent-\{\alpha\}}.$$

Since we know that, for any group Γ, the set $Choice^m_\Gamma$ partitions the collection H_m of possible outcomes, it follows that $State^m_\alpha$ is likewise a partitioning. And as a special case of our earlier definition of $Choice^m_\Gamma(h)$ as the particular action from $Choice^m_\Gamma$ containing the history h, we now let $State^m_\alpha(h)$ stand for the particular state from $State^m_\alpha$ that is realized at h.

These various definitions can be illustrated by application to Figure 4.1. For simplicity, we suppose that there are only two agents involved: $Agent = \{\alpha, \beta\}$. Then, of course, $Agent - \{\alpha\} = \{\beta\}$, so that

$$
\begin{aligned}
State^m_\alpha &= Choice^m_{Agent-\{\alpha\}} \\
&= Choice^m_\beta \\
&= \{K_3, K_4\}.
\end{aligned}
$$

As desired, the states confronting the agent α at the moment m are the actions simultaneously available to β, the only other agent. It is evident that the states belonging to $State^m_\alpha$ partition the histories through m, and since K_3 is the unique member of $State^m_\alpha$ containing h_2, for example, we have $State^m_\alpha(h_2) = K_3$.

In addition to situations presenting an agent with the kind of substantial states depicted in Figure 4.1, two special cases should be mentioned. First, we often focus on single-agent stit frames, where α, say, is the only member of $Agent$. And second, even if agents other than α are present, it may be that all of these other individuals face only vacuous choices at some moment m—that is, we may have $Choice^m_\beta = \{H_m\}$ for every other agent β. In each of these two cases it is easy to see that $State^m_\alpha = \{H_m\}$, and this is as it should be: since the states confronting any agent at a moment are defined as the patterns of action available to other agents, a situation in which there are no other agents, or in which they face only vacuous choices, should confront the agent only with a vacuous partitioning of outcomes into states.

Having characterized the states facing an agent at a given moment, we now turn to the task of defining an ordering on the actions available to the agent through a state-by-state comparison of their results; and as an initial step, we must first specify a standard for comparing the possible results of two actions against the background of a particular state. The example depicted in Figure 4.1 is deceptively simple in this regard, for in this situation, once a particular state from $State_\alpha^m$ is fixed, each action available to the agent α then determines a unique outcome, so that these actions can simply be ranked along with their outcomes. In the more general case, of course, even against the background of a fixed state, the actions available to an agent may determine only sets of outcomes, or propositions, rather than unique outcomes—but here, we can nevertheless compare the results of different actions in a state through the preference defined earlier on propositions. More exactly, where S is a state belonging to $State_\alpha^m$, and where K and K' are actions available to α at m, we can say that the results of K' are at least as good as those of K in the state S whenever the proposition $K' \cap S$, determined by performing the action K' in the state S, is weakly preferred to the proposition $K \cap S$, determined by performing K in S, and likewise, that the results of K' are better than those of K in S whenever the proposition $K' \cap S$ is strongly preferred to the proposition $K \cap S$.

We are now in a position to introduce our value orderings on actions—described here as *dominance* orderings—as follows.

Definition 4.5 (Dominance; $\preceq$, $\prec$) Let α be an agent and m a moment from a utilitarian stit frame, and let K and K' be members of $Choice_\alpha^m$. Then $K \preceq K'$ (K' *weakly dominates* K) if and only if $K \cap S \leq K' \cap S$ for each state $S \in State_\alpha^m$; and $K \prec K'$ (K' *strongly dominates* K) if and only if $K \preceq K'$ and it is not the case that $K' \preceq K$.

The idea, of course, is that K' weakly dominates K whenever the results of performing K' are at least as good as those of performing K in every state, and that K' strongly dominates K whenever K' weakly dominates but is not weakly dominated by K.

This concept of strong dominance can be reformulated to highlight the fact that K' strongly dominates K just in case the results of K' are at least as good as those of K in every state, and better in some.

Proposition 4.6 Let α be an agent and m a moment from a utilitarian stit frame, and let K and K' be members of $Choice_\alpha^m$. Then $K \prec K'$ if and only if (1) $K \cap S \leq K' \cap S$ for each state $S \in State_\alpha^m$, and (2) $K \cap S < K' \cap S$ for some state $S \in State_\alpha^m$.

And the reformulation can again be illustrated through the example depicted in Figure 4.1, where, as we have seen, $State_\alpha^m = \{K_3, K_4\}$. Of the actions K_1 and K_2 belonging to $Choice_\alpha^m$, then, it is clear that $K_1 \prec K_2$, since (1) we have both $K_1 \cap K_3 \leq K_2 \cap K_3$ and $K_1 \cap K_4 \leq K_2 \cap K_4$, and since (2) $K_1 \cap K_3 < K_2 \cap K_3$, for example.

It is easy to see that the preference orderings defined earlier on propositions, when applied to actions, are stronger than the dominance orderings now defined on actions. Where K and K' are actions available to an agent α at the moment m, we are guaranteed to have $K \preceq K'$ whenever $K \leq K'$; but of course, the converse need not hold, as illustrated by Figure 4.1, where we have $K_1 \preceq K_2$ without $K_1 \leq K_2$. The preference and dominance orderings on actions do coincide, however, in the two special cases considered earlier, where α is either the only agent under consideration, or at least the only agent facing a nonvacuous choice at m: here, since $State_\alpha^m = \{H_m\}$, we have $K \preceq K'$ just in case $K \leq K'$.[4]

The dominance orderings on actions satisfy the following properties, analogous to those set out in Proposition 4.3 concerning preference on propositions.

Proposition 4.7 Let α be an agent and m a moment from a utilitarian stit frame, and let K, K', and K'' be members of $Choice_\alpha^m$. Then:

1. If $K \prec K'$, then $K \preceq K'$.

2. If $K \preceq K'$ and $K' \preceq K''$, then $K \preceq K''$.

3. If $K \preceq K'$ and $K' \prec K''$, then $K \prec K''$.

4. If $K \prec K'$ and $K' \preceq K''$, then $K \prec K''$.

5. If $K \prec K'$ and $K' \prec K''$, then $K \prec K''$.

6. If $K \prec K'$, then it is not the case that $K' \prec K$.

7. It is not the case that $K \prec K$.

And again, it is important to note that, like the preference ordering on propositions, but unlike an ordering on actions that might be derived from a comparison of expected value, the dominance orderings are not linear. Different actions might be incomparable with respect even to weak dominance—a point that can be illustrated again by our first gambling example, depicted in Figure 3.9, where we have neither $K_1 \preceq K_2$ nor $K_2 \preceq K_1$.

4.2 Dominance act utilitarianism

4.2.1 Optimal actions

Although the central topic of this chapter is the design of a deontic logic for representing an agent's oughts, it will be useful first to see how a variant of act utilitarianism might be developed in the present framework.

---

[4]A preliminary version of the theory developed here can be found in Horty [1996]; this preliminary version concentrates on single-agent models, and therefore ranks the agent's actions through the propositional preference orderings $\leq$ and $<$.

The general goal of any utilitarian theory is to specify standards for classifying actions as right or wrong; and in its usual formulation, act utilitarianism defines an agent's action in some situation as right just in case the consequences of that action are at least as great in value as those of any of the alternatives open to the agent, and wrong otherwise.[5] We have already discussed the treatment of utility, or value, in the present setting; the notion is represented through the *Value* function introduced in Section 3.2. In order to arrive at a precise statement of the utilitarian idea, then, it seems necessary only to identify the alternative actions available to an agent in a given situation, and then to specify the consequences of those various actions.

Although the task of identifying the alternative actions open to an agent in a given situation has been a vexed issue in the philosophical literature, a natural and intuitively compelling solution to this problem is already built into the present analysis of agency: we can simply identify the alternatives open to an agent α at a moment m with the actions belonging to $Choice_\alpha^m$.[6]

In the framework of indeterministic time, however, the matter of specifying the consequences of an action does seem to present a real difficulty: when a particular action might lead, indeterministically, to a variety of possible outcomes—histories perhaps markedly different in value—how could any particular one of these outcomes be singled out as representing the consequences of that action? This difficulty in specifying an action's consequences in an indeterministic setting, as well as the impact of the difficulty on utilitarian thought, were both emphasized by Prior in his contribution to a symposium on the topic:

> Suppose that determinism is *not* true. Then there may indeed be a number of alternative actions which we could perform on a given occasion, but none of these actions can be said to have any "total consequences," or to bring about a definite state of the world which is better than any other that might be brought about by other choices. For we may presume that other agents are free beside the one who is on the given occasion deciding what he ought to do, and the total future state of the world depends on how these others choose as well as on how the given person chooses; and even if there were not other people to spoil one's

---

[5] A careful contemporary formulation of act utilitarianism can be found, for example, in Section 1.21 of Bergström [1966]; this formulation is closely related to the theory described in Chapters 1 and 2 of Moore [1912].

[6] The most important sustained discussion of the problem of identifying the alternative actions open to an agent is contained in Chapter 2 of Bergström [1966], which is summarized also in his [1971]; other work bearing on the issue includes, for example, Åqvist [1969], Castañeda [1968], Castañeda [1969], Prawitz [1968], Prawitz [1970], and Sobel [1971]. Anyone familiar with Bergström's work will see that the present proposal agrees with his at least to the extent of requiring that the set of alternative actions open to an agent at a moment should be agent-identical, time-identical, performable, incompatible in pairs, and jointly exhaustive.

> calculations there would still be oneself, with one's own future
> choices, or some of them, undetermined like this present one ....
> And while I speak here of one's calculations being spoilt, the
> trouble of course goes deeper than that—it's not merely that one
> cannot calculate the totality of what will happen if one decides
> in a certain way; the point is rather that there *is* no such totality.
> [Prior, 1956, pp. 91–92]

Prior concentrates in this passage on the role of other agents, and also on
the role of a single agent's own future choices, in influencing the outcomes
to which the agent's present actions might lead. But the general point
concerning the difficulty of specifying the consequences of actions, and so
applying the usual formulation of act utilitarianism, can be made even apart
from these complications, by considering only the momentary actions of a
single agent.

To see this, we need only return to our initial gambling example from
Figure 3.9. As we recall, the agent here is faced with a choice between
the option K_1 of gambling and the option K_2 of refraining; if he chooses
to gamble, he then receives ten dollars if he wins and nothing if he loses,
but if he chooses to refrain, he is sure to retain five dollars. Now, how
could the consequences of the alternative actions open to the agent in this
situation be identified and compared? If the agent gambles and wins, the
resulting outcome will be better than any outcome that might result from
his refraining. If he gambles and loses, the resulting outcome will be worse.
But if the agent gambles, he cannot determine whether he wins or loses;
and so he cannot determine whether the resulting outcome will be better
or worse than that of refraining. It seems to be impossible to decide which
of the two available actions—gambling or refraining—could be said to have
the better consequences, and so impossible to apply the usual formulation
of act utilitarianism to the case at hand.

Of course, if we were provided with the kind of probabilistic information alluded to earlier—information concerning the probability with which
various outcomes might result from the actions available to the agent—it
would be easy to adapt the usual formulation of act utilitarianism to an
indeterministic setting. For we could then assign an expected value to each
of the available actions, and the ordering of actions based on their expected
values would allow us to define a form of act utilitarianism that does not
rely on some definite notion of an action's consequences: an agent's action
in a situation could then be defined as right whenever its expected value
is at least as great as that of any alternative, or equivalently, whenever no
alternative holds a greater expected value.

In fact, this approach—leading to a theory that might be described as
expected value act utilitarianism—is the solution that Prior himself proposes
in [1956] to the problem of formulating utilitarianism in an indeterministic

setting, where definite consequences of actions cannot be identified.[7] But
again, this approach cannot be implemented in the current framework, where
the kind of probabilistic information necessary for defining expected values
is unavailable. Our strategy, instead, is to modify the schematic approach
underlying expected value act utilitarianism by appealing to dominance comparisons among actions rather than comparisons of expected value, and so
classifying an action as right whenever it is not strongly dominated by any
alternative.

As a first step, we define the set $Optimal_\alpha^m$ containing the *optimal* actions
available to an agent α at a moment m, those actions available to the agent
that are not strongly dominated by any others.

Definition 4.8 ($Optimal_\alpha^m$) Where α is an agent and m a moment from a
utilitarian stit frame,

$$Optimal_\alpha^m = \{K \in Choice_\alpha^m : \text{there is no } K' \in Choice_\alpha^m \,.\, K \prec K'\}.$$

It is then a simple matter to formulate the theory naturally characterized
as *dominance act utilitarianism*, a form of act utilitarianism applicable in
the presence of both indeterminism and uncertainty, and based on the dominance ordering among actions. According to this theory, an action available
to an agent α at a moment m is classified as *right* at an index m/h just in
case it is among the optimal actions available to that agent—just in case it
belongs to $Optimal_\alpha^m$—and classified as *wrong* at m/h otherwise. We can
say also that α *satisfies* this version of act utilitarianism at the index m/h
whenever the action performed by α at that index is classified there as right,
and that he *violates* the theory otherwise.

It is important to note that, although the classification of actions as right
or wrong offered by this dominance theory is officially relativized to full
indices—moment/history pairs—this classification does not, in fact, depend
on histories at all: any action that is classified as right at the index m/h
must be classified as right also at the index m/h', for each history h' from
H_m. Because the classification depends only on moments, we will extend the
terminology introduced in Section 2.1 to describe the classification of actions
offered by the dominance theory as *moment determinate*, and we will often
speak of the theory as classifying an action as right or wrong simply at a
moment.[8]

The theory of dominance act utilitarianism can be illustrated through
our two gambling examples from Section 3.4. In the first of these examples,

---

[7] Of course, this probabilistic approach is not unique to Prior, but can be found in any
number of discussions of utilitarianism; we concentrate here on Prior's remarks simply
because this book is cast within his logical framework.

[8] Section 5.4 describes an act utilitarian theory that is not moment determinate, a
theory in which the classification of actions as right or wrong varies from one history
through a moment to another.

depicted in Figure 3.9, we have $Optimal^m_\alpha = \{K_1, K_2\}$. Here, both actions available to the agent are classified as right, since neither dominates the other, and so the agent satisfies act utilitarianism at every index. In the case of Figure 3.10, by contrast, we have only one undominated action: $Optimal^m_\alpha = \{K_2\}$. The action K_2 alone is thus classified as right, and so the agent is said to satisfy act utilitarianism only at the indices m/h_3 and m/h_4. Since the action K_1 is dominated by K_2, this action is classified as wrong, and the agent is said to violate act utilitarianism at m/h_1 and m/h_2.

4.2.2 The finite choice condition

Before concluding our discussion of act utilitarianism, one remaining complication must be attended to. Until now, our treatment of the framework underlying action has been very general, allowing not only for situations in which an infinite number of histories pass through a moment m, but also for situations in which an agent α is faced with an infinite number of actions or choices at m—that is, situations in which $Choice^m_\alpha$ is itself infinite. The possibility that the agent might have to choose from among an infinite number of available actions introduces an interesting complication into utilitarian theory, for it is then conceivable that each available action might be dominated by another. In that case, the set $Optimal^m_\alpha$ would be empty: none of the actions available to the agent α would be classified as right by dominance act utilitarianism, and so α would violate this theory no matter which action he chose to perform.

Somewhat more concrete examples of this abstract possibility have been discussed by John Pollock in [1984, pp. 417–420], and by Michael Slote in [1989, pp. 110–115]. One of Pollock's examples involves a thrill-seeking individual who derives progressively greater excitement by leaning farther and farther out over an abyss, approaching ever more closely the point at which he would lose balance and fall to his death. If we imagine that this individual has continuous control over his position, and that there is indeed a first point at which he can no longer maintain balance (rather than a last point at which he can maintain balance), then the situation fits our abstract characterization. No matter how far the individual chooses to lean out over the abyss, he can derive a slightly greater thrill by leaning even farther, still without falling to his death; each action available to the individual is thus dominated by another, and so he cannot satisfy dominance act utilitarianism. Slote imagines a situation in which an agent can, in effect, persuade God to create i more happy people, for any number i chosen by the agent. On a total utility view, according to which a world with more happy people is better than a world with fewer, the agent is again faced with a situation in which he cannot satisfy act utilitarianism: no matter how many happy people he asks God to create, he could have achieved a greater utility by asking for more.

These examples are puzzling, for in both cases it is hard to see what the agents involved should do—how far should the first lean out over the abyss; how much additional utility should the second ask God to add to the world? The issues posed by these puzzling examples, however, are largely orthogonal to those under consideration in this book.[9] And here, we need only note that examples such as these simply cannot arise as long as we limit our attention to the class of utilitarian models in which agents face only a finite number of choices.

Definition 4.9 (Finite choice utilitarian stit frames/models) A *finite choice utilitarian stit frame* is a utilitarian stit frame in which, for each agent α and moment m, the set $Choice_\alpha^m$ is finite. A *finite choice utilitarian stit model* is a model based on a finite choice utilitarian stit frame.

Within this finite choice framework, of course, the set $Optimal_\alpha^m$ of undominated actions available to an agent α at a moment m must be nonempty, so that it will always be possible for the agent to satisfy act utilitarianism.

Proposition 4.10 Let α be an agent and m a moment from a finite choice utilitarian stit frame. Then $Optimal_\alpha^m \neq \emptyset$.

And in fact, we can establish a slightly stronger result—that each nonoptimal action available to the agent will be dominated by an optimal action.

Proposition 4.11 Let α be an agent and m a moment from a finite choice utilitarian stit frame. Then for each action $K \in Choice_\alpha^m - Optimal_\alpha^m$, there is an action $K' \in Optimal_\alpha^m$ such that $K \prec K'$.

This result will later be useful in the proof of Proposition 4.13.

4.3   A new deontic operator

4.3.1   The definition

At this point, we can return to our central project of defining a deontic operator to represent what an agent ought to do in a way that avoids the difficulties with the Meinong/Chisholm analysis. In order to capture this notion, we now introduce a new two-place operator $\odot[\ldots \; cstit: \ldots]$, allowing for the construction of statements of the form

$$\odot[\alpha \; cstit: A],$$

with the intuitive meaning: α ought to see to it that A.

---

[9]Pollock suggest that, in these cases, rationality simply cannot serve as a guide to action; Slote appeals to such situations in motivating the need for a satisficing, rather than maximizing, version of utilitarianism.

The simplest way to understand the semantics of this new operator is to focus, first, on finite choice situations, where the set of optimal actions available to an agent α at any moment m is guaranteed to be nonempty. In these situations, it seems reasonable to suppose that α ought to see to it that A just in case the truth of A is guaranteed by each of the optimal actions available to the agent—formally, that $\bigodot[\alpha \ cstit: A]$ should be settled true at a moment m just in case $K \subseteq |A|_m$ for each $K \in Optimal_\alpha^m$.

This suggestion can be viewed as an agentive analogue to the idea underlying standard deontic logic: in standard deontic logic, where we are concerned with what ought to be the case, the statement $\bigcirc A$ is defined as true whenever A holds in each of the best worlds; and likewise, according to the present suggestion, where we are concerned with what an agent ought to do, the statement $\bigodot[\alpha \ cstit: A]$ should be defined as true whenever A is guaranteed by each of the agent's best actions. It is easy to see also that this proposal yields the correct results at least in the two gambling cases that forced us to abandon the Meinong/Chisholm analysis. In the case of Figure 3.9, as we recall, we did not wish to conclude either that the agent should or should not gamble; and here, since both K_1 and K_2 are optimal, yet neither A nor $\neg A$ is guaranteed by both these actions, the present suggestion would yield neither $\bigodot[\alpha \ cstit: A]$ nor $\bigodot[\alpha \ cstit: \neg A]$. In the case of Figure 3.10, we did want to conclude that the agent should refrain from gambling; and here, since the only optimal action is K_2, which guarantees the truth of $\neg A$, the statement $\bigodot[\alpha \ cstit: \neg A]$ would be true.

Unfortunately, this simple proposal fails in situations such as those described by Pollock and Slote, where the set of optimal actions available to an agent is empty. If the statement $\bigodot[\alpha \ cstit: A]$ were actually defined as true whenever A is guaranteed by each of the optimal actions available to α, then in situations like these, with no optimal actions available, we would be forced to conclude that $\bigodot[\alpha \ cstit: A]$ must be true for any arbitrary formula A—so that all deontic distinctions among propositions would disappear. In fact, this conclusion may even hold some initial attractions, perhaps as reflecting the perplexing quality of these situations, in which it is, after all, impossible for the agent to satisfy act utilitarianism. However, even though none of the actions available to the agent in these situations can be classified as right, it still seems that there are deontic distinctions to be preserved concerning the propositions that might result from the agent's actions, the complements of agentive ought statements.

To see this, let us return to Slote's example, in which the agent must choose to ask God to create i happy people for some natural number i. This example can be illustrated as in Figure 4.2, where the series $K_0, K_1, K_2, \ldots$ depicts the actions available to the agent α at the moment m. Each action K_i, leading to the unique history h_i, is supposed to represent the choice of asking God to create i happy people, and in keeping with the assumption

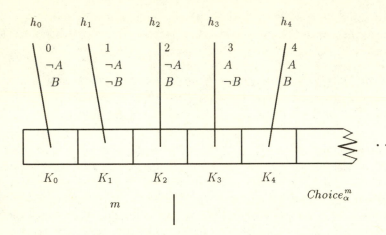

Figure 4.2: No optimal action

that it is always better to have more people than fewer, we suppose that each history h_i carries a utility of i. Finally, we suppose that A is true at the index m/h_i whenever i is greater than two, and that B is true at m/h_i whenever i is even. The statement A thus expresses the proposition that α asks for at least three happy people, while B expresses the proposition that α asks for an even number of happy people.

In this situation, of course, none of the actions available to the agent is optimal: each action K_i is dominated by the action K_{i+1}. But even so, it seems reasonable to register deontic distinctions among the propositional complements of agentive ought statements. It is natural to expect, for example, that the statement $\odot[\alpha\ cstit\colon A]$ should be true and the statement $\odot[\alpha\ cstit\colon \neg A]$ false: the agent ought to ask for at least three happy people, since the actions that lead to this result uniformly dominate those that do not, and the agent ought not to ask for fewer than three happy people, since the actions leading to this result are uniformly dominated by those that do not. And it is natural to expect that both $\odot[\alpha\ cstit\colon B]$ and $\odot[\alpha\ cstit\colon \neg B]$ should be false: it is neither the case that the agent ought to ask for an even number of happy people nor that the agent ought to ask for an odd number of happy people, since any action leading to either of these results is dominated by some action leading to the other.

We have seen this kind of problem before, in Figure 3.3. And in fact, the general evaluation rule presented in Definition 3.4 for the $\odot$ operator was formulated to apply sensibly in situations containing histories of ever-increasing value; but there, as we recall, it was necessary to impose a linear value ordering on the histories in order to secure a normal deontic logic. In the present case, because the dominance ordering among actions is not linear, we are forced to define our new deontic operator through a more complicated evaluation rule.

Definition 4.12 (Evaluation rule: $\odot[\alpha \; cstit: A]$) Where α is an agent and m/h an index from a utilitarian stit model $\mathcal{M}$,

- $\mathcal{M}, m/h \models \odot[\alpha \; cstit: A]$ if and only if, for each action $K \in Choice_\alpha^m$ such that $K \not\subseteq |A|_m^{\mathcal{M}}$, there is an action $K' \in Choice_\alpha^m$ such that (1) $K \prec K'$, and (2) $K' \subseteq |A|_m^{\mathcal{M}}$, and (3) $K'' \subseteq |A|_m^{\mathcal{M}}$ for each action $K'' \in Choice_\alpha^m$ such that $K' \preceq K''$.

Still, although this rule is somewhat intricate in its formulation, the underlying idea is straightforward. Let us say that a statement A is *safely guaranteed* by an action K available to an agent whenever the truth of A is guaranteed by K and also by any other action available to the agent that weakly dominates K. Then the idea behind the evaluation rule is that $\odot[\alpha \; cstit: A]$ should be true at an index m/h just in case: for every action K available to α at m that does not guarantee the truth of A, there is another action K' available to α at m that both strongly dominates K and safely guarantees A.

With the deontic operator defined in this way, we again get the correct results in our two gambling examples: both $\odot[\alpha \; cstit: A]$ and $\odot[\alpha \; cstit: \neg A]$ are settled false in Figure 3.9, while $\odot[\alpha \; cstit: \neg A]$ is settled true in Figure 3.10. But this more complex evaluation rule now yields the correct results also in more complex cases, such Figure 4.2. Here, the statement $\odot[\alpha \; cstit: A]$ is settled true, since each of the three actions K_0, K_1, and K_2 that do not guarantee the truth of A is strongly dominated by the action K_3, which safely guarantees A. On the other hand, the statement $\odot[\alpha \; cstit: B]$, for instance, is not true, since, although each action K_i that does not guarantee B is strongly dominated by an action K_{i+1} that does guarantee B, the guarantee is never safe: K_{i+1} is itself always dominated by another action K_{i+2} that does not guarantee B.

4.3.2 Deontic logic and act utilitarianism

We first approached the semantics of our new deontic operator through a consideration of finite choice situations, where the set of optimal actions available to the agent is nonempty; and in these situations, we were initially drawn to a simple proposal according to which statements of the form $\odot[\alpha \; cstit: A]$ would be defined as true just in case the truth of A was guaranteed by each of the optimal actions available to the agent. However, we were compelled to abandon this simple proposal in order to allow for appropriate deontic distinctions among the complements of agentive ought statements even in situations in which the set of optimal actions available to the agent might be empty, and we settled instead on a more complicated evaluation rule. It is now necessary to ask whether this more complicated rule agrees with the simple proposal in the finite choice case, and fortunately, the answer is positive.

Proposition 4.13 Let α be an agent and m/h an index from a finite choice utilitarian stit model $\mathcal{M}$. Then $\mathcal{M}, m/h \models \odot[\alpha\ cstit\colon A]$ if and only if $K \subseteq |A|_m^{\mathcal{M}}$ for each $K \in Optimal_\alpha^m$.

From a technical standpoint, this result shows that our official evaluation rule is, in a sense, a conservative generalization of the idea underlying the simple proposal; in addition, it legitimizes the use of the simple proposal as a kind of streamlined evaluation rule for our deontic operator, applicable in finite choice cases. But the result can also be given a broader interpretation, concerning the connection between deontic logic and act utilitarianism.

In the past, the task of mapping the relations between deontic logic and act utilitarianism has resulted in surprising difficulties, leading some writers to suggest the possibility of a conflict in the fundamental principles underlying the two theories.[10] One source of these difficulties, I believe, is the gap between the subjects of normative evaluation involved in the two areas: while deontic logic has been most successfully developed as a theory of what ought or ought not to be, utilitarianism is concerned with classifying actions, rather than states of affairs, as right or wrong. The present account closes this gap, developing a deontic logic designed to represent what agents ought to do within a framework that allows, also, for the formulation of a particular variant of act utilitarianism, the dominance theory. As Proposition 4.13 shows, a precise connection can then be established between the two subjects: at least in a finite choice setting, a statement of the form $\odot[\alpha\ cstit\colon A]$ is true just in case α guarantees the truth of A whenever α performs an action that satisfies dominance act utilitarianism.

4.3.3 Logic of the dominance ought

Turning now to the logic of our new deontic operator, it is clear from the structure of the evaluation rule, first of all, that any statement of the form $\odot[\alpha\ cstit\colon A]$ is always either settled true or settled false; and also that the current version of the characteristic deontic formula,

$$D_\alpha\odot.\quad \odot[\alpha\ cstit\colon A] \supset \Diamond[\alpha\ cstit\colon A],$$

---

[10] The matter of relating deontic logic to act utilitarianism is discussed in Åqvist's survey article [1984, pp. 661–662], and in the papers referred to there; an especially useful study of the issue can be found in Åqvist's own [1969]. The suggestion of a fundamental conflict between the principles underlying deontic logic and act utilitarianism occurs in Castañeda [1968].

is valid. The new deontic operator is, moreover, a normal modal operator, satisfying the principles

$RE_\alpha \odot$. $\quad A \equiv B \ / \ \odot[\alpha \ cstit: A] \equiv \odot[\alpha \ cstit: B],$

$N_\alpha \odot$. $\quad \odot[\alpha \ cstit: \top],$

$M_\alpha \odot$. $\quad \odot[\alpha \ cstit: A \wedge B] \supset . \odot[\alpha \ cstit: A] \wedge \odot[\alpha \ cstit: B],$

$C_\alpha \odot$. $\quad \odot[\alpha \ cstit: A] \wedge \odot[\alpha \ cstit: B] \supset \odot[\alpha \ cstit: A \wedge B].$

Although it is a straightforward matter to verify $RE_\alpha \odot$, $N_\alpha \odot$, and $M_\alpha \odot$, the argument establishing $C_\alpha \odot$—presented in Validity A.2 (see Appendix)—is considerably more complex.

Since our new operator validates both $C_\alpha \odot$ and $D_\alpha \odot$, it must, of course, also support the principle

$D_\alpha^* \odot$. $\quad \neg(\odot[\alpha \ cstit: A] \wedge \odot[\alpha \ cstit: \neg A]),$

which rules out the possibility of conflicts in what a single agent ought to do.[11] And an argument analogous to that set out in Section 3.3 for the principle $D_{\alpha,\beta}^* \bigcirc$ can be used to establish the validity of

$D_{\alpha,\beta}^* \odot$. $\quad \neg(\odot[\alpha \ cstit: A] \wedge \odot[\beta \ cstit: \neg A]),$

ruling out the possibility of a conflict among the oughts of distinct agents.

We have now, of course, abandoned the Meinong/Chisholm strategy of attempting to explicate what an agent ought to do as what it ought to be that the agent does; but it is still possible to use the formula $\bigcirc[\alpha \ cstit: A]$ as a representation of the idea that it ought to be that the agent α sees to it that A, and to explore the relations between this idea and the distinct idea that α ought to see to it that A, now represented by the distinct formula $\odot[\alpha \ cstit: A]$.

Although perhaps already apparent, it is worth noting explicitly that the notion carried by the new operator of what an agent ought to do is logically neither weaker nor stronger than the notion of what it ought to be that the agent does, but incomparable. Even if it ought to be that α sees to it that A, we cannot necessarily conclude that α ought to see to it that A; and even

---

[11] This result suggests a terminological point. Slote argues in [1989, pp. 109–110] that situations of the sort he and Pollock describe—situations in which an agent cannot satisfy act utilitarianism because, for each available action, there is another available that is still better—show that contemporary act utilitarianism allows for the possibility of "moral dilemmas." A situation is generally not classified as a moral dilemma, however, unless it presents the agent with conflicting oughts, and as the validity of $D_\alpha^* \odot$ shows, even in situations like those described by Pollock and Slote, where the set of optimal actions available to the agent is empty, there is nevertheless no conflict among the oughts presented to the agent. It is perhaps misleading, then, to classify these situations as moral dilemmas; they present, instead, moral anomalies of a different sort.

if α ought to see to it that A, we cannot necessarily conclude that it ought
to be the case that α sees to it that A: both the formulas

$$\bigcirc[\alpha \; cstit\text{: } A] \supset \odot[\alpha \; cstit\text{: } A],$$
$$\odot[\alpha \; cstit\text{: } A] \supset \bigcirc[\alpha \; cstit\text{: } A]$$

are invalid in the class of utilitarian stit models. A countermodel to the first
is provided by Figure 3.9; a countermodel to (an instance of) the second is
provided by Figure 3.10.

It is interesting to observe, however, that if we limit our attention to
the class of utilitarian stit models that can be taken to represent standard
deontic stit models—those utilitarian models, defined earlier, in which the
space of values is limited to 1 and 0—then the first of these two formulas is
valid in this more restricted class. Thus, while the notion of what it ought
to be that an agent does is incomparable in a utilitarian setting with the
notion of what the agent ought to do, it is a logically stronger notion in a
standard deontic setting.

Even in the more general utilitarian setting, though, where the notion of
what an agent ought to do is incomparable to the notion of what it ought
to be that the agent does, these two notions are guaranteed at least not to
conflict. The principle

$$D_{\alpha}^{*}\odot\bigcirc. \neg(\bigcirc[\alpha \; cstit\text{: } A] \wedge \bigcirc[\alpha \; cstit\text{: } \neg A]),$$

established as Validity A.3 (see Appendix), guarantees that we will never
come across a situation in which the agent ought to see to it that A even
though it ought to be that he sees to it that $\neg A$.

In addition to comparing our new formula $\odot[\alpha \; cstit\text{: } A]$ with the previous $\bigcirc[\alpha \; cstit\text{: } A]$, representing the idea that it ought to be the case that α
sees to it that A, it is useful to compare this statement also to formulas of
the form $\bigcirc A$, representing the idea that it ought to be that A. Of course,
the formula $\bigcirc A \supset \odot[\alpha \; cstit\text{: } A]$ is invalid, as shown by Figure 3.9, our first
gambling example: even though A is true in the best histories, the agent
need not see to it that A. More interesting, however—and in contrast to
the validity of $\bigcirc[\alpha \; cstit\text{: } A] \supset \bigcirc A$, mentioned in Section 3.3—we can now
see that the formula $\odot[\alpha \; cstit\text{: } A] \supset \bigcirc A$ is invalid. A countermodel to an
instance is provided by Figure 3.10, our second gambling example, where
$\odot[\alpha \; cstit\text{: } \neg A]$ is settled true but $\bigcirc \neg A$ settled false: even though the agent
ought not to gamble, some of the best histories are those in which he gam-
bles. (This same example shows that $\bigcirc(\odot[\alpha \; cstit\text{: } A] \supset [\alpha \; cstit\text{: } A])$, whose
analogue was also noted as valid in Section 3.3, is now invalid: it need not be
the case that, in all the best histories, the agent does what he ought to do.)
Again, however, although what an agent ought to see to and what ought to
be the case are incomparable, these two ideas must at least be consistent,
as shown by the validity of $\neg(\odot[\alpha \; cstit\text{: } A] \wedge \bigcirc \neg A)$.

4.4 Independence

The deontic logic developed in this chapter is based upon a dominance relation among the actions available to an agent, which in turn relies upon a preliminary analysis of the notion of causal independence—both set out in Section 4.1. As promised there, we now return to examine this analysis of causal independence more closely, first describing some connections between the current approach and the kind of conditional treatment found in Gibbard and Harper [1978], next reconsidering sure-thing reasoning from a conditional perspective, and finally exploring some ways in which the preliminary analysis developed here might be refined and generalized.

4.4.1 Independence and conditionals

Gibbard and Harper rely in their treatment of causal independence on a background logic of counterfactual conditionals. Although they do not formulate this background logic explicitly, it is clear that the conditional statements involved are themselves supposed to be given their meaning in terms of a primitive similarity relation on temporally extended possible worlds [1978, Section 2]—so that it is this similarity relation that must ultimately be taken to encode whatever causal information is present in a model. We now show that the causally independent states introduced here play roughly the same role, allowing us to define a similarity relation on histories from which a conditional treatment of causal independence can then be recovered.

In order to motivate the connection between causal independence and conditionals, let us first return to Figure 4.1, where, as we recall, the agent α is forced to choose at m between placing a nickel on the table either heads up or tails up, performing either the action K_1 or the action K_2, while the agent β faces the simultaneous, and so causally independent, choice of placing a dime on the table either heads up or tails up, performing either K_3 or K_4. Suppose that, in fact, both α and β place their coins on the table heads up, so that the resulting history, determined by the combination of K_1 and K_3, is h_2. As the diagram shows, the statement B, expressing the proposition that the dime is placed heads up, is true at the index m/h_2. But we can also ask a counterfactual question: at this index, determined by this particular pattern of action, would the statement B have been true even if α had placed his nickel on the table tails up rather than heads up, selecting K_2 rather than K_1?

Since the actions of α and β are causally independent, the choice made by α cannot influence that of β. At the index m/h_2, then, where β does in fact select the action K_3, it thus seems reasonable to conclude—since this selection cannot be influenced by the action selected by α—that β would have selected K_3 regardless of the action chosen by α, and in particular, that β would still have selected K_3 even if α had selected K_2. In that case, the resulting outcome, determined by the combination of K_2 and K_3, would have been the history h_3. And since B holds also at m/h_3, the answer to our counterfactual question appears to be yes: relative to the index m/h_2, the statement B would have been true even if α had selected K_2 rather than K_1.

This example should be contrasted with the situation depicted in Figure 4.3, which is to be interpreted much like Figure 4.1. Again, we imagine that the agent α must choose at m to place his nickel on the table heads up or tails up, performing either the action K_1 or K_2, while β simultaneously chooses to place his dime heads up or tails up, performing either K_3 or K_4; but in this case the statement B—now true at m/h_2 and m/h_4—represents the proposition that the two coins match, that they are either both placed heads up or both placed tails up. (The situations depicted in Figures 4.1 and 4.3 differ also in the utilities assigned to h_3 and h_4, but this difference does not bear on our current discussion.) Let us suppose again that both α and β place their coins on the table heads up, so that the resulting history, again determined by the combination of K_1 and K_3, is h_2, where the statement B is true—the coins match. Again, however, we can ask the counterfactual question: at this index m/h_2, would the statement B have been true even if α had placed his nickel tails up, selecting K_2 rather than K_1? But in this case, the answer is a clear no. If α had placed his nickel tails up, the resulting history, determined by the combination of K_2 and K_3, would have been h_3, where B fails.

As we recall from Section 4.1, the basic intuition guiding the present analysis of causal independence is that a proposition is supposed to be causally independent of the actions available to a particular agent whenever its truth or falsity is guaranteed by a source of causality other than the actions of that agent. At any index at which such a proposition is true, then, since its truth must be guaranteed by an independent source of causality, the proposition will have to be true regardless of the action selected by the agent in question—and it is because of this, as our two examples show, that the notion of independence is naturally correlated with counterfactuals. In the case of Figure 4.1, the proposition that the dime is placed heads up is indeed independent of the actions available to α, since, at every index, either its truth or its falsity is guaranteed by β, a different source of causality. As a result, at any index at which the dime is placed heads up, then no matter how α places the nickel at that index, we can conclude that the dime would still have been placed heads up even if α had placed the nickel otherwise. But in the case of Figure 4.3, the proposition that the two coins match is not independent of the actions available to α, since its truth or falsity at an index is determined, in part, by the action that α selects. And here, as we have seen, there are indices at which the two coins match, but at which we cannot say that they would still have matched if α had placed his

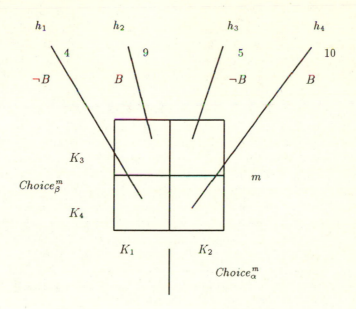

Figure 4.3: The second coin example

coin otherwise.

We now introduce a conditional operator—represented through the $\Box\!\!\rightarrow$ symbol—in terms of which the connections sketched so far between independence and counterfactual conditionals can be made precise.

In our informal discussion, the antecedents of the counterfactual conditionals under consideration have been taken to express claims to the effect that agents perform certain actions; and since our conditional operator belongs to the object language, we have to make sure that the object language itself is rich enough to express these claims. Therefore, for each agent α and for each action K open to α at some moment m, we introduce a special propositional constant A_α^K, governed by the following evaluation rule.

Definition 4.14 (Evaluation rule: A_α^K) Where α is an agent and m/h an index from a stit model $\mathcal{M}$, and where K is some action from $Choice_\alpha^m$,

- $\mathcal{M}, m/h \models A_\alpha^K$ if and only if $Choice_\alpha^m(h) = K$.

The idea, of course, is that the statement A_α^K is supposed to mean that the agent α performs the action K, and so this statement is defined as true at an index m/h just in case the action performed by α at that index is K. In fact, our conditional operator, like that of Gibbard and Harper, will be restricted so as to accept only these action statements as antecedents. We thus limit our attention to statements of the form $A_\alpha^K \Box\!\!\rightarrow B$, carrying the intuitive meaning: if α had performed the action K, then B would hold.

The semantic account of these conditional statements follows what is, by now, the standard format, but with one new twist. A conditional of the form $A_\alpha^K \square\!\!\rightarrow B$ is regarded as true at an index m/h whenever B is true along each of the histories through m most similar to h at which A_α^K holds—but here the set of "most similar" histories is taken as defined, rather than primitive.

At any index m/h, each of the various agents must, of course, perform some action or another. Where K is an action available to the agent α at the moment m, we can thus define the histories through m most similar to h at which A_α^K holds quite simply, as those in which, although α now guarantees the truth of A_α^K, all of the other agents perform exactly the same actions they did at the original index. As we have seen, the set of histories in which the group of agents other than α perform the same actions they did at m/h is $State_\alpha^m(h)$, and of course, the set of histories at which A_α^K holds is simply K. The histories through m most similar to h at which A_α^K holds— those at which α performs the action K but all other agents perform the same actions they did at the original index—can therefore be characterized formally as $f_m(h, K)$, the output of the conditional selection function f, defined as follows.

Definition 4.15 ($f_m(h, K)$) Where α is an agent and m/h an index from a stit model, and where K is some action from $Choice_\alpha^m$,

$$f_m(h, K) = State_\alpha^m(h) \cap K.$$

Given this selection function, the evaluation rule for our conditional can then be framed in the usual way, with $A_\alpha^K \square\!\!\rightarrow B$ defined as true at the index m/h whenever B is true at each history from $f_m(h, K)$.

Definition 4.16 (Evaluation rule: $A_\alpha^K \square\!\!\rightarrow B$) Where α is an agent and m/h an index from a stit model $\mathcal{M}$, and where K is some action from $Choice_\alpha^m$,

- $\mathcal{M}, m/h \models A_\alpha^K \square\!\!\rightarrow B$ if and only if $f_m(h, K) \subseteq |B|_m^\mathcal{M}$.

And the conditional so defined allows us to capture the results suggested by our motivating cases. In the case of Figure 4.1, for example, we have $f_m(h_2, K_2) = \{h_3\}$ and $|B|_m = \{h_2, h_3\}$. Therefore, $f_m(h_2, K_2) \subseteq |B|_m$, and so the statement $A_\alpha^{K_2} \square\!\!\rightarrow B$—here expressing the idea that the dime would have been placed heads up even if α had placed the nickel otherwise— holds at m/h_2. But in the case of Figure 4.3, where $f_m(h_2, K_2) = \{h_3\}$ and $|B|_m = \{h_2, h_4\}$, we do not have $f_m(h_2, K_2) \subseteq |B|_m$, and so the statement $A_\alpha^{K_2} \square\!\!\rightarrow B$—now expressing the claim that the coins would have matched even if α had placed the nickel otherwise—fails at m/h_2.

It follows immediately from the structure of its evaluation rule that our conditional is normal, validating the principles

$$RCEC. \quad B \equiv C \ / \ A_\alpha^K \,\square\!\!\rightarrow\! B \equiv A_\alpha^K \,\square\!\!\rightarrow\! C,$$
$$CN. \quad A_\alpha^K \,\square\!\!\rightarrow\! \top,$$
$$CM. \quad A_\alpha^K \,\square\!\!\rightarrow\! (B \wedge C) \supset (A_\alpha^K \,\square\!\!\rightarrow\! B \wedge A_\alpha^K \,\square\!\!\rightarrow\! C),$$
$$CC. \quad A_\alpha^K \,\square\!\!\rightarrow\! B \wedge A_\alpha^K \,\square\!\!\rightarrow\! C \supset A_\alpha^K \,\square\!\!\rightarrow\! (B \wedge C).$$

And since the selection function in terms of which the conditional is defined always satisfies both the requirement that $f_m(h, K) \subseteq K$ and the requirement that $h \in f_m(h, K)$ whenever $h \in K$, we can conclude also that this conditional validates the further principles

$$I. \quad A_\alpha^K \,\square\!\!\rightarrow\! A_\alpha^K,$$
$$MP. \quad A_\alpha^K, \ A_\alpha^K \,\square\!\!\rightarrow\! B \ / \ B.$$

Unlike the conditional underlying the analysis of Gibbard and Harper, however, the present operator does not validate the principle that $\neg(A_\alpha^K \,\square\!\!\rightarrow\! B)$ entails $A_\alpha^K \,\square\!\!\rightarrow\! \neg B$.

Having introduced a counterfactual conditional, we now use this operator to provide a conditional treatment of causal independence.

In the present setting, causal independence is viewed as a relation between propositions at a moment and the actions available to an agent at that moment. The paradigms of propositions that are causally independent of the actions available to an agent at a moment are, of course, the states, the patterns of action simultaneously available to all other agents; but these are not the only independent propositions. If the propositions X and Y are causally independent of the actions available to an agent at a moment m—if the truth or falsity of these propositions is guaranteed by a source of causality other than the actions of that agent—then the propositions $X \cap Y$, $X \cup Y$, and $H_m - X$ must be independent as well, their truth or falsity must be likewise guaranteed; and in general, the propositions that are causally independent of the actions available to an agent at a moment are those that can be defined as unions of the states facing that agent.

Definition 4.17 (Causal independence) Let α be an agent and m a moment from a stit frame, and let X be a proposition at m. Then the proposition X is *causally independent* of the actions available to α at m if and only if there is some set $\mathcal{S}$ such that $\mathcal{S} \subseteq State_\alpha^m$ and $X = \bigcup_{S \in \mathcal{S}}$.

Whenever such an independent proposition is true at an index, it is reasonable to suppose, since its truth must be guaranteed by a source of causality other than the actions available to the agent, that the proposition would have to be true regardless of the particular action performed by the agent. This idea   that a proposition would be true regardless of the action

performed by the agent—can be taken to mean that, for each action available
to the agent, the proposition would be true even if the agent were to perform
that action. And, moving to the object language, it is now natural to express
the counterfactual element involved in this claim with our counterfactual
conditional: the idea that the proposition expressed by a statement B would
be true regardless of the action selected by an agent α can be captured as
the claim that the formula $A_\alpha^K \,\square\!\!\rightarrow B$ holds for each action K available to
α. Any statement B expressing a proposition independent of the actions
available to the agent α, then, must entail all appropriate conditionals of
the form $A_\alpha^K \,\square\!\!\rightarrow B$, and indeed, the converse holds as well: any statement
that entails all the appropriate conditionals must express an independent
proposition.

Proposition 4.18 Let α be an agent and m a moment from a stit model
$\mathcal{M}$. Then the proposition $|B|_m^{\mathcal{M}}$ expressed by the statement B at the moment
m is causally independent of the actions available to α at m if and only if,
for each action $K \in Choice_\alpha^m$, the statement $B \supset (A_\alpha^K \,\square\!\!\rightarrow B)$ is settled true
at m.

As this result shows, the independent propositions could just as easily have
been defined as those that are true regardless of the agent's action whenever
they are true at all.

4.4.2   Conditionals and sure-thing reasoning

The conditional treatment of causal independence set out here provides us
with a new perspective on the distinction between those situations in which
sure-thing reasoning is allowed and those in which it is blocked; we illustrate
by contrasting the situations depicted in our two motivating examples, Figures 4.1 and 4.3.

Considered from the point of view of the agent α, these two situations
are remarkably similar: both present the agent with a choice between the
action K_1, with two possible outcomes having values of 4 and 9, and the
action K_2, with two possible outcomes having values of 5 and 10; and in both
cases, the statement B holds at the two outcomes having values of 9 and 10,
while the statement $\neg B$ holds at the two outcomes having values of 4 and 5.
Because of these similarities, it might seem that these two situations should
agree on—either both allowing or both blocking—the following sure-thing
argument in favor of the choice of K_2 over K_1. Either B holds or $\neg B$ holds.
If B holds, then it is better to perform K_2 than K_1, since the unique outcome
that would result from performing K_2 given that B holds has a value of 10,
while the unique outcome that would result from performing K_1 given that
B holds has a value of only 9. It is likewise better to perform K_2 than K_1
if $\neg B$ holds, since the unique outcome that would result from performing
K_2 given that $\neg B$ holds has a value of 5, while the unique outcome that

would result from performing K_1 given that $\neg B$ holds has a value of only 4. Therefore, since K_2 is a better action than K_1 to perform in each of these two cases, which exhaust the possibilities, K_2 is simply a better action than K_1 to perform.

In fact, an argument along these lines is acceptable in Figure 4.1, where the proposition expressed by the statement B—the proposition that the dime is placed heads up—is causally independent of the actions available to the agent; and we can conclude on the basis of this argument that, in this situation, $K_1 \prec K_2$. As we have seen, however, this kind of sure-thing reasoning is not allowed in situations like Figure 4.3, where the statement B expresses the proposition that the two coins match, which is not causally independent of the actions available to α; and indeed, in this situation, we do not have $K_1 \prec K_2$. But it is now reasonable to ask: why not? At least on the face of it, the argument set out above says nothing about causal dependence or independence. So why should the fact that the proposition expressed by the statement B is independent in one situation but not the other have any bearing at all on the argument's validity?

Fortunately, we can answer this question with the aid of our conditional treatment of causal independence. Although it is true that the sure-thing argument set out above makes no explicit reference to independence, it turns out that the independence assumption is carried implicitly by the conditional reasoning through which we are supposed to decide which outcomes would result from the different actions available to the agent; and proper attention to this reasoning shows why the argument is valid in one case but not the other. To establish this point, we now review the sure-thing argument in each of these two situations, focusing particularly on the principles of conditional reasoning involved.

We begin with Figure 4.1. Since either B or $\neg B$ must be true at any index, it is permissible to reason by cases. Suppose, then, that B is true. Now, in the situation depicted, B expresses a proposition causally independent of the available actions; hence, B would be true no matter which action the agent were to perform, and in particular, B would be true if the agent were to perform the action K_1. Formally, this conclusion is guaranteed by Proposition 4.18, which tells us, since B expresses a causally independent proposition, that B entails $A_\alpha^{K_1} \square\rightarrow B$. From the conditional principle listed as I above, we know that $A_\alpha^{K_1} \square\rightarrow A_\alpha^{K_1}$, and so the principle CC allows us to combine these results in the conclusion $A_\alpha^{K_1} \square\rightarrow (A_\alpha^{K_1} \wedge B)$—telling us that, if the agent were to perform the action K_1, then $A_\alpha^{K_1} \wedge B$ would be true. Of course, the proposition expressed by $A_\alpha^{K_1} \wedge B$ in this situation is $K_1 \cap |B|_m$, which contains the unique history h_2, with a value of 9. Hence, under the assumption that B is true, we can legitimately conclude that performing the action K_1 would lead to an outcome of value 9. A similar argument tells us, again under the assumption B, that performing the action K_2 would result in the history h_3, with value 10—so that, under the assumption that B is true, we can indeed conclude that it is better to perform the action K_2 than K_1. Since the proposition expressed by $\neg B$ is likewise independent of the actions available to the agent, this overall pattern of reasoning can be duplicated to show that it is better to perform K_2 than K_1 also under the assumption that $\neg B$. And then, since it is better to perform K_2 than K_1 both when B is true and when $\neg B$ is true, simple truth-functional reasoning—in the form of the principle of constructive dilemma—allows us to conclude that it is better to perform K_2 than K_1. The sure-thing argument is valid.

Now what about Figure 4.3? We can again reason by cases, since we know that either B or $\neg B$ must be true at any index. So again, let us first assume that B is true. In the previous situation, where the statement B expressed a causally independent proposition, we were able to use Proposition 4.18 to conclude, under this assumption, that $A_\alpha^{K_1} \square \!\!\rightarrow B$—that B would still be true even if the agent were to perform the action K_1. But that result cannot be applied in the present situation, since the proposition expressed by B is no longer causally independent; and in fact, the inference from B to $A_\alpha^{K_1} \square \!\!\rightarrow B$ must itself now be rejected: the statement B is true at the index m/h_4, for example, but $A_\alpha^{K_1} \square \!\!\rightarrow B$ fails at that same index. Since we cannot conclude, even given B as an assumption, that B would still be true if the agent were to perform the action K_1, we cannot conclude that the outcome resulting from the performance of K_1 would belong to $K_1 \cap |B|_m$: all we know is that the outcome resulting from the performance of K_1 must belong to K_1, with a value of either 4 or 9. For similar reasons—because B does not entail $A_\alpha^{K_2} \square \!\!\rightarrow B$—we cannot conclude in this situation, even given B as an assumption, that the outcome resulting from the performance of K_2 would belong to $K_2 \cap |B|_m$: all we know is that the outcome resulting from the performance of K_2 must belong to K_2, with a value of either 5 or 10. Even given B as an assumption, then, there is no longer any clear reason to favor K_2 over K_1, since it is no longer a matter of selecting an action leading to a unique outcome of value 10 over an action leading to a unique outcome of value 9. Because we cannot conclude that K_2 is a better action than K_1 when B is true (or, in fact, when $\neg B$ is true), we can no longer apply the principle of constructive dilemma to reach the conclusion that K_2 is better than K_1.[12]

---

[12] This argument is designed to show that the assumption that B holds does not semantically entail the conclusion that K_2 is a better action than K_1 for the agent to perform. Stalnaker [1975] defines a pragmatic notion of "reasonable inference" according to which this conclusion may be said to follow from the assumption that B, and also from the assumption that $\neg B$. But this still does not allow us to conclude unconditionally that K_2 is a better action than K_1 in Figure 4.3, since, as Stalnaker notes, the principle of constructive dilemma that is needed to reach the unconditional conclusion is not applicable to the concept of reasonable inference.

4.4.3 Refining the analysis

Rather than simply postulating a set of causally independent states confronting each agent at each moment, we based the theory developed here on a preliminary analysis of causal independence. The motivating intuition behind this analysis is that a proposition is to be taken as causally independent of the actions available to an agent at a moment whenever its truth or its falsity is always, at each history through that moment, guaranteed by a source of causality other than the actions of that agent. But in the present setting, where the only sources of causality represented at all are the actions of the various agents, this general intuition reduces to the more specific idea that a proposition is independent of the actions available to a particular agent at a moment whenever its truth or its falsity is always guaranteed by some pattern of action simultaneously available to all the others.

This preliminary analysis of causal independence is meant to be helpful in the present setting, providing at least an initial approximation. And as long as we are willing to assume that simultaneous events are causally unrelated, we can safely conclude that the preliminary analysis does not mislead through overclassification: each proposition that is classified by the analysis as causally independent of the actions available to an agent at a moment—each proposition whose truth or falsity is guaranteed by some pattern of action simultaneously available to all other agents—will actually be causally independent. The preliminary analysis does, however, mislead through underclassification, for it is easy to imagine situations in which certain propositions are naturally viewed as causally independent of an agent's actions even though their truth or falsity is not, in fact, guaranteed by patterns of action simultaneously available to other agents.

We consider two such cases here. Each presents a proposition that is apparently independent of the actions available to an agent. But in the first, although the truth or falsity of the proposition is simultaneously guaranteed, it is not guaranteed by a pattern of action available to other agents, and in the second, although the truth or falsity of the proposition is guaranteed by actions available to other agents, the guarantee is not simultaneous. The point of this discussion is not to elaborate our preliminary analysis into an account capable of handling cases like these—which would be a substantial research task—but simply to illustrate some of the issues that would arise in attempting to do so.

Beginning with the first case, then, let us imagine that an agent must choose at some particular moment—as he approaches a highway exit, perhaps—whether to spend his day at the park or the beach. We will suppose that, at the time of the agent's choice, it is not yet settled whether or not the day will be sunny, and that the agent's preferences are as follows: if it is sunny, he prefers a day at the beach to a day at the park; if it is not sunny, he prefers a day at the beach to a day at the park; but he prefers a

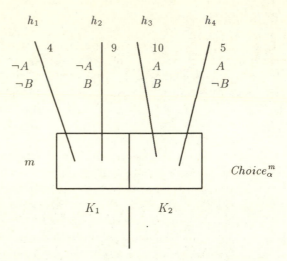

Figure 4.4: A simultaneous choice by nature

sunny day at the park to a day at the beach that is not sunny. And we will suppose also that the moment at which the agent must choose whether to spend his day at the park or the beach is also the final moment at which the weather for the day is still unsettled. Just as the agent chooses to spend his day at the park or the beach, it is as if nature simultaneously chooses whether or not the day will be sunny.

Within the present framework, of course, only the choices available to actual agents are allowed as choice partitions, and so the best representation of this situation currently available is depicted in Figure 4.4, where m is the moment at which the agent α must choose between the park and the beach, K_1 and K_2 are the actions of choosing the park or the beach respectively, and the statement B expresses the proposition that the day will be sunny (the statements A and $\neg A$ are included only for later reference). Since the history h_3 carries a value of 10 while h_2 carries a value of 9, the beach is better than the park on a sunny day; since the history h_4 carries a value of 5 while h_1 carries a value of 4, the beach is better than the park on a day that is not sunny; but a comparison between the histories h_2 and h_4 shows that a sunny day at the park is better than a day at the beach that is not sunny.

Now, based on our intuitive description of the situation, we would expect the proposition that the day will be sunny to be causally independent of the agent's choice between the park and the beach. We would expect to be able to conclude, if the day is going to be sunny, that the day will then be sunny no matter which action the agent chooses. And since the agent is better off choosing the beach over the park both when the day is sunny and when the day is not sunny, we would expect to be able to conclude, through sure-thing reasoning, that the agent is simply better off choosing the beach over the park. But these desirable results do not follow when our preliminary analysis is applied to the situation as depicted in Figure 4.4. There, according to our analysis, the proposition expressed by the statement B is not classified as independent of the actions available to α, since the truth or falsity of this statement is not guaranteed by actions available to other agents. We cannot conclude from B either that $A_\alpha^{K_1} \square{\rightarrow} B$ or that $A_\alpha^{K_2} \square{\rightarrow} B$. And we do not have $K_1 \prec K_2$.

When the situation is depicted as in Figure 4.4, then, our preliminary analysis of causal independence yields the wrong results, failing to classify the proposition expressed by B as independent of the actions available to α; but in this case, both the root of the problem and at least the general lines of a solution are plain. The problem arises because, although the truth or falsity of the proposition that the day will be sunny does seem to be guaranteed by some source of causality other than the actions available to α, this source of causality is not represented within the current setting, which recognizes only agents and their actions. And the solution, of course, is to realize that, if we wish to treat accurately those propositions whose truth or falsity is guaranteed by sources of causality other than the actions of agents, the background framework will have to be enriched to represent these other sources of causality as well.

As far as the present example goes, it would suffice, from a technical point of view, at least, simply to introduce a designated "agent" representing nature—ν, say—into the set $Agent$. The fact that it is decided at the moment m by an act of nature whether or not the day is sunny could be then represented by setting $Choice_\nu^m = \{K_3, K_4\}$, with $K_3 = \{h_2, h_3\}$ and $K_4 = \{h_1, h_4\}$. (The situation would no longer be depicted through Figure 4.4, but instead through a diagram like the earlier Figure 4.1, with $Choice_\nu^m$ replacing $Choice_\beta^m$.) And with the situation represented in that way, the preliminary analysis, without further modification, would then yield the correct results. The proposition expressed by B would be classified as causally independent of the actions available to α at m, since its truth or its falsity is always guaranteed by the actions simultaneously available to another "agent." We would be able to conclude from B both that $A_\alpha^{K_1} \square{\rightarrow} B$ and that $A_\alpha^{K_2} \square{\rightarrow} B$. And we would have $K_1 \prec K_2$.

Stepping back from this particular example, it would probably be best, more generally, to modify the underlying framework so as to segregate nonagentive from agentive sources of causal influence, and also to distinguish between the various different nonagentive causal sources, rather than lumping them all together simply as "nature." The proper definition of this more elaborate framework, however, would require us to resolve a number of fundamental issues. For example: is it reasonable to suppose that the product

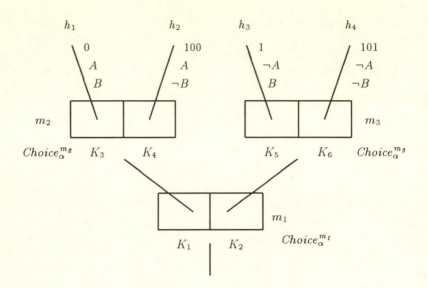

Figure 4.5: Later choices by another agent

of the various causal influences from all sources should determine a unique history?

Having considered some of the problems for our preliminary analysis of causal independence presented by causation that is simultaneous but nonagentive, we now turn to our second case: an example of causal influence that is agentive in source but not simultaneous. The basic scenario is found in Figure 4.5, which depicts a situation in which the agent α first chooses at m_1 between the actions K_1 and K_2, and then the agent β later chooses—at m_2 or m_3, depending on the initial choice of α—either between K_3 and K_4 or between K_5 and K_6. The statement B is true at the indices m_1/h_1, m_2/h_1, m_1/h_3, and m_3/h_3.

It will be useful to provide this schematic scenario with two separate interpretations. The first is based on Jeffrey's well-known war and peace example from [1965]. In this case, we suppose that α must choose at m_1 between arming or disarming: K_1 is the choice of arming, K_2 the choice of disarming. Later, at either m_2 or m_3, the agent β, an aggressor, must decide whether or not to attack α: K_3 and K_5 represent the choice to attack, K_4 and K_6 the choice to refrain from attacking. The statement B can now be interpreted as expressing the proposition that β attacks. Values are assigned to histories in such a way that the benefits of disarming are given a weight of 1 while the benefits of avoiding an attack are given a weight of 100; thus, for example, the history h_4 carries a value of 101, since it is a history in which both benefits are realized.

When the situation depicted in Figure 4.5 is interpreted in this way, the preliminary analysis seems to yield the right results. The proposition expressed by B—the proposition that β attacks—is classified as not independent of the actions available to α at m_1, since, although the truth or the falsity of B is guaranteed by the actions of another agent, this guarantee is not simultaneous with the choice available to α. Because the proposition expressed by B is not independent of the actions available to α, we cannot conclude, where B is true, that B would still have been true no matter which action α performed, and likewise where B is false. (For example, although B is true at the index m/h_3, where α chooses to disarm, the statement $A_\alpha^{K_1} \,\square\!\!\rightarrow B$ fails; we cannot conclude that β would have attacked even if α had chosen to arm.) And so we cannot conclude by sure-thing reasoning, just because disarming is a better choice than arming both when B is true and when B is false, that disarming is a better choice than arming: we do not have $K_1 \prec K_2$.

The reason that the results of the preliminary analysis seem appropriate in this case, of course, is that, in the situation as described, it really does seem natural to suppose that the later choice by β would be influenced by the earlier choice of α; the interpretation suggests, in particular, that β would be more likely to attack if α chooses to disarm. Often, things are like this: the later actions of other agents, and certainly many of our own later actions, are often influenced by our present choices. And in these cases, the preliminary analysis will seem accurate, since it does not classify a proposition as independent of our actions unless its truth or falsity is guaranteed by the simultaneous choices of other agents. In many other cases, however, it is more natural to think of the later choices of other agents— although later, and so in principle susceptible to the causal influence of our present choices—as in fact independent; and in these cases, the results of the preliminary analysis will seem incorrect.

To illustrate, we consider an academic example which can also be seen, as it turns out, as an interpretation of the abstract scenario depicted in Figure 4.5. In this case, we are to suppose that the agent α must choose at m_1 whether to spend the day at his office in an American university, or to stay home: K_1 represents the choice of staying home, K_2 the choice of going to the office. Later in the day, the agent β, a journal editor in Europe, must decide whether or not to accept a paper submitted by α: K_3 and K_5 represent the editor's decision to reject the paper, K_4 and K_6 the decision to accept it. The statement B is now interpreted as expressing the proposition that β will accept the paper, and the values assigned to the various histories reflect the assumption that α receives some slight benefit from going to the office (perhaps there are some administrative tasks to be taken care of), but a great benefit if the paper is accepted.

When the abstract scenario is interpreted in this way, it appears that the

preliminary analysis is again incorrect. Even though the truth or falsity of
the proposition expressed by B is not guaranteed by a simultaneous action
of β, but only by a later action, it is nevertheless most natural to regard
this proposition as independent of the actions available to α at m_1. (We
can suppose that, at the time of his decision, the editor does not even know,
let alone care, whether or not the agent has gone to his office.) Since the
proposition is independent, we should again be able to conclude, if β is going
to reject the paper, that he is going to reject the paper whether or not α
goes to the office. And since α is better off going to the office both if β
rejects the paper and if β does not, we should again be able to conclude
that α is better off going to the office.

As our two interpretations of Figure 4.5 show, it seems best to view some,
but not all, later actions by other agents as causally independent of a given
agent's present actions. The preliminary analysis fails, then, by neglecting
this distinction: since it requires simultaneity for independence, it groups all
later actions together as not causally independent. And indeed, this failure
is, in a sense, a necessary consequence of the current representational setting.
For the preliminary analysis to function as an analysis at all, it must define
the notion of causal independence entirely in terms of the concepts available
within the current analytic framework—roughly, in terms of what can be
depicted in our diagrams. But as we have seen, the same diagram, Figure
4.5, supports two different interpretations, in one of which the proposition
expressed by B seems to be independent of the actions available to α at m_1,
and in one of which it does not. It is reasonable to conclude, therefore, that
whatever it is about the two interpretations of this diagram that suggests
causal independence in one case, but not the other, is not contained in the
diagram itself, so that it is impossible for any analysis based only on the
concepts represented in the diagram to capture the distinction.

It is interesting to note that the differences between our two interpretations of Figure 4.5 could be captured through the postulational approach,
hinted at and then put aside in Section 4.1, according to which the meaning
of the *State* function is stipulated rather than defined. Suppose, for example, that we were to suspend Definition 4.4, which embodies our preliminary
analysis. We could then represent the two interpretations by stipulating that
in the first, the war and peace interpretation, $State_\alpha^{m_1} = \{H_{m_1}\}$, while in
the second, the academic interpretation, $State_\alpha^{m_1} = \{|B|_{m_1}, |\neg B|_{m_1}\}$. And
in that case, Definitions 4.16 and 4.5, without further change, would yield
the desired results: under the war and peace interpretation, the statement
B would imply neither $A_\alpha^{K_1} \square\!\!\rightarrow B$ nor $A_\alpha^{K_2} \square\!\!\rightarrow B$, and we would not have
$K_1 \prec K_2$; but under the academic interpretation, we would have B implying
both $A_\alpha^{K_1} \square\!\!\rightarrow B$ and $A_\alpha^{K_2} \square\!\!\rightarrow B$, and also $K_1 \prec K_2$. On this postulational
approach, however, each of the two interpretations supplements the abstract
scenario depicted in Figure 4.5 with additional information, by stipulating

that the agent is confronting a different state partition in the two cases. And any attempt to extend the preliminary analysis to capture the distinction between these two interpretations would likewise require a more expressive formalism, capable of representing the difference between the causal relations suggested by each.[13]

---

[13] A graphical notation for representing these causal relations is sketched in Thomason and Horty [1996], but the details of this proposal have not been worked out.

Chapter 5

Conditional oughts

5.1 Conditionally optimal actions

The previous chapter defined a notion of what an agent ought to do absolutely, without reference to any particular background conditions, but the techniques developed there can be extended to yield an account of the agent's conditional oughts as well.

To motivate this kind of extension, consider the situation depicted in Figure 5.1. Here, the agent α must choose from among the actions K_1, K_2, and K_3, where the possible outcomes of these various choices are the histories h_1 through h_5, with their indicated utilities. The agent is able to guarantee the truth of the statement A by choosing the action K_1, but as the diagram shows, it is not possible for the agent to guarantee the truth of B. Each of the actions available to α in this situation is optimal; and so we cannot say that α ought to see to it that A, since there are optimal actions, K_2 and K_3, that do not guarantee the truth of this statement. But suppose we are given B as a background assumption—suppose, that is, we can assume that the outcome will be some history in which B is true. Then, under these conditions, it does seem reasonable to say that α ought to see to it that A; for if we restrict our consideration only to those histories in which B holds, the action K_1, guaranteeing A, does seem to promise the best result.

As this example shows, the oughts governing an agent at a moment can usefully be thought of as conditioned on the truth of certain background propositions, sets of histories through that moment; and as these background sets shift, the agent's oughts may then shift as well. In order to make precise sense of this idea, we must first generalize some of the concepts underlying our analysis of an agent's oughts to the conditional setting.

We begin with the notion of choice itself. Let us take X as a proposition at the moment m, some set of histories through m. Then the set of actions available to an agent α at m under the condition that X holds—expressed

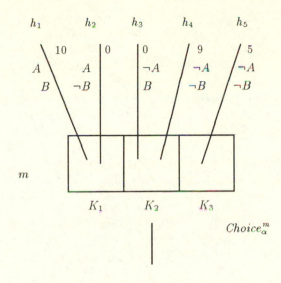

Figure 5.1: $Optimal_\alpha^m/|B|_m = \{K_1\}$

here as $Choice_\alpha^m/X$—is simply the set containing those actions open to α at m that are consistent with X.

Definition 5.1 ($Choice_\alpha^m/X$) Where α is an agent and m a moment from a stit frame, and where X is a proposition at m,

$$Choice_\alpha^m/X = \{K \in Choice_\alpha^m : K \cap X \neq \emptyset\}.$$

In the case of Figure 5.1, for example, where we take $|B|_m = \{h_1, h_3\}$ as a background proposition, the set of actions available to α at m under the condition $|B|_m$ is then $Choice_\alpha^m/|B|_m = \{K_1, K_2\}$.

It is equally straightforward to arrive at conditional analogues of our earlier concepts of weak and strong dominance, as follows.

Definition 5.2 (Conditional dominance; $\preceq_X, \prec_X$) Let α be an agent and m a moment from a utilitarian stit frame, and let K and K' be members of $Choice_\alpha^m$, and X a proposition at m. Then $K \preceq_X K'$ (K' *weakly dominates K under the condition X*) if and only if $K \cap X \cap S \leq K' \cap X \cap S$ for each state $S \in State_\alpha^m$; and $K \prec K'$ (K' *strongly dominates K under the condition X*) if and only if $K \preceq_X K'$ and it is not the case that $K' \preceq_X K$.

This conditional analysis follows the pattern of the absolute treatment from Definition 4.5, except that, in comparing the results of two actions K and K' in a given state S, our attention is now restricted only to those outcomes that are consistent with the background proposition X. And the analysis can be illustrated again through an application to Figure 5.1. Here, since

α is the only agent facing a nontrivial choice at the moment m, we have $State_\alpha^m = \{H_m\}$. It is thus easy to see, for example, that $K_2 \preceq_{|B|_m} K_1$ since $K_2 \cap |B|_m \cap H_m \leq K_1 \cap |B|_m \cap H_m$; and since it is not the case that $K_1 \cap |B|_m \cap H_m \leq K_2 \cap |B|_m \cap H_m$, we have $K_2 \prec_{|B|_m} K_1$ as well. Even though the two actions K_1 and K_2 are incomparable with respect to absolute dominance, K_1 does strongly dominate K_2 under the condition $|B|_m$.

The notion of strong conditional dominance can be reformulated along the lines suggested for absolute dominance in Proposition 4.6. In this case, the idea of the reformulation is that K' strongly dominates K under the condition X just in case, as long as our attention is restricted to those outcomes consistent with X, the results of K' are at least as good as those of K in every state, and better in some.

Proposition 5.3 Let α be an agent and m a moment from a utilitarian stit frame, and let K and K' be members of $Choice_\alpha^m$, and X a proposition at m. Then $K \prec_X K'$ if and only if (1) $K \cap X \cap S \leq K' \cap X \cap S$ for each state $S \in State_\alpha^m$, and (2) $K \cap X \cap S < K' \cap X \cap S$ for some state $S \in State_\alpha^m$.

And ordering properties can then be established for our conditional dominance relations analogous to those set out for absolute dominance in Proposition 4.7.

Proposition 5.4 Let α be an agent and m a moment from a utilitarian stit frame, and let K, K', and K'' be members of $Choice_\alpha^m$, and X be a proposition at m. Then:

1. If $K \prec_X K'$, then $K \preceq_X K'$.

2. If $K \preceq_X K'$ and $K' \preceq_X K''$, then $K \preceq_X K''$.

3. If $K \preceq_X K'$ and $K' \prec_X K''$, then $K \prec_X K''$.

4. If $K \prec_X K'$ and $K' \preceq_X K''$, then $K \prec_X K''$.

5. If $K \prec_X K'$ and $K' \prec_X K''$, then $K \prec_X K''$.

6. If $K \prec_X K'$, then it is not the case that $K' \prec_X K$.

7. It is not the case that $K \prec_X K$.

Having generalized the notions of both choice and dominance to the conditional setting, we can now combine these ideas to arrive at a concept of conditional optimality. Again taking X as a proposition at m, we can define the set of optimal actions available to α at m under the condition X—expressed as $Optimal_\alpha^m / X$—to be the set of those actions available to α at m under the condition X that are not strongly dominated under this condition by any other such action.

Definition 5.5 ($Optimal_\alpha^m/X$) Where α is an agent and m a moment from a utilitarian stit frame, and where X is a proposition at m,

$$Optimal_\alpha^m/X = \{K \in Choice_\alpha^m/X : \text{there is no } K' \in Choice_\alpha^m/X.K \prec_X K'\}.$$

And returning to Figure 5.1 for illustration, we can now see that $Optimal_\alpha^m/|B|_m = \{K_1\}$. Even though each of the actions available to the agent in this situation is optimal in the absolute sense, only K_1 is optimal under the condition specified by B.

It is worth noting explicitly that the conditional notions of choice, dominance, and optimality introduced here are, in fact, generalizations of our earlier concepts; when the background condition X is identified with the trivial proposition H_m, each of these three conditional notions coincides with its absolute counterpart. At the other extreme, when X is identified with the inconsistent proposition $\emptyset$, then $Choice_\alpha^m/X$ and $Optimal_\alpha^m/X$ are both empty; and in this case, $K \preceq_X K'$ holds and $K \prec_X K'$ fails regardless of K and K'.

As long as the background condition X is consistent, the set $Choice_\alpha^m/X$ must be nonempty, but it is possible for $Optimal_\alpha^m/X$ to be empty even when X is consistent; for it is easy to imagine a situation along the lines of the Pollock/Slote examples discussed earlier, in which each action available to α at m under the condition X is dominated under this condition by another such action. As before, however, given a consistent background condition, the existence of conditionally optimal actions is guaranteed at least in finite choice situations.

Proposition 5.6 Let α be an agent and m a moment from a finite choice utilitarian stit frame, and let X be a consistent proposition at m. Then $Optimal_\alpha^m/X \neq \emptyset$.

Again, it is best to establish this fact by way of a slightly more general result—that, in a finite choice situation, any action available but not optimal under some background condition must be dominated under that condition by an optimal action.

Proposition 5.7 Let α be an agent and m a moment from a finite choice utilitarian stit frame, and let X be a proposition at m. Then for each action $K \in Choice_\alpha^m/X - Optimal_\alpha^m/X$, there is an action $K' \in Optimal_\alpha^m/X$ such that $K \prec_X K'$.

For it is this more general result that is needed as a lemma in the proof of Proposition 5.9, which simplifies the evaluation rule to be set out for our conditional deontic operator.

5.2   A conditional ought operator

5.2.1   The definition

With these preliminaries aside, we can now turn to the task of analyzing statements concerning what an agent ought to do under specified background conditions.

In order to represent these conditional oughts, we first introduce a three-place deontic operator allowing us to construct statements of the form

$$\odot([\alpha \ cstit\colon A] \ / \ B),$$

which expresses the idea: under the condition that B holds, α ought to see to it that A. As with the absolute oughts, the evaluation rule governing this conditional deontic operator is formulated to apply in the general case, even when the set of conditionally optimal actions open to an agent is empty.

Definition 5.8 (Evaluation rule: $\odot([\alpha \ cstit\colon A] \ / \ B)$) Where α is an a-gent and m/h an index from a utilitarian stit model $\mathcal{M}$,

- $\mathcal{M}, m/h \models \odot([\alpha \ cstit\colon A] \ / \ B)$ if and only if, for each action $K \in Choice_\alpha^m/|B|_m^{\mathcal{M}}$ such that $K \nsubseteq |A|_m^{\mathcal{M}}$, there is an action $K' \in Choice_\alpha^m/|B|_m^{\mathcal{M}}$ such that (1) $K \prec_{|B|_m^{\mathcal{M}}} K'$, and (2) $K' \subseteq |A|_m^{\mathcal{M}}$, and (3) $K'' \subseteq |A|_m^{\mathcal{M}}$ for each action $K'' \in Choice_\alpha^m/|B|_m^{\mathcal{M}}$ such that $K' \preceq_{|B|_m^{\mathcal{M}}} K''$.

In fact, this evaluation rule is itself a generalization of that presented in Definition 4.12 for the absolute ought, and it can be motivated in a similar way. Where X is some background proposition, let us say that a statement A is *safely guaranteed under the condition* X by an action K available to an agent whenever the truth of A is guaranteed by K, and also by any other action that is available to the agent under the condition X and that weakly dominates K under this condition. The idea behind the current evaluation rule, then, is that $\odot([\alpha \ cstit\colon A] \ / \ B)$ should be true at an index m/h just in case: for every action K available to α at m under the condition $|B|_m$ that does not guarantee A, there is another action K' also available to α at m under the condition $|B|_m$ that both strongly dominates K under this condition and safely guarantees A under this condition.

Although the formulation of the evaluation rule for conditional oughts is complicated, most of the complications—forced by a treatment of the general case—can be avoided in the special case of finite choice situations. Here, much as with absolute oughts, conditional ought statements can be evaluated by reference to the set of conditionally optimal actions; for it can be shown that an agent ought to see to it that A under the conditions specified by B whenever seeing to it that A is a necessary condition for performing an action that is optimal under these conditions.

Proposition 5.9 Let α be an agent and m/h an index from a finite choice utilitarian stit model $\mathcal{M}$. Then $\mathcal{M}, m/h \models \odot([\alpha \; cstit \colon A] \, / \, B)$ if and only if $K \subseteq |A|_m^{\mathcal{M}}$ for each $K \in Optimal_\alpha^m / |B|_m^{\mathcal{M}}$.

This result can again be illustrated through Figure 5.1, where, as we have seen, $Optimal_\alpha^m / |B|_m = \{K_1\}$. In this situation, then, the result allows us to reach the conclusion that $\odot([\alpha \; cstit \colon A] \, / \, B)$ holds at m simply by noting that K_1—the unique optimal action under the conditions specified by B—guarantees the truth of A.

5.2.2   Some logical considerations

Let us now consider some logical features of the conditional ought operator defined here, noting first that it is normal in its consequent, supporting the principles

$RCEC_\alpha \odot$. $A \equiv C$ / $\odot([\alpha \; cstit \colon A] \, / \, B) \equiv \odot([\alpha \; cstit \colon C] \, / \, B)$,

$CN_\alpha \odot$. $\odot([\alpha \; cstit \colon \top] \, / \, B)$,

$CM_\alpha \odot$. $\odot([\alpha \; cstit \colon A \wedge C]/B) \supset (\odot([\alpha \; cstit \colon A]/B) \wedge \odot([\alpha \; cstit \colon C]/B))$,

$CC_\alpha \odot$. $\odot([\alpha \; cstit \colon A]/B) \wedge \odot([\alpha \; cstit \colon C]/B) \supset \odot([\alpha \; cstit \colon A \wedge C]/B)$,

and that, as with the other deontic operators defined so far, any statement of the form $\odot([\alpha \; cstit \colon A] \, / \, B)$ is moment determinate, always either settled true or settled false.

The conditional ought operator fails to validate the formula

$$\odot([\alpha \; cstit \colon A] \, / \, B) \supset \Diamond[\alpha \; cstit \colon A],$$

an extremely strong version of the characteristic deontic idea that ought implies can, according to which an agent must have the ability to do anything he that he ought to do under any antecedent conditions whatsoever. The reason for this failure is that our evaluation rule for this operator embodies the assumption that, under impossible antecedent conditions, an agent is required to see to the truth of every statement, including inconsistent statements; the formula $\odot([\alpha \; cstit \colon \bot] \, / \, \bot)$ is thus valid, while of course $\Diamond[\alpha \; cstit \colon \bot]$ is unsatisfiable. It is easy to see, however, that the conditional ought operator does validate the formula

$CD_\alpha \odot$. $\Diamond B \supset (\odot([\alpha \; cstit \colon A] \, / \, B) \supset \Diamond[\alpha \; cstit \colon A])$,

a weaker and more plausible version of the idea that ought implies can, according to which the agent must have the ability to do whatever he ought to do under any possible antecedent conditions.[1] Because the strong version

---

[1] Our treatment thus agrees with the approach advocated by Chellas [1980, Section 10.2] to the problem of generalizing the characteristic deontic idea to a conditional setting.

of the characteristic deontic idea fails, we cannot rule out the possibility of a conflict among the oughts governing an agent under any antecedent conditions whatsoever: the agent will, of course, face conflicting oughts under impossible conditions. But the principles $CC_\alpha \odot$ and $CD_\alpha \odot$ lead in the usual way to the validity of

$$CD_\alpha^* \odot . \quad \Diamond B \supset \neg(\odot([\alpha \; cstit: A] \, / \, B) \wedge \odot([\alpha \; cstit: \neg A] \, / \, B)),$$

which rules out the possibility of a conflict among the oughts governing an agent under any conditions that might actually occur.

Concerning the behavior of the conditional ought operator in its antecedent, we can see at once that it satisfies the reassuring principles

$$RCEA_\alpha \odot . \quad B \equiv C \quad / \quad \odot([\alpha \; cstit: A] \, / \, B) \equiv \odot([\alpha \; cstit: A] \, / \, C),$$

$$DEF_\alpha \odot . \quad \odot([\alpha \; cstit: A] \, / \, \top) \equiv \odot[\alpha \; cstit: A].$$

The first of these principles tells us that our analysis of what an agent ought to do under antecedent conditions is sensitive only to the proposition determined by those antecedent conditions, not the particular sentence that happens to express the proposition. The second principle tells us that what an agent ought to do under antecedent conditions that are trivially satisfied coincides with what the agent ought to do absolutely; as a result, we could, if we wished, define our absolute ought operator in terms of the conditional ought operator together with a trivially true sentence.

Even though our analysis of conditional oughts avoids any appeal to the kind of similarity relations among indices that underlie so many conditional deontic logics, we are nevertheless able to falsify the formula

$$\odot([\alpha \; cstit: A] \, / \, B) \supset \odot([\alpha \; cstit: A] \, / \, B \wedge C),$$

expressing the principle of antecedent strengthening, or monotonicity. A formal counterexample to (an instance of) this formula is provided in Figure 5.2. Here, it is clear that $\odot[\alpha \; cstit: A]$ is settled true at m, since $Optimal_\alpha^m = \{K_1\}$, and K_1 guarantees the truth of $[\alpha \; cstit: A]$; and from $\odot[\alpha \; cstit: A]$, we can conclude by $DEF_\alpha \odot$ that $\odot([\alpha \; cstit: A] \, / \, \top)$ must also be settled true. However, $Optimal_\alpha^m / |B|_m = \{K_1, K_2\}$, and since K_2 is a conditionally optimal action that does not guarantee the truth of $[\alpha \; cstit: A]$, we know that $\odot([\alpha \; cstit: A] \, / \, B)$ is settled false; and from this, since $B \equiv \top \wedge B$, the principle $RCEA_\alpha \odot$ leads us to the conclusion that $\odot([\alpha \; cstit: A] \, / \, \top \wedge B)$ must be settled false as well.

Finally, let us consider the issue of detachment in conditional oughts: if an agent ought to see to it that A under the condition B, and B is true, can we conclude from this that the agent ought to see to it that A? It is not difficult to see that this inference is unwarranted if what we mean by truth is mere truth at an index: the statement

$$\odot([\alpha \; cstit: A] \, / \, B) \wedge B \supset \odot[\alpha \; cstit: A]$$

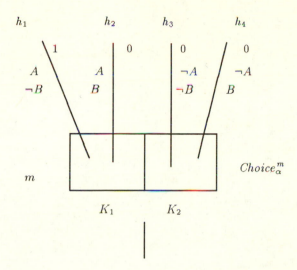

Figure 5.2: $\odot([\alpha \ cstit: A] \ / \ \top)$ without $\odot([\alpha \ cstit: A] \ / \ \top \wedge B)$

is invalid. A counterexample is already provided by our motivating case of Figure 5.1, where both $\odot([\alpha \ cstit: A]/B)$ and B are true at the index m/h_1, for example, but $\odot[\alpha \ cstit: A]$ is false. However, the matter is different if what we mean by truth is settled truth, or necessity: for it is easy to see, in this case, that the statement

$$\odot([\alpha \ cstit: A] \ / \ B) \wedge \Box B \supset \odot[\alpha \ cstit: A]$$

is valid. If B is settled true at a moment—that is, if $\Box B$ holds—then it is settled true at that moment also that $B \equiv \top$. From this and the truth of $\odot([\alpha \ cstit: A] \ / \ B)$, the principle $RCEA_\alpha \odot$ yields $\odot([\alpha \ cstit: A] \ / \ \top)$, and then $DEF_\alpha \odot$ allows us to conclude that $\odot[\alpha \ cstit: A]$. Our current treatment of detachment thus accords with the idea—first advocated, as far as I know, by Patricia Greenspan [1975]—that an absolute ought should be derivable from a conditional ought together with the necessity, though not the mere truth, of its antecedent condition.

Greenspan also argues, however, that an absolute ought should be derivable from a conditional ought along with a "prescription of the conditional statement's antecedent" [1978, p. 81]; but of course, this idea bifurcates in the present setting. It can be interpreted, first, as the suggestion that an absolute ought should be derivable from a conditional ought whenever the antecedent of the conditional is something that ought to be the case, as in the statement

$$\odot([\alpha \ cstit: A] \ / \ B) \wedge \bigcirc B \supset \odot[\alpha \ cstit: A];$$

or second, it can be interpreted as the suggestion that an absolute ought should be derivable from a conditional ought whenever the antecedent is something that the agent ought to see to, as in the statement

$$\odot([\alpha \; cstit: A] \, / \, B) \wedge \odot[\alpha \; cstit: B] \supset \odot[\alpha \; cstit: A].$$

The first of these two statements is again invalid. And a counterexample is provided, again, by Figure 5.1, where $\bigcirc B$ holds at m/h_1, since h_1 is the history of greatest value, but as we have seen, although $\odot([\alpha \; cstit: A] \, / \, B)$ also holds at this index, $\odot[\alpha \; cstit: A]$ fails. The second statement, however, is valid—established here as Validity A.7 (see Appendix)—and there is also reason to regard this formula as a more accurate representation of Greenspan's suggestion: although she does not work with a semantic theory that allows for a formal distinction between the two ideas, it is clear from her preliminary discussion in [1975] that she means to interpret the deontic operator as representing what an agent ought to do, rather than what ought to be. The present framework, with the notion of what an agent ought to do carefully separated from the notion of what ought to be, thus provides the machinery necessary for distinguishing the valid deontic detachment principle suggested by Greenspan from its invalid cousin.

5.3   Two patterns of argument

We have now introduced a notion of conditional dominance, and also a new deontic operator for describing what an agent ought to do under given conditions. The purpose of the present section is to examine two plausible patterns of argument relating these new conditional concepts to the corresponding unconditional, or absolute, notions.

The first of these arguments is nonlinguistic, concerning dominance relations among actions themselves. Suppose that X is a proposition at a moment m, and that $\overline{X}$ is its complement (that is, $\overline{X} = H_m - X$), and let K and K' be actions available to an agent at m. Then since X and $\overline{X}$ partition the possible outcomes, it is tempting to suppose that, if K' dominates K under the condition X, and if K' dominates K also under the condition $\overline{X}$, then K' should dominate K absolutely. Let us call this pattern of reasoning the *action argument*; formally, it leads from the premises $K \prec_X K'$ and $K \prec_{\overline{X}} K'$ to the conclusion $K \prec K'$.

The second argument is a kind of linguistic counterpart to the action argument, involving statements about an agent's oughts. Suppose that an agent α ought to see to it that A under the condition B, and also that α ought to see to it that A under the condition $\neg B$. Then it is tempting to conclude that α ought to see to it that A. Let us call this pattern of reasoning the *ought argument*; it can be represented formally as an inference from the premises $\odot([\alpha \ cstit: A] \ / \ B)$ and $\odot([\alpha \ cstit: A] \ / \ \neg B)$ to the conclusion $\odot[\alpha \ cstit: A]$.

In fact, both of these arguments are invalid in the present framework, as illustrated by the earlier Figure 4.4 (the reader should now ignore the intuitive interpretation that was supplied for that example, and consider it simply as a formal model). To see the invalidity of the action argument, take $X = \{h_2, h_3\}$ and $\overline{X} = \{h_1, h_4\}$, so that X and $\overline{X}$ partition the possible outcomes at m. Then, because α faces only a vacuous state partition at m, it is clear that $K_1 \prec_X K_2$, since $K_1 \cap X < K_2 \cap X$, and likewise clear that $K_1 \prec_{\overline{X}} K_2$; but we do not have $K_1 \prec K_2$, or even the weaker $K_1 \preceq K_2$. Thus, although K_2 strictly dominates K_1 under both the conditions X and $\overline{X}$, these two actions are incomparable when considered from an unconditional point of view. To see the invalidity of the ought argument, note first that $Optimal_\alpha^m / |B|_m = \{K_2\}$, and that $Optimal_\alpha^m / |\neg B|_m = \{K_2\}$ as well. Because K_2 guarantees the truth of A, we thus have both $\odot([\alpha \ cstit: A] / B)$ and $\odot([\alpha \ cstit: A] / \neg B)$ settled true at m. But since $Optimal_\alpha^m = \{K_1, K_2\}$, and K_1 does not guarantee the truth of A, the statement $\odot[\alpha \ cstit: A]$ is settled false. This situation thus supports the statement that α ought to see to it that A under the condition B, and also the statement that α ought to see to it that A under the condition $\neg B$, but it does not allow us to conclude unconditionally that α ought to see to it that A.

Although the action argument and the ought argument are both invalid, however, these two arguments nevertheless carry a good deal of persuasive force, and are frequently employed in practice. Both arguments are, moreover, closely related to valid patterns of reasoning. In the case of the ought argument, for instance, it is easy to see that the validity of this argument would follow at once from the principle

$DIL_\alpha \odot .$ $\odot([\alpha \ cstit: A] / B) \wedge \odot([\alpha \ cstit: A] / C) \supset \odot([\alpha \ cstit: A] / B \vee C).$

For this principle would lead us from the premises of the ought argument to the statement $\odot([\alpha \ cstit: A] \ / \ B \vee \neg B)$ as an intermediate result; and then, since, as we have seen, an absolute ought can be derived from a conditional ought together with the necessity of its antecedent, and since the statement $B \vee \neg B$ is, of course, necessary, the intermediate result would yield the conclusion $\odot[\alpha \ cstit: A]$. In rejecting the ought argument, then, we must also reject the principle $DIL_\alpha \odot$. But this principle is simply the analogue in the current setting of a commonly accepted validity in conditional deontic logic—the statement $\bigcirc(A/B) \wedge \bigcirc(A/C) \supset \bigcirc(A/B \vee C)$, in which $\bigcirc(.../...)$ is read as "It ought to be the case that ..., given that ...."[2]

---

[2] This statement is validated, for instance, in the conditional deontic logics advanced by Hansson [1971], Føllesdal and Hilpinen [1971], van Fraassen [1972], and Lewis [1973]. A useful comparison of these various logics can be found in Lewis [1974], where the statement at hand occurs as axiom A6.

Because both the action argument and the ought argument, though themselves invalid, are persuasive and closely related to valid patterns of reasoning, the goal of the present section is to isolate conditions under which these two arguments can be safely employed.

5.3.1   The action argument

We begin with the action argument, the inference from $K \prec_X K'$ and $K \prec_{\overline{X}} K'$ to $K \prec K'$, where K and K' are actions available to an agent at the moment m and the propositions X and $\overline{X}$ partition the possible outcomes at m.

It should be plain that the issues presented by this inference run parallel to those confronted earlier, in our discussion of sure-thing reasoning. In both cases, two actions are evaluated against the background of a partition of the possible outcomes; in both cases, we focus on a situation in which one action K' seems preferable to another action K when our attention is restricted to outcomes belonging to each member of the partition, and we face the question of concluding from this that K' is preferable to K absolutely.

Our treatment of sure-thing reasoning in Section 4.1 was based on the view that such a conclusion could be drawn as long as the propositions belonging to the background partition were causally independent of the actions available to the agent; and we identified the states—the patterns of action simultaneously available to all other agents—as paradigms of causally independent propositions. Later, in Section 4.4, we generalized the notion of causal independence so that propositions consisting of unions of states, as well as individual states, were then classified as causally independent, and it is this more general notion that provides the key to the current issue: as it turns out—perhaps no surprise—the action argument is valid whenever the propositions belonging to the background partition are, in this general sense, causally independent of the actions available to the agent.

In order to state this result precisely, and in full generality, we first introduce the notion of an independent partition as a partition of the possible outcomes at a moment that is causally independent of an agent's actions.

Definition 5.10 (Independent partition) Let α be an agent and m a moment from a stit frame, and let $X_1, \ldots, X_n$ be propositions at m. Then the set $\{X_1, \ldots, X_n\}$ is a *partition of H_m that is independent of* the actions available to α at m if and only if $\{X_1, \ldots, X_n\}$ is a partition of H_m and each of the propositions $X_1, \ldots, X_n$ is independent of the actions available to α at m.

It can then be shown that, against the background of an independent partition, an analogue to the action argument holds for weak dominance relations: if one action weakly dominates another under the conditions specified by each proposition from the partition, then the weak dominance relation holds absolutely.

Proposition 5.11 Let α be an agent and m a moment from a utilitarian stit frame; let K and K' be members of $Choice_\alpha^m$; and let $\{X_1, \ldots, X_n\}$ be a partition of H_m that is independent of the actions available to α at m. Then $K \preceq K'$ if and only if $K \preceq_X K'$ for each $X \in \{X_1, \ldots, X_n\}$.

From this we can conclude that the strong dominance relation holds absolutely whenever weak dominance holds under each of the independent conditions and strong dominance holds under some.

Proposition 5.12 Let α be an agent and m a moment from a utilitarian stit frame; let K and K' be members of $Choice_\alpha^m$; and let $\{X_1, \ldots, X_n\}$ be a partition of H_m that is independent of the actions available to α at m. Then $K \prec K'$ if and only if (1) $K \preceq_X K'$ for each $X \in \{X_1, \ldots, X_n\}$, and (2) $K \prec_X K'$ for some $X \in \{X_1, \ldots, X_n\}$.

And the validity of the action argument itself, against the background of an independent partition, follows at once from this result—for of course, the result entails that strong dominance holds absolutely whenever strong dominance holds under each condition from an independent partition.

5.3.2 The ought argument

We now turn to the ought argument, the linguistic counterpart to the action argument leading from the premises $\odot([\alpha\ cstit\colon A]\ /\ B)$ and $\odot([\alpha\ cstit\colon A]\ /\ \neg B)$ to the conclusion $\odot[\alpha\ cstit\colon A]$.

As we have seen, the key to guaranteeing validity in the case of the action argument is the requirement that the background partition should be independent of the choices available to the agent. Let us begin, then, simply by lifting the notion of an independent partition introduced in our consideration of the action argument from the level of propositions to the level of sentences. Thinking of a set of sentences as representing the set of propositions expressed by those sentences, we will say that the sentences represent an independent partition whenever the partition formed by the propositions they express is itself independent.

Definition 5.13 (Representing an independent partition) Let α be an agent and m a moment from a stit model $\mathcal{M}$. Then the set of sentences $\{B_1, \ldots, B_n\}$ *represents a partition of H_m that is independent of* the actions available to α at m if and only if the proposition set $\{|B_1|_m^{\mathcal{M}}, \ldots, |B_n|_m^{\mathcal{M}}\}$ is a partition of H_m that is independent of the actions available to α at m.

Now, since independence of the background partition was sufficient to guarantee the validity of the action argument, it might seem reasonable to expect, having lifted independence to the level of sentences, that we should be able to guarantee the validity of the ought argument in a similar way, simply by requiring the set of conditioning statements to represent an independent partition. That is: it might seem reasonable to expect the premises $\odot([\alpha \; cstit: A]/B)$ and $\odot([\alpha \; cstit: A]/\neg B)$ to entail the conclusion $\odot[\alpha \; cstit: A]$ as long as the statement set $\{B, \neg B\}$ represents a partition that is independent of the actions available to the agent α.

Surprisingly, however, this is not so. The ought argument can fail even in situations in which the set of conditioning statements does represent an independent partition. To see this, consider the situation depicted in Figure 5.3, which is interpreted as follows. At the moment m, the agent β must place a coin on the table, either heads up or tails up: K_4 is the action of placing the coin heads up, and K_5 the action of placing the coin tails up. Simultaneously, the agent α must either bet that the coin is placed heads up, bet that the coin is placed tails up, or refrain from gambling: K_1 is the action of betting on heads, K_2 the action of betting on tails, and K_3 the action of refraining. If α chooses to gamble on the coin's placement, the resulting utility is 10 if he bets correctly and 0 if he bets incorrectly; but a utility of 5 is guaranteed if α chooses not to gamble at all. The statement B, true at h_2, h_4, and h_6, expresses the proposition that β places the coin on the table heads up, and so $\neg B$, true elsewhere, the proposition that β places the coin tails up. The statement A expresses the proposition that α gambles. Since α gambles just in case he bets either heads or tails, performing either the action K_1 or the action K_2, the statement A is true at h_1 through h_4, and false only at h_5 and h_6, where α performs the action K_3.

Now in this situation, the optimal action for α to perform under the condition that β places the coin heads up is, of course, to bet heads, and likewise, the optimal action for α under the condition that β places the coin tails up is to bet tails; that is, we have $Optimal^m_\alpha/|B|_m = \{K_1\}$ and $Optimal^m_\alpha/|\neg B|_m = \{K_2\}$. No matter whether α bets heads or tails, however, we know at least that he gambles; that is, both K_1 and K_2 guarantee the truth of A. We can therefore conclude that both $\odot([\alpha \; cstit: A] / B)$ and $\odot([\alpha \; cstit: A] / \neg B)$ are settled true at m—that α ought to gamble given the coin is placed heads up, and also that α ought to gamble given the coin is placed tails up. The present situation thus supports both premises of the ought argument; and of course, the situation is one in which the set of conditioning statements $\{B, \neg B\}$ does, in fact, represent a partition that is independent of the actions available to α. Nevertheless, the situation does not support the conclusion of the ought argument. For each of the three actions available to the agent is, in fact, optimal under absolute conditions; that is, we have $Optimal^m_\alpha = \{K_1, K_2, K_3\}$. And since one of these optimal actions, K_3, does not guarantee the truth of A, we cannot conclude that $\odot[\alpha \; cstit: A]$. Even though α ought to gamble under the condition that the

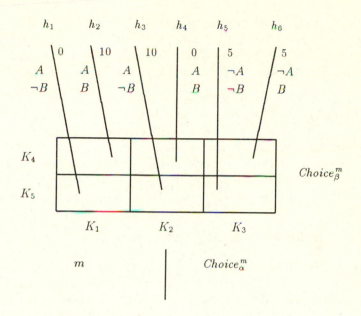

Figure 5.3: The third coin example

coin is placed heads up, and also under the condition that the coin is placed tails up—and even though the coin must be placed either heads up or tails up, and its placement is independent of the actions available to α—we still cannot conclude absolutely that α ought to gamble.

In the present example, the consequent statements of the conditional oughts involved—here, the statement A, representing the proposition that α gambles—is guaranteed by more than one action available to the agent: both K_1 and K_2 guarantee the truth of A. As it happens, it is this feature that allows our ought argument to fail, even though its conditioning statements represent an independent partition; the validity of an ought argument can be ensured as long as its consequent statements are restricted to those whose truth can be guaranteed only by a single action available to the agent.

In order to effect this restriction formally, let us recall the action statements of the form A_α^K introduced in Section 4.4, taken to mean that the agent α performs the action K, and so true at an index m/h just in case α performs the action K at that index. Each of these action statements is guaranteed, of course, only by a single one of the actions available to the agent; and when the consequent statements of the conditionals involved in the ought argument are so restricted, and the independence restriction on their antecedent statements remains in place as well, the argument can then be shown to be valid.

Proposition 5.14 Let α be an agent and m/h an index from a utilitarian stit model $\mathcal{M}$, and let $\{B_1, \ldots, B_n\}$ represent a partition of H_m that is independent of the actions available to α at m. Then if $\mathcal{M}, m/h \models \odot([\alpha \; cstit: A_\alpha^K] \,/\, B_i)$ for each $1 \leq i \leq n$, it follows that $\mathcal{M}, m/h \models \odot[\alpha \; cstit: A_\alpha^K]$.

Even though the ought argument is persuasive, and can be shown to follow from $DIL_\alpha\odot$, which is analogous to a principle generally accepted in conditional deontic logics, the validity of this argument can be guaranteed only under very special circumstances, governing both the antecedent and the consequent statements of the conditional oughts involved: the set of antecedent statements must represent an independent partition of the possible outcomes, and the consequent must be equivalent to an action statement.

5.4   Orthodox act utilitarianism

The goal of this section is to show how the notion of conditional optimality developed in the present chapter can be used to explicate a version of act utilitarianism different from the theory of dominance act utilitarianism defined in Section 4.2, and much more representative of the literature. In order to distinguish it from the dominance theory, and in deference to the literature, I refer to the version of act utilitarianism defined here as *orthodox act utilitarianism*.

5.4.1   An example

We begin by illustrating the difference between the orthodox and dominance theories with an example that has figured prominently in the controversy over forms of utilitarianism. Although this example first appeared in Gibbard's [1965], and was elaborated on shortly thereafter by J. Howard Sobel [1968], we take the later but more extensive discussion in Donald Regan's [1980] as our primary text:

> Suppose that there are only two agents in the moral universe, called Whiff and Poof. Each has a button in front of him which he can push or not. If both Whiff and Poof push their buttons, the consequences will be such that the overall state of the world has a value of ten units. If neither Whiff nor Poof pushes his button, the consequences will be such that the overall state of the world has a value of 6 units. Finally, if one and only one of the pair pushes his button (and it does not matter who pushes and who does not), the consequences will be such that the overall state of the world has a value of 0 (zero) units. Neither agent, we assume, is in a position to influence the other's choice. [Regan, 1980, p. 19]

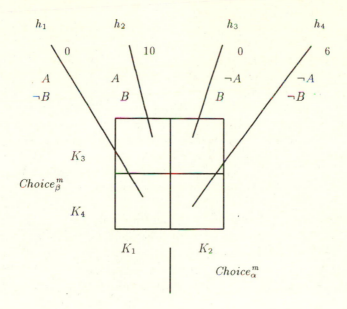

Figure 5.4: Whiff and Poof

Like Gibbard and Sobel before him, Regan introduces this example in order to make a general point about act utilitarianism—that universal satisfaction of this theory, satisfaction of the theory by every member of a group, still may not guarantee the best results achievable by that group. Rather than considering the morals to be drawn from this general point, however, we concentrate here on the more basic question of what it might mean to say, in this situation, that act utilitarianism is satisfied.

In the present setting, Regan's example can be depicted as in Figure 5.4, where α represents Whiff, β represents Poof, and m is the moment at which each of these two agents must choose whether or not to push his button.[3] The action K_1 represents Whiff's option of pushing his button, and K_2 his option of refraining; likewise, K_3 and K_4 represent Poof's options of pushing or refraining; and the possible outcomes resulting from the choices by these agents are represented by the histories h_1 through h_4, which are assigned the values indicated in Regan's description. (The sentence letters A and B, representing, respectively, the statements that Whiff pushes his button and that Poof pushes his button, do not figure in the current discussion, but are included for later reference.)

Now, when Regan's example is set out in this way, it is easy to see that both agents must satisfy our previous theory of dominance act utilitarian-

---

[3]Regan does not actually require that these choices must be simultaneous (though simultaneity is part of Gibbard's earlier description), but he does require the choices to be independent, and we guarantee independence through simultaneity.

ism no matter what they do. Neither action available to either agent is dominated, and so we have both $Optimal_\alpha^m = \{K_1, K_2\}$ and $Optimal_\beta^m = \{K_3, K_4\}$. Since both of the actions K_1 and K_2 available to Whiff are optimal, both must be classified as right by the dominance theory; and both of the actions K_3 and K_4 available to Poof must likewise be classified as right. Of course, against the background of this dominance theory, it is a trivial matter to establish Regan's general point that even universal satisfaction of act utilitarianism does not guarantee the best results. Since the dominance theory is universally satisfied no matter which patterns of action the agents perform, it is satisfied at the index m/h_1, for example, where Whiff pushes his button but Poof does not; and the resulting outcome here has a value of 0.

In its application to Regan's example, then, the theory of dominance act utilitarianism yields results that are at least definite, even if not particularly constraining: each of the two agents can satisfy the theory by selecting either of the available actions. Regan's own conclusions—based on his own theory of act utilitarianism or, as he calls it, AU—are strikingly different:

> Now, if we ask what AU directs Whiff to do, we find that we cannot say. If Poof pushes, then AU directs Whiff to push. If Poof does not push, then AU directs Whiff not to push. Until we specify how Poof behaves, AU gives Whiff no clear direction. The same is true, *mutatis mutandis*, of Poof. [Regan, 1980, p. 18]

In saying that act utilitarianism gives Whiff no clear direction, Regan does not simply mean that this theory, like the dominance theory, classifies multiple actions as right, allowing the agents to choose among these. Instead, he seems to mean that, on the basis only of the information provided so far, the theory is, in fact, unable to generate any results at all: no actions can be classified either as right or as wrong. In order to arrive at a situation in which act utilitarianism is able to yield definite results, Regan feels that it is necessary to supplement the description of the example provided so far, and depicted in Figure 5.4, with additional information concerning the actions actually performed by the individuals involved:

> If we shift our attention to patterns of behaviour for the pair, we can decide whether each agent satisfies AU in any specified pattern. [Regan, 1980, p. 18]

And he illustrates the kind of reasoning allowed by this additional information as follows:

> Suppose, for example, Whiff and Poof both push their buttons. The total value thereby achieved is ten units. Does Whiff satisfy AU? Yes. The only other thing he might do is not push his button. But under the circumstances, which include the fact

that Poof pushes his button, Whiff's not pushing would result in a total utility of zero. Therefore Whiff's pushing his button has at least as good consequences as any other action available to him under the circumstances. Therefore, it is right according to AU. [Regan, 1980, pp. 18–19]

Evidently, Regan is unwilling to classify the actions available to Whiff and Poof as either right or wrong absolutely, but only as right or wrong under conditions determined by the actions of the other.[4] It therefore seems natural, in the present framework, to represent the theory of act utilitarianism guiding Regan's judgments through the notion of conditional, rather than absolute, optimality. When both agents push their buttons, the action performed by Whiff is right because it is optimal under the conditions determined by Poof's actions; that is, we have $Optimal_\alpha^m/K_3 = \{K_1\}$. And of course, under these same conditions, given that Poof pushes his button, Whiff's choice not to push would be wrong, since it would not then be conditionally optimal.

On this view, the universal satisfaction of act utilitarianism is a kind of equilibrium condition, requiring, not just that each agent should perform an optimal action, but that each should perform an action that is optimal given the actions performed by the others. When both agents push their buttons, as we have seen, Whiff's action is right because it is optimal under the conditions determined by Poof's, but since $Optimal_\beta^m/K_1 = \{K_3\}$, Poof's action is also right, optimal under the conditions determined by Whiff's; and so the equilibrium condition is met. Regan's general point that even universal satisfaction of act utilitarianism does not guarantee an optimal outcome is now considerably more interesting than the similar claim for the dominance theory, since it means that even patterns of action satisfying this equilibrium condition may lead to suboptimal results. When both Whiff and Poof refrain from pushing their buttons, for example, each performs the right action according to Regan; each performs the unique action that is optimal given what the other does, since we have both $Optimal_\alpha^m/K_4 = \{K_2\}$ and $Optimal_\beta^m/K_2 = \{K_4\}$. But the utility of the resulting outcome is only 6.

---

[4] And this idea—that situations such as that depicted in Figure 5.4 must be supplemented with information concerning the actions performed by various agents before act utilitarianism can even be applied—is not unique to Regan. Gibbard adopts a similar strategy in his original discussion of this example, evaluating each agent's selection only under an assumption about the action selected by the other [1965, p. 215]. And Sobel defends Gibbard's strategy as follows: "It is perhaps natural to feel that Gibbard's first case is objectionable just because it includes assumptions concerning what agents will and would do. But this can be no objection since it is obvious that such assumptions are essential to the application of AU; without such assumptions the dictates of AU could not be determined ..." [1968, p. 152].

5.4.2   The definition

Let us now generalize from this particular example to arrive at a formal explication, in the present setting, of the orthodox theory of act utilitarianism underlying Regan's work.

In formulating this new theory, it is important to bear in mind a fundamental point of contrast with the earlier dominance account: while the dominance theory associates with any moment a single classification of the actions available to an agent as right or wrong, the orthodox theory will allow an action to be classified as right at some histories through a moment but wrong at others. Unlike the classification of actions generated by the dominance account, that is, the results of the new theory will not be moment determinate. This feature is crucial for allowing the evaluation of actions to vary appropriately, as Regan suggests, with the patterns of behavior to which they might belong. In the case of Figure 5.4, for example, the orthodox theory will have to classify the action K_1, representing Whiff's pushing his button, as right at the index m/h_2, when Poof pushes as well, but as wrong at the index m/h_1, when Poof does not.

Regan's characterization of act utilitarianism proceeds in the usual way—requiring an agent, in any given situation, to perform some action leading to "the best consequences he can possibly produce in that situation"—but the real key to his understanding of the theory can be in a gloss provided for the final term in this formula:

> Note that the 'situation' of the agent includes all causally relevant features of the rest of the world. In particular, it includes the behaviour of other agents whose behavior the agent in question is not able to influence, and it includes the facts about the way other agents whom the agent in question is able to influence would respond to various choices on his part. [Regan, 1980, pp. 3–4]

Let α be the agent in question. Of course, the only sources of causality represented at all in the present framework are the actions of the various agents, and if we confine our attention to a single moment m, we can safely assume that the particular action selected by α at m cannot influence the choices of any of these other agents. Where h is some history through the moment m, then, the situation of α at the index m/h—the causally relevant features of the rest of the world—can be identified with the patterns of action exhibited at m/h by the entire set of agents other than α; and this pattern, of course, is simply $State_\alpha^m(h)$, the particular state confronting α at m/h. Regan's situations can thus be represented, in the present framework, by our states.

Having identified the situations against which actions are to be evaluated, we are now in a position to define the set of actions classified by act utilitarianism as right for an agent α at an index m/h—expressed here as $AU\text{-}right_\alpha^{m/h}$. In keeping with the idea that satisfying act utilitarianism entails producing the best consequences possible in any given situation, it is natural to define these right actions as those that are optimal in the situation determined by that index.

Definition 5.15 ($AU\text{-}right_\alpha^{m/h}$) Where α is an agent and m/h an index from a utilitarian stit frame,

$$AU\text{-}right_\alpha^{m/h} = Optimal_\alpha^m / State_\alpha^m(h).$$

We can then define *orthodox act utilitarianism*—our formal reconstruction of the theory underlying Regan's work—as the view that an action available to an agent α at a moment m is *right* at the index m/h just in case it belongs to $AU\text{-}right_\alpha^{m/h}$, and *wrong* otherwise. And we can say that α *satisfies* this theory at a particular index m/h whenever the action performed by α at that index is classified by the theory as right at that index, and that he *violates* the theory otherwise.

This version of act utilitarianism can be illustrated by returning to Figure 5.4, and considering again the index m/h_2, where both Whiff and Poof push their buttons. At this index, the situation confronting Whiff, determined by Poof's action, is K_3; that is, $State_\alpha^m(h_2) = K_3$. We therefore have

$$
\begin{aligned}
AU\text{-}right_\alpha^{m/h_2} &= Optimal_\alpha^m / State_\alpha^m(h_2) \\
&= Optimal_\alpha^m / K_3 \\
&= \{K_1\},
\end{aligned}
$$

so that the action K_1 is classified as right at m/h_2; and since K_1 is likewise the action that Whiff performs at m/h_2, he satisfies the orthodox theory at that index. We can also see, however, that $AU\text{-}right_\alpha^{m/h_1} = \{K_2\}$. As a result, the action K_1 is classified as wrong at m/h_1 and Whiff must be said to violate orthodox act utilitarianism at this index, where he again performs the action K_1. Our definitions thus provide us with a formal recapitulation of the point emphasized earlier—that the classification of actions provided by the orthodox theory is not moment determinate. Here, the same action, K_1, is classified as right at the index m/h_2 but wrong at the index m/h_1; although Whiff performs the same action at each of these two indices, he satisfies orthodox act utilitarianism at the first but violates this theory at the second.

We have now defined two act utilitarian theories—the orthodox theory, which an agent α satisfies at an index m/h by performing some action belonging to $AU\text{-}right_\alpha^{m/h}$, and the dominance theory, which α satisfies at m/h by performing an action belonging to $Optimal_\alpha^m$. What are the relations between the two?

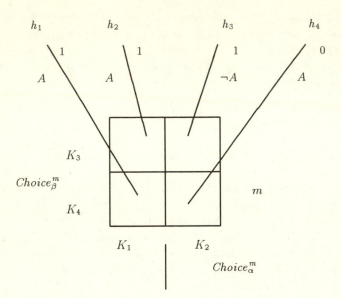

Figure 5.5: $A U\text{-}right_\alpha^{m/h_3} = \{K_1, K_2\}$, but $Optimal_\alpha^m = \{K_1\}$

From a formal standpoint, the matter is straightforward. As Figure 5.4 already shows, it is possible to satisfy the dominance theory while violating the orthodox theory. For even though, as noted earlier, Whiff and Poof both satisfy the dominance theory at every index from this example, we have just seen that Whiff violates the orthodox theory at the index m/h_1. Somewhat more surprising, it is also possible to satisfy the orthodox theory while violating the dominance theory, as illustrated by Figure 5.5 (in which the statement A is, again, included only for future reference). Here, we have $A U\text{-}right_\alpha^{m/h_3} = \{K_1, K_2\}$, so that the agent α satisfies the orthodox theory at the index m/h_3, where he performs the action K_2. But it is easy to see that $Optimal_\alpha^m = \{K_1\}$, so that α violates the dominance theory at the same index.

Simply because the dominance and orthodox theories of act utilitarianism are distinct theories—because there are indices at which they classify different sets of actions as right—there is a sense, of course, in which they must be inconsistent: considered as theoretical specifications of the right actions, these two theories cannot both be correct. But there is also another, weaker sense in which these theories are consistent, as shown by the following result.

Proposition 5.16 Let α be an agent and m a moment from a finite choice utilitarian stit frame. Then $A U\text{-}right_\alpha^{m/h} \cap Optimal_\alpha^m \neq \emptyset$ for each $h \in H_m$.

Because there is always, at any index, some overlap between the actions classified as right by orthodox and dominance act utilitarianism, it is always possible for both theories, though distinct, to be jointly satisfied.

When we turn from the formal standpoint to matters of intuitive adequacy, however, the question concerning the relations between the orthodox and dominance theories is considerably more complex; these two utilitarian theories reflect sharply different views of moral evaluation. The difference has its roots in the idea, central to Regan's view, that act utilitarianism must evaluate an agent's action against the background of the pattern of independent actions of which it is a part. It is this idea that allows Regan to judge that Whiff's pushing his button is right in the situation in which Poof pushes as well, but wrong in the situation in which Poof does not push; and it is this idea also that forces us to relativize our formal reconstruction of the theory to full indices, rather than moments, classifying Whiff's pushing action as right at the index m/h_2 but wrong at the index m/h_1. But if the evaluation of an agent's action depends on the pattern of independent actions of which it is a part—and particularly if, as in Regan's own example, the same action is judged as right in the context of one pattern but wrong in the context of another—then the agent himself cannot always determine whether the action he performs is right or wrong; the matter is, to some extent, outside of the agent's own control.

This feature of the orthodox theory—that it subjects agents to moral assessment on the basis of factors over which they have no control—may appear to be objectionable to some, and to contrast unfavorably with the moment determinateness of the dominance theory, where the assessment of an agent's actions at a moment is independent of the choices made by others. But there is also reason to think that, at times, our assessment of an agent's actions actually does depend on factors beyond his control, so that the orthodox theory's treatment of this matter is correct. (We tend to judge a speeding driver that hits a child more harshly than a speeding driver that does not, even if the actions of the two drivers are otherwise identical, and the only factor that influences which one actually hits the child is the child's own decision as to when to cross the street.) These issues—concerning the extent to which the moral character of an agent and his actions can legitimately be thought of as influenced by factors outside of his control—are discussed in the extensive literature on *moral luck*.[5] Of course, the present account does not contribute anything substantial to this discussion, but it does provide a framework in which two utilitarian theories exemplifying the opposing points of view can be teased apart, formulated explicitly, and compared.

---

[5] Although the idea that the moral evaluation of an agent may be influenced by external factors goes back at least to Aristotle's *Nicomachean Ethics*, much of the recent discussion of this topic was inspired by a pair of influential articles: Nagel [1976] and Williams [1976]. A useful collection of contemporary work on the topic can be found in Statman [1993].

5.4.3   An orthodox deontic operator

Just as the deontic operator introduced in Section 4.3 reflects the ideas underlying dominance act utilitarianism, we can now define a new operator representing the orthodox perspective on an agent's oughts. We motivated our
earlier treatment by supposing, in the finite choice case, that $\bigodot[\alpha \; cstit: A]$
should be settled true at a moment m whenever the truth of A is guaranteed by each of the optimal actions available to α. And likewise, where we
represent the claim that α ought to see to it that A in the orthodox sense
through the statement

$$\bigoplus[\alpha \; cstit: A],$$

we will now suppose that this statement should be true at the index m/h
just in case the truth of A is guaranteed by each of the actions available to
the agent that are optimal given the circumstances—that is, the particular
state—in which he finds himself at this index.

As before, the official evaluation rule for this orthodox ought operator
is formulated to apply even when the set of optimal actions available to an
agent in some state may be empty.

Definition 5.17 (Evaluation rule: $\bigoplus[\alpha \; cstit: A]$) Where α is an agent
and m/h an index from a utilitarian stit model $\mathcal{M}$,

- $\mathcal{M}, m/h \models \bigoplus[\alpha \; cstit: A]$ if and only if, for each action $K \in Choice_\alpha^m$
  such that $K \nsubseteq |A|_m^{\mathcal{M}}$, there is an action $K' \in Choice_\alpha^m$ such that (1)
  $K \prec_{State_\alpha^m(h)} K'$, and (2) $K' \subseteq |A|_m^{\mathcal{M}}$, and (3) $K'' \subseteq |A|_m^{\mathcal{M}}$ for each
  action $K'' \in Choice_\alpha^m$ such that $K' \preceq_{State_\alpha^m(h)} K''$.

This official rule tells us, then, that $\bigoplus[\alpha \; cstit: A]$ holds at an index m/h
just in case: for every action K available to α at m that does not guarantee
the truth of A, there is another action K' also available to α at m that both
strongly dominates K under the condition $State_\alpha^m(h)$ and safely guarantees
A under this condition.

Again, however, the meaning of the orthodox ought operator is most
perspicuous in the finite choice setting, where the official evaluation rule
coincides with our motivating intuition that $\bigoplus[\alpha \; cstit: A]$ should hold at an
index m/h whenever the truth of A is guaranteed by each available action
that is optimal under the circumstances in which the agent finds himself at
this index.

Proposition 5.18 Let α be an agent and m/h an index from a finite choice
utilitarian stit model $\mathcal{M}$. Then $\mathcal{M}, m/h \models \bigoplus[\alpha \; cstit: A]$ if and only if
$K \subseteq |A|_m^{\mathcal{M}}$ for each $K \in AU\text{-}right_\alpha^{m/h}$.

And again, just as the earlier Proposition 4.13 established a link between the
dominance ought operator and the theory of dominance act utilitarianism,

this result confirms a similar connection in the orthodox case, showing that the statement $\bigoplus[\alpha \ cstit : A]$ holds at an index m/h from a finite choice model whenever A is guaranteed by each of the actions available to α that the orthodox theory classifies at m/h as right.

It would be possible to illustrate our new deontic operator with the Whiff and Poof example, but for the sake of variety we now introduce another, due to Holly Goldman [1976], but also discussed by Humberstone in [1983], a paper that sets out in a different context some of the fundamental ideas underlying the orthodox ought defined here. In this example, two drivers are traveling toward each other on a one-lane road, with no time to stop or communicate, and with a single moment at which each must choose, independently, either to swerve or to continue along the road. There is only one direction in which the drivers might swerve, and so a collision can be avoided only if one of the drivers swerves and the other does not; if neither swerves, or both do, a collision occurs. This example is depicted in Figure 5.6, where α and β represent the two drivers, K_1 and K_2 represent the actions available to α of swerving or continuing along the road, K_3 and K_4 likewise represent the swerving or continuing actions available to β, and m represents the moment at which α and β must make their choice. The histories h_1 and h_3 are the ideal outcomes, resulting when one driver swerves and the other does not; collision is avoided. The histories h_2 and h_4, resulting either when both drivers swerve or both continue along the road, represent nonideal outcomes; collision occurs. The statement A, true at h_1 and h_2, expresses the proposition that α swerves.

Now, considering this example, first, from the dominance point of view, it is clear that $Optimal_\alpha^m = \{K_1, K_2\}$; both actions available to α are classified as optimal. Evidently, then, because one of the optimal actions available to α guarantees the truth of A and the other guarantees the truth of $\neg A$, both $\bigodot[\alpha \ cstit : A]$ and $\bigodot[\alpha \ cstit : \neg A]$ are settled false at m. When we adopt the orthodox point of view, by contrast, the truth or falsity of ought statements can now vary from index to index. At the index m/h_1, for example, where β continues along the road, the optimal action available to α under these conditions is to swerve; that is, we have $AU\text{-}right_\alpha^{m/h_1} = \{K_1\}$. Thus, since K_1 guarantees the truth of A, the statement $\bigoplus[\alpha \ cstit : A]$ holds at m/h_1. But at the index m/h_2, where β swerves, the optimal action available to α under these new conditions is to continue along the road; that is, $AU\text{-}right_\alpha^{m/h_2} = \{K_2\}$. And so, since K_2 guarantees $\neg A$, the statement $\bigoplus[\alpha \ cstit : \neg A]$ holds at m/h_2. As before, what α ought to do at an index depends on what β does.

Turning briefly to logic, it is easy to see that our orthodox ought operator validates the principles $D_\alpha \bigoplus$, $RE_\alpha \bigoplus$, $N_\alpha \bigoplus$, $M_\alpha \bigoplus$, and $C_\alpha \bigoplus$ (analogues of $D_\alpha \bigodot$, $RE_\alpha \bigodot$, $N_\alpha \bigodot$, $M_\alpha \bigodot$, and $C_\alpha \bigodot$, but with $\bigoplus$ for $\bigodot$), but differs

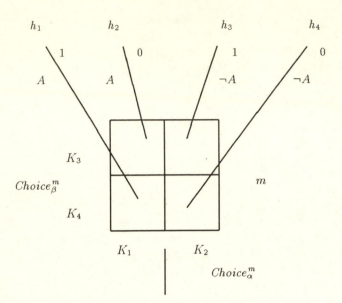

Figure 5.6: The driving example

from the dominance ought in not being moment determinate.[6] Because of this difference, the two oughts interact differently with the historical necessity and possibility operators: for example, the dominance ought validates the formula $\odot[\alpha\ cstit\colon A] \supset \square \odot[\alpha\ cstit\colon A]$; but the corresponding validity fails for the orthodox ought, and indeed, as Figure 5.6 shows, the formula $\oplus[\alpha\ cstit\colon A] \wedge \diamond \oplus[\alpha\ cstit\colon \neg A]$ is satisfiable. Neither of these two oughts entails the other; both

$$\oplus[\alpha\ cstit\colon A] \supset \odot[\alpha\ cstit\colon A],$$
$$\odot[\alpha\ cstit\colon A] \supset \oplus[\alpha\ cstit\colon A]$$

are invalid. A countermodel to the first of these statements is again provided by Figure 5.6, where, as we have seen, $\oplus[\alpha\ cstit\colon A]$ holds at m/h_1 but $\odot[\alpha\ cstit\colon A]$ is settled false; a countermodel to the second is provided by Figure 5.5, where $\odot[\alpha\ cstit\colon A]$ is settled true but $\oplus[\alpha\ cstit\colon A]$ fails at m/h_2. Although incomparable in strength, however, the two oughts are at least consistent, due to the validity of

$$D_\alpha^* \odot \oplus.\quad \neg(\odot[\alpha\ cstit\colon A] \wedge \oplus[\alpha\ cstit\colon \neg A]).$$

In the finite choice setting, this principle follows at once from Propositions 4.13, 5.16, and 5.18, though a general verification, omitted here, would

---

[6]Within the stit framework, both Bartha [1993] and Wansing [1998] have argued for the advantages of an ought operator that is not moment determinate.

require us to unwind the evaluation rules for the two operators.

From the standpoint of intuitive adequacy, the contrast between the orthodox and dominance deontic operators provides us with another perspective on the issue of moral luck, the role of external factors in our moral evaluations; for here, both operators seem to capture a legitimate sense of the ought used in our ordinary judgments. Returning to Figure 5.6 for illustration, imagine that what actually happens is that both agents continue along the road, so that the resulting outcome is the history h_4, in which there is a collision. Now, looking back at the matter from some moment $m' \in h_4$ such that $m < m'$—perhaps while recovering in the hospital bed— there does seem to be a sense in which the agent α can correctly regret his choice, saying to himself: I ought to have swerved. This sense is captured by the orthodox ought, which yields $P \oplus [\alpha \ cstit: A]$ as true at m'/h_4, since $\oplus [\alpha \ cstit: A]$ holds at the earlier m/h_4. Still, we are tempted to say, even though the agent might legitimately regret his choice, it is not one for which he should be blamed—it is not really as if he failed to do something he ought to have done, since either choice, at the time, could equally well have led to a collision, with the outcome determined only by matters over which the agent had no control. This sense is captured by the dominance account: $P \odot [\alpha \ cstit: A]$ fails at m'/h_4 because there is no prior moment along h_4 at which $\odot [\alpha \ cstit: A]$ holds.

Chapter 6

Group oughts

6.1 Optimal group actions

This chapter extends certain aspects of the normative account from the previous Chapters 4 and 5 in two ways—first, to an account governing groups of agents as well as individuals, and then to an account governing individual agents viewed as acting in cooperation with the members of a group. The general idea that group actions might be subject to normative evaluation is not new; it has been suggested by a number of writers.[1] Often, however, these suggestions have remained at a programmatic level, without providing the kind of machinery necessary for assessing the validity of particular arguments. The primary contribution of the present discussion, by contrast, is the articulation of a precise account of group normative concepts, cast against a precise background notion of group agency.

This notion of group agency lying in the background, of course, is that set out in Section 2.4, where the partition $Choice_\Gamma^m$ is introduced to represent the actions available to the group Γ at the moment m, and the statement $[\Gamma \; cstit: A]$ is then defined to mean that, through the choice of one or another of its available actions, the group Γ guarantees the truth of A. Once the shift is made to a group setting, our development of the normative concepts governing groups largely parallels the individual case, and so we begin simply by generalizing the familiar concepts of states, dominance, and optimality.

In the individual case, the set $State_\alpha^m$ of states confronting an agent α at a moment m was defined to contain the patterns of action simultaneously available to $Agent - \{\alpha\}$, the set of agents other than α. A natural generalization of this idea leads us now to define $State_\Gamma^m$, the set of states confronting the group Γ at the moment m, as containing the patterns of action simultaneously available to $Agent - \Gamma$, the set of agents other than those belonging to Γ.

---

[1] A partial list includes Carlson [1995], Conee [1983], Feldman [1986], Jackson [1988], McKinsey [1981], Parfit [1984], Postow [1977], Rabinowicz [1989], and Tännsjö [1989].

Definition 6.1 (*$State_\Gamma^m$*) Where Γ is a group of agents and m a moment from a stit frame,

$$State_\Gamma^m = Choice_{Agent-\Gamma}^m.$$

And, as in the individual case, we let $State_\Gamma^m(h)$ stand for the particular state from $State_\Gamma^m$ that is realized at the index m/h.

Once the appropriate states have been identified, the dominance relations among the actions available to a group can be specified through a definition that mirrors the account for individuals.

Definition 6.2 (Group dominance; $\preceq, \prec$) Let Γ be a group of agents and m a moment from a utilitarian stit frame, and let K and K' be members of $Choice_\Gamma^m$. Then $K \preceq K'$ (K' *weakly dominates* K) if and only if $K \cap S \leq K' \cap S$ for each state $S \in State_\Gamma^m$; and $K \prec K'$ (K' *strongly dominates* K) if and only if $K \preceq K'$ and it is not the case that $K' \preceq K$.

And it is then easy to show that the ordering relations established for individual dominance in Proposition 4.7 hold for group dominance as well.

With the notions of dominance among group actions in place, we can define the set of optimal actions available to a group Γ at the moment m—represented as $Optimal_\Gamma^m$—in the expected way, as the set of actions available to Γ at m that are not strongly dominated by any others.

Definition 6.3 (*$Optimal_\Gamma^m$*) Where Γ is a group of agents and m a moment from a utilitarian stit frame,

$$Optimal_\Gamma^m = \{K \in Choice_\Gamma^m : \text{there is no } K' \in Choice_\Gamma^m. K \prec K'\}.$$

And the theory of dominance act utilitarianism introduced in Section 4.2 for individual agents can now be extended to groups as well. As in the individual case, the theory will now classify an action available to the group Γ as *right* at an index m/h just in case that action belongs to $Optimal_\Gamma^m$, and *wrong* at m/h otherwise; and we can say also that Γ *satisfies* dominance act utilitarianism at m/h whenever the action performed by Γ at that index is classified there as right, and that Γ *violates* the theory otherwise. Again, it should be noted that the dominance classification of group actions as right or wrong, like the classification of individual actions, is moment determinate: any group action that is classified as right at the index m/h must be classified as right also at the index m/h', for every history h' from H_m.

These concepts can be illustrated by returning to the Whiff and Poof example, depicted in Figure 5.4. Here, where $\Gamma = \{\alpha, \beta\}$, it is clear that this group is faced at m with a choice from among four actions: $Choice_\Gamma^m = \{K_1 \cap K_3, K_1 \cap K_4, K_2 \cap K_3, K_2 \cap K_4\}$. But only the first of these—the group action performed by Γ when both of its individual members push their buttons—is optimal: $Optimal_\Gamma^m = \{K_1 \cap K_3\}$. The group Γ thus satisfies dominance act utilitarianism only at the index m/h_2; it violates the dominance theory at m/h_1, m/h_3, and m/h_4.

We saw in Section 2.4 that the notion of group agency presented there could be thought of as including individual agency as a special case: since $Choice^m_{\{\alpha\}} = Choice^m_\alpha$, the actions available to the group $\{\alpha\}$ coincide with those available to the individual α. And it is now worth noting that the concepts of states, dominance, and optimality defined here for groups likewise generalize the corresponding concepts for individuals. Since $State^m_{\{\alpha\}} = State^m_\alpha$, the states confronting the group $\{\alpha\}$ are identical with those confronting the individual α. The dominance relations among the actions available to $\{\alpha\}$ agree with those among the actions available to α. And so, of course, since $Optimal^m_{\{\alpha\}} = Optimal^m_\alpha$, the set of optimal actions available to $\{\alpha\}$ and α coincide as well.

In Section 4.2, we saw that the existence of optimal actions for individual agents is guaranteed in the finite choice framework, where the choices available to each agent are restricted at any given moment to a finite number of actions. Even in the finite choice framework, however, it is still possible for a group of agents to face an infinite number of available actions, if the group is itself infinite; and in that case, as with the Pollock/Slote situations described earlier, each action available to the group might be dominated by another. Imagine, for example, a committee containing a countably infinite number of members, each of whom must choose at the designated moment to vote either for or against some proposal. And suppose that the utility of each possible outcome is identified with the number of committee members voting for the proposal, unless the committee happens to favor the proposal unanimously, in which case the resulting outcome has a utility of 0. In such a situation, each individual member of the committee has available only two choices—voting for or against the proposal—and so each individual member is guaranteed an optimal action. But the group as a whole faces an infinite number of available actions, each of which is dominated by another: if any finite number of members vote for the proposal, it would be better if one more had done so, but if all members do so, it would be better if only a few had. Hence, the set of optimal actions available to the committee itself is empty.

In order to guarantee the existence of optimal group actions, then, we must limit our attention, not only to finite choice frames, but also to finite groups of agents—not an entirely unreasonable restriction.

Proposition 6.4 Let Γ be a finite group of agents and m a moment from a finite choice utilitarian stit frame. Then $Optimal^m_\Gamma \neq \emptyset$.

Again, it is best to derive this fact from the slightly more general result that each nonoptimal group action is dominated by some optimal action.

Proposition 6.5 Let Γ be a finite group of agents and m a moment from a finite choice utilitarian stit frame. Then for each action $K \in Choice_\Gamma^m - Optimal_\Gamma^m$, there is an action $K' \in Optimal_\Gamma^m$ such that $K \prec K'$.

For again, it is this more general result that is needed in the proof of Proposition 6.14, which provides us with a simplified evaluation rule for group ought statements.

6.2   Individual and group act utilitarianism

Having formulated dominance act utilitarianism for both individuals and groups, we can now explore the relations between these two versions of the theory. Does the satisfaction of dominance act utilitarianism by each member of a group entail that the group itself satisfies this theory? Does satisfaction by a group entail satisfaction by its individual members?

It is easy to see that the answer to the first of these questions is no. A counterexample is provided already by the Whiff and Poof case, from Figure 5.4. As noted in our initial discussion of this example, each action available to each of the agents α and β is optimal—that is, we have $Optimal_\alpha^m = \{K_1, K_2\}$ and $Optimal_\beta^m = \{K_3, K_4\}$—so that each of these agents individually satisfies dominance act utilitarianism at every index. But as we have just seen, only one of the four actions available to the group $\Gamma = \{\alpha, \beta\}$ is optimal—we have $Optimal_\Gamma^m = \{K_1 \cap K_3\}$—and so this group itself satisfies dominance act utilitarianism only at the index m/h_2, where it performs the action $K_1 \cap K_3$. At each of the other indices, m/h_1, m/h_3, and m/h_4, even though both α and β satisfy dominance act utilitarianism as individuals, the group Γ violates this theory.[2]

Although satisfaction of dominance act utilitarianism by each member of a group does not entail satisfaction of this theory by the group itself, then, it is frequently claimed that the converse implication holds for act utilitarian theories—that satisfaction by a group entails satisfaction by each of its members. Regan, for example, claims that "for any group of agents in any situation, any pattern of behaviour by that group of agents in that situation which produces the best consequences possible is a pattern in which the members of the group all satisfy AU," and supports this claim with the following argument:

> Consider a group of agents who are behaving in such a way as to produce the best consequences possible [in the circumstances].

---

[2]Of course, the possibility that a normative theory might be violated by a group of individuals each of whom satisfies that theory leads to a number of difficulties. One might wonder, for example, under what circumstances the blame (or even liability) for doing what is wrong can be allocated among the individual members of a group that violates the theory; interesting discussions of this problem can be found in Feinberg [1968] and Held [1970].

Suppose that some member of the group is not satisfying AU.
Call the member Smith. To say Smith is not satisfying AU is to
say there is something he could do which would have better consequences in the circumstances than what he is doing. In other
words, by altering only this behaviour . . . , we could improve the
overall consequences produced. But that means that from the
point of view of the group, the consequences of their behaviour
as a group could be improved by altering Smith's behaviour in
the same way. This contradicts our original assumption. We
conclude that a group which is producing the best consequences
possible cannot include any agent who is not satisfying AU. [Re-
gan, 1980, pp. 54-55][3]

And though he offers no argument for the conclusion, Frank Jackson is even
more explicit on the point:

if the right group action is actually performed, then that group
action's constituent individual actions must be right (or at least
not wrong). Although the right prescription for a group cannot
in general be obtained by conjoining the right prescriptions for
the individuals in the group, if the right prescription should actually be followed by the group, then the actions by the individuals in the group which together constitute the group following
that prescription, cannot be incompatible with what would then
be the right prescriptions for those individuals. [Jackson, 1988,
p. 264]

Now, the first thing to note about this entailment—from group to individual satisfaction of act utilitarianism—is that it fails for the dominance
theory. A counterexample can be found in our earlier Figure 5.5. Here, it is
easy to see that three of the four actions available to the group $\Gamma = \{\alpha, \beta\}$
are optimal: $Optimal_\Gamma^m = \{K_1 \cap K_3, K_1 \cap K_4, K_2 \cap K_3\}$. But as noted in the
discussion of that example, the agent α has available only one optimal action: $Optimal_\alpha^m = \{K_1\}$. Consider, then, the index m/h_3, where the group
Γ performs the action $K_2 \cap K_3$ and the individual α performs the action K_2.
Since the action performed by Γ at this index is an optimal group action, the
group satisfies dominance act utilitarianism; but even though α belongs to
Γ, the action performed at this index by α is not among the optimal actions
available to this individual, and so α violates the theory.

In the case of the dominance act utilitarianism, then, there are no strong
links between individual and group satisfaction: it is possible for each agent
belonging to a group to satisfy the theory even though the group itself does

---

[3]A similar argument is presented by Parfit [1984, p. 54]; both Regan's and Parfit's
arguments are studied in some detail by Rabinowicz [1989].

not, and likewise possible for a group to satisfy the theory even though some of its individual members do not. But what of the claim, by Regan and Jackson, among others, that group satisfaction of act utilitarianism entails satisfaction by the individual members of the group, and what of Regan's argument in support of this claim? In the passages cited, Regan and Jackson are writing, of course, not about dominance act utilitarianism, but about the form of utilitarian theory described here as orthodox: their claim concerns the relations between individual and group orthodox act utilitarianism. We have already formulated the individual version of this orthodox theory, but in order to evaluate the claim, we must first extend the orthodox theory to cover groups as well.

Once again, the extension is routine: since the orthodox theory is defined in terms of the conditional concepts introduced for individual agents in the previous chapter, it is simply a matter of generalizing some of these ideas to the group setting. We begin with the notions of conditional choice and conditional dominance from Definitions 5.1 and 5.2. These are now extended to characterize the actions available to a group of agents under some particular background condition, as well as conditional dominance relations among those group actions.

Definition 6.6 (*Choice$_\Gamma^m/X$*) Where Γ is a group of agents and m a moment from a stit frame, and where X is a proposition at m,

$$Choice_\Gamma^m/X = \{K \in Choice_\Gamma^m : K \cap X \neq \emptyset\}.$$

Definition 6.7 (Conditional group dominance; $\preceq_X, \prec_X$) Let Γ be a group of agents and m a moment from a utilitarian stit frame, and let K and K' be members of *Choice$_\Gamma^m$*, and X a proposition at m. Then $K \preceq_X K'$ (K' *weakly dominates* K *under the condition* X) if and only if $K \cap X \cap S \leq K' \cap X \cap S$ for each state $S \in State_\Gamma^m$; and $K \prec_X K'$ (K' *strongly dominates* K *under the condition* X) if and only if $K \preceq_X K'$ and it is not the case that $K' \preceq_X K$.

The two ideas of conditional group choice and conditional group dominance can be combined, as in Definition 5.5, to yield a specification of the optimal actions available to a group under some background condition.

Definition 6.8 (*Optimal$_\Gamma^m/X$*) Where Γ is a group of agents and m a moment from a utilitarian stit frame, and where X is a proposition at m,

$$Optimal_\Gamma^m/X = \{K \in Choice_\Gamma^m/X : \text{there is no } K' \in Choice_\Gamma^m/X.K \prec_X K'\}.$$

Following the pattern of Definition 5.15, the set $AU\text{-}right_\Gamma^{m/h}$ can be defined as containing those actions available to the group Γ that are optimal given the state in which Γ finds itself at the index m/h.

Definition 6.9 ($AU\text{-}right_\Gamma^{m/h}$) Where Γ is a group of agents and m/h an index from a utilitarian stit frame,

$$AU\text{-}right_\Gamma^{m/h} = Optimal_\Gamma^m / State_\Gamma^m(h).$$

Finally, the theory of orthodox act utilitarianism can be extended from individuals to groups by defining an action available to Γ as *right* at the index m/h just in case it belongs to $AU\text{-}right_\Gamma^{m/h}$, and *wrong* at m/h otherwise; and as before, Γ can be said to *satisfy* the orthodox theory at the index m/h just in case the action performed by Γ at m/h is classified there as right, and to *violate* the theory otherwise.

As might be expected, this group version of the orthodox theory generalizes that set out earlier for individuals: it is easy to see that $AU\text{-}right_{\{\alpha\}}^{m/h} = AU\text{-}right_\alpha^{m/h}$ for any index m/h, so that the group $\{\alpha\}$ satisfies the orthodox theory just in case the individual α does so as well. And this observation is sufficient to establish a general distinction between the dominance and orthodox theories of act utilitarianism as applied to arbitrary groups—for we already know both that satisfaction of the dominance theory by a group $\{\alpha\}$ also coincides with satisfaction by the individual α, and also that there are cases in which the individual α can satisfy either the dominance or the orthodox theory while violating the other. It is interesting to note, however, that there is one particular group—the group *Agent*, containing the entire set of agents—for which the dictates of these two utilitarian theories agree.

Proposition 6.10 Let *Agent* be the set of agents and m/h an index from a utilitarian stit frame. Then $AU\text{-}right_{Agent}^{m/h} = Optimal_{Agent}^m$.

Formally, this result follows at once from Definition 6.9 together with the observation that $State_{Agent}^m(h) = H_m$, since we know that $Optimal_\Gamma^m / H_m = Optimal_\Gamma^m$ for any group Γ. But it is also worth tracing out the meaning of this identity through a more discursive route, by reflecting, first, that the orthodox theory defines an action available to the group Γ as right at an index m/h just in case that action is optimal in the state in which Γ finds itself at that index, where this state is determined by the pattern of action performed by the group of agents other than those belonging to Γ. Since there are no agents other than those belonging to *Agent*, however, the state confronting the group *Agent* itself at the index m/h is entirely undetermined, or determined only by the trivial proposition H_m; and so the orthodox theory must classify an action available to the group *Agent* as right just in case it is optimal for this group under the conditions determined by the trivial proposition—or simply, optimal.

With the orthodox theory of act utilitarianism extended to cover groups as well as individuals, we can now return to consider the relations supported by this theory between individual and group satisfaction. Again, the Whiff and Poof example from Figure 5.4 suffices to show that individual satisfaction of orthodox act utilitarianism by each member of a group does not entail satisfaction by the group itself. At the index m/h_4, where α performs the action K_2 and β performs the action K_4, each of these individual agents satisfies the orthodox theory, since $AU\text{-}right_{\alpha}^{m/h_4} = \{K_2\}$ and $AU\text{-}right_{\beta}^{m/h_4} = \{K_4\}$; but the group $\Gamma = \{\alpha, \beta\}$ itself violates the theory at this index, since the group action performed there by Γ is $K_2 \cap K_4$, while $AU\text{-}right_{\Gamma}^{m/h_4} = \{K_1 \cap K_3\}$.

However, when we turn to the converse implication, from group to individual satisfaction, we now find that the claim advanced by Regan and Jackson is indeed correct: at any index at which a group satisfies the orthodox theory of act utilitarianism, this theory must be satisfied also by each individual belonging to that group. To say that a group Γ satisfies the orthodox theory at an index m/h, of course, is to say that $Choice_{\Gamma}^m(h)$—the action selected by Γ at that index—belongs to $AU\text{-}right_{\Gamma}^{m/h}$; and likewise, an individual α satisfies the theory whenever $Choice_{\alpha}^m(h)$ belongs to $AU\text{-}right_{\alpha}^{m/h}$. The implication from group satisfaction of the orthodox theory to individual satisfaction by the members of the group can therefore be expressed as follows.

Proposition 6.11 Let Γ be a group of agents and m/h an index from a utilitarian stit frame. Then whenever $Choice_{\Gamma}^m(h) \in AU\text{-}right_{\Gamma}^{m/h}$, we have $Choice_{\alpha}^m(h) \in AU\text{-}right_{\alpha}^{m/h}$ for each $\alpha \in \Gamma$.

And the proof of this fact follows the general lines of Regan's argument, but requires a more detailed treatment of the states confronting the individual and the group.

The dominance and orthodox theories of act utilitarianism differ, therefore, not only in their evaluation of particular actions by individuals and groups—allowing both individuals and groups to satisfy either theory without satisfying the other—but also in supporting different logical relations between individual and group satisfaction. In the case of the dominance theory, as we have seen, individual and group satisfaction are independent: satisfaction of the dominance theory by the individuals belonging to a group does not entail satisfaction by the group itself, and satisfaction by a group does not entail satisfaction by the individuals it contains. But in the case of the orthodox theory, while satisfaction by each individual in a group is again possible even when the group itself violates the theory, satisfaction of the orthodox theory by a group does, in fact, entail satisfaction by the individuals it contains.

6.3   Deontic operators for group oughts

6.3.1   Definitions

We now turn to the task of generalizing the dominance and orthodox ought operators defined in Chapters 4 and 5 for individual agents so as to apply also to groups, allowing us to construct statements of the form

$$\odot[\Gamma \ cstit\!: A],$$
$$\oplus[\Gamma \ cstit\!: A],$$

carrying, respectively, the dominance and orthodox senses of: the group Γ ought to see to it that A. Our treatment is brief, since it follows the same path mapped out in Chapter 4 and then traced again, twice, in Chapter 5.

Again, the official evaluation rules for the two group ought operators are formulated for the most general case, applying even when the set of optimal actions open to a group is empty (either because the group itself is infinite or because some of its individual members face infinitely many choices).

Definition 6.12 (Evaluation rule: $\odot[\Gamma \ cstit\!: A]$) Where Γ is a group of agents and m/h an index from a utilitarian stit model $\mathcal{M}$,

- $\mathcal{M}, m/h \models \odot[\Gamma \ cstit\!: A]$ if and only if, for each action $K \in Choice_\Gamma^m$ such that $K \not\subseteq |A|_m^{\mathcal{M}}$, there is an action $K' \in Choice_\Gamma^m$ such that (1) $K \prec K'$, and (2) $K' \subseteq |A|_m^{\mathcal{M}}$, and (3) $K'' \subseteq |A|_m^{\mathcal{M}}$ for each action $K'' \in Choice_\Gamma^m$ such that $K' \preceq K''$.

Definition 6.13 (Evaluation rule: $\oplus[\Gamma \ cstit\!: A]$) Where Γ is a group of agents and m/h an index from a utilitarian stit model $\mathcal{M}$,

- $\mathcal{M}, m/h \models \oplus[\Gamma \ cstit\!: A]$ if and only if, for each action $K \in Choice_\Gamma^m$ such that $K \not\subseteq |A|_m^{\mathcal{M}}$, there is an action $K' \in Choice_\Gamma^m$ such that (1) $K \prec_{State_\Gamma^m(h)} K'$, and (2) $K' \subseteq |A|_m^{\mathcal{M}}$, and (3) $K'' \subseteq |A|_m^{\mathcal{M}}$ for each action $K'' \in Choice_\Gamma^m$ such that $K' \preceq_{State_\Gamma^m(h)} K''$.

But again, the complexities involved in these general rules can be avoided if we limit our attention to finite groups of agents in finite choice frames, so that optimal actions are guaranteed to exist; for in this case it can be shown that a group ought to see to it that some statement holds just in case guaranteeing the truth of that statement is a necessary condition for satisfying the group version of either dominance or orthodox act utilitarianism.

Proposition 6.14 Let Γ be a finite group of agents and m/h an index from a finite choice utilitarian stit model $\mathcal{M}$. Then $\mathcal{M}, m/h \models \odot[\Gamma \ cstit\!: A]$ if and only if $K \subseteq |A|_m^{\mathcal{M}}$ for each $K \in Optimal_\Gamma^m$.

Proposition 6.15 Let Γ be a finite group of agents and m/h an index from a finite choice utilitarian stit model $\mathcal{M}$. Then $\mathcal{M}, m/h \models \bigoplus[\Gamma\ cstit: A]$ if and only if $K \subseteq |A|_m^{\mathcal{M}}$ for each $K \in AU\text{-}right_\Gamma^{m/h}$.

As before, these two results can be taken to provide simplified evaluation rules for our two group ought operators in a finite setting, which can again be illustrated through Figure 5.4, the Whiff and Poof case. Here, taking Γ as the group $\{\alpha, \beta\}$, we have seen that $Optimal_\Gamma^m = \{K_1 \cap K_3\}$. We can thus conclude that $\bigodot[\Gamma\ cstit: A]$ is settled true at the moment m, since $K_1 \cap K_3$—the unique optimal action available to the group Γ—guarantees the truth of A. If we suppose further that Γ above can be identified with the entire set $Agent$, we know from Proposition 6.10 that $AU\text{-}right_\Gamma^{m/h} = \{K_1 \cap K_3\}$ for each history h through the moment m. In this particular case, then, we also have $\bigoplus[\Gamma\ cstit: A]$ settled true at m, so that the dominance and orthodox accounts coincide.

6.3.2 Some logical points

It is easy to see that, for a fixed group, the logic of these two group ought operators is identical with that of their individual counterparts. The dominance group ought is moment determinate, the orthodox group ought is not; both satisfy the appropriate analogues of the principles $D_\alpha \bigodot$, $RE_\alpha \bigodot$, $N_\alpha \bigodot$, $M_\alpha \bigodot$, and $C_\alpha \bigodot$ (replacing α by Γ for the dominance account, replacing α by Γ and $\bigodot$ by $\bigoplus$ for the orthodox account). And of course, the oughts governing the group $\{\alpha\}$ can be identified, in each case, with those governing the individual α, due to the validity of the principles

$$\bigodot[\{\alpha\}\ cstit: A] \equiv \bigodot[\alpha\ cstit: A],$$
$$\bigoplus[\{\alpha\}\ cstit: A] \equiv \bigoplus[\alpha\ cstit: A].$$

But the introduction of precisely defined group deontic operators gives us the ability to explore a number of issues concerning the relations among the oughts governing different groups, and also among the oughts governing groups and their individual members.

We consider here only the matter of *inheritance* (both downward and upward) of oughts between groups and the individuals. Do individuals inherit oughts from the groups to which they belong? Do groups inherit oughts from their individual members? Let us begin with the question of downward inheritance, from groups to individuals. Suppose, for example, that the group Γ ought to see to it that A, and that it is a necessary condition for Γ to see to it that A that α sees to it that B, where α is an individual belonging to the group Γ. Can we conclude, then, that α ought to see to it that B?

Some writers think so. Derek Parfit, for instance, argues in [1984, p. 70] that "even if some act benefits no one, it can be what someone ought to do,

because it is one of a set of acts [by a group of agents] that together benefit other people"—that is, the individual ought to perform the act simply
because it is his necessary contribution to what some group of agents ought
to do. This downward inheritance view of Parfit's has been criticized by
Torbjörn Tännsjö, who writes to the contrary that, "even if it is true that
you and I constitute a group of people who together ought to do something,
it does not follow that *each* of us ought to 'do his share' ," and supports his
claim with the following example:

> Even if it is true of you and me that we ought to perform the
> collective action consisting in my pouring water into the pool
> and your jumping into it, it does not follow logically that you
> ought to jump .... To think otherwise is a mistake in deontic
> logic. [Tännsjö, 1989, p. 223]

Now, although Tännsjö describes the argument suggested by this example as a mistake in deontic logic, he does not attempt to specify the particular
deontic logic in which the argument is mistaken; and it turns out that the
matter depends on the underlying strategy for representing what groups and
individuals ought to do. Suppose that α and β are the two agents involved
in the example (α = you, β = me), that A expresses the proposition that
α jumps into the pool, and that B expresses the proposition that β fills the
pool. And suppose we assume, with Tännsjö, that the group $\Gamma = \{\alpha, \beta\}$
ought to see to it that $A \wedge B$ (that β fills the pool and α jumps in), and
that it is a necessary condition for Γ to see to it that $A \wedge B$ that α sees to
it that A (that α jumps in). Can we then draw the conclusion that α ought
to see to it that A?

Let us consider this question, first, from the perspective of a generalized
version of the Meinong/Chisholm analysis—a theory that identifies what
both groups and individuals ought to do with what it ought to be that they
do. From this perspective, the argument in Tännsjö's example would have
to be classified as acceptable; for according to such a theory, it would be
represented as an inference from the two premises $\bigcirc[\Gamma \; cstit: A \wedge B]$ and
$\square([\Gamma \; cstit: A \wedge B] \supset [\alpha \; cstit: A])$ to the conclusion $\bigcirc[\alpha \; cstit: A]$, which is
easily seen to be valid. (The validity follows at once from the fact that what
ought to be is closed under necessary consequence: $\bigcirc A$ and $\square(A \supset B)$ imply
$\bigcirc B$, for any formulas A and B.) On the other hand, both the dominance
and orthodox theories developed here allow us to agree with Tännsjö that
the argument is mistaken; for it can now be seen that both the inference
from the premises $\odot[\Gamma \; cstit: A \wedge B]$ and $\square([\Gamma \; cstit: A \wedge B] \supset [\alpha \; cstit: A])$ to
the conclusion $\odot[\alpha \; cstit: A]$ and the inference from the premises $\oplus[\Gamma \; cstit:$
$A \wedge B]$ and $\square([\Gamma \; cstit: A \wedge B] \supset [\alpha \; cstit: A])$ to the conclusion $\oplus[\alpha \; cstit: A]$
are invalid.

In order to demonstrate the invalidity of these inferences, we elaborate
the situation described by Tännsjö into the stit model depicted as Figure 6.1.

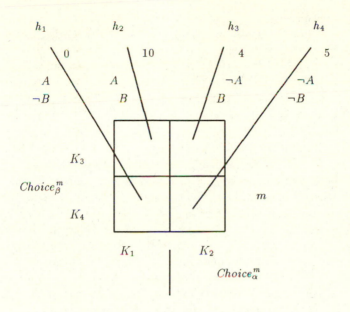

Figure 6.1: The swimming pool example

Here, the vertical partitions represent the actions available to you at the moment m: K_1 represents the action of jumping into the pool, K_2 the action of refraining. The horizontal partitions represent the actions available to me: K_3 represents the action of filling the pool, K_4 the action of refraining. The history h_2, in which I fill the pool and you jump in, receives a utility of 10, the greatest available; the history h_1, in which you jump into an empty pool, receives the lowest utility of 0. The history h_4, in which I do not fill the pool and you do not jump in, receives an intermediate utility of 5; and the history h_3, in which I fill the pool but you do not jump in, receives a slightly reduced utility of 4, because the effort of filling the pool is wasted unless you actually bother to jump in.[4]

It is then easy to see that this situation functions as a formal counter-model to the above inferences; we begin with the dominance account. Since $Optimal_\Gamma^m = \{K_1 \cap K_3\}$ and $K_1 \cap K_3$, the unique optimal action available to Γ, guarantees the truth of $A \wedge B$, the premise $\odot[\Gamma \ cstit: A \wedge B]$ is settled true: the best thing for the pair of us to do is for me to fill the pool and for you to jump in. And of course, the premise $\Box([\Gamma \ cstit: A \wedge B] \supset [\alpha \ cstit: A])$ holds as well: any history in which I fill the pool and you jump in is a history in which you jump in. But since $Optimal_\alpha^m = \{K_1, K_2\}$, there is at least one

---

[4] Tännsjö himself does not actually assign cardinal utilities to outcomes in the situation he describes, and in fact, the only ordinal information provided is that the outcome in which β fills the pool and α jumps in is better than any other.

optimal action available to you—namely, K_2—that does not guarantee the truth of A, and so the statement $\odot[\alpha\ cstit: A]$ is settled false: according to the dominance theory, you need not jump in.

Turning now to the orthodox account, we again suppose for simplicity that Γ can be identified with the entire set *Agent*, so that Proposition 6.10 leads us to conclude that $A U\text{-}right_\Gamma^{m/h_1} = \{K_1 \cap K_3\}$. We thus have $\bigoplus[\Gamma\ cstit: A \wedge B]$ true at the index m/h_1: even at this index—where I do not fill the pool but you jump in anyway—the best thing for the pair of us to do would nevertheless have been for me to fill the pool and for you to jump in. On the other hand, it is easy to see that $A U\text{-}right_\alpha^{m/h_1} = \{K_2\}$: under the conditions in which you actually find yourself at this particular index—where I choose not to fill the pool—it is not best for you to jump in, and in fact, is much better for you not to. Since K_2, your unique best action at the index m/h_1, does not guarantee the truth of A, and in fact guarantees the truth of $\neg A$, we have $\bigoplus[\alpha\ cstit: \neg A]$ true at that index.[5]

Let us now consider the question of upward inheritance, from individuals to groups. Suppose that some individual α ought to see to it that A, and that it is a necessary condition for α to see to it that A that the group Γ sees to it that B, where α belongs to Γ. Can we conclude that Γ ought to see to it that B?

Again, this kind of upward inheritance of oughts from individuals to groups is supported by the generalized version of the Meinong/Chisholm analysis, which identifies what both groups and individuals ought to do with what it ought to be that they do; for according to this view, the issue concerns the inference from the premises $\bigcirc[\alpha\ cstit: A]$ and $\square([\alpha\ cstit: A] \supset [\Gamma\ cstit: B])$ to the conclusion $\bigcirc[\Gamma\ cstit: B]$, which is valid. But again, upward inheritance is not supported by either the dominance or the orthodox account: even given $\square([\alpha\ cstit: A] \supset [\Gamma\ cstit: B])$, both the inference from $\odot[\alpha\ cstit: A]$ to $\odot[\Gamma\ cstit: B]$ and the inference from $\bigoplus[\alpha\ cstit: A]$ to $\bigoplus[\Gamma\ cstit: B]$ fail.

To illustrate the invalidity of (an instance of) the dominance inference, we return to the earlier Figure 5.5. Here, the statement $\odot[\alpha\ cstit: A]$ is

---

[5]McKinsey [1981, p. 321] also seems to reject downward inheritance in concluding that there is "no obvious way, once we know what a group's obligations are, of reading off the resulting obligations of individual members of the group," but he then goes on to qualify his conclusion: "One thing which I think we can definitely say is at least that if a group has an obligation to do an action, then every member of the group is obligated not to *block* the group's doing that action." Our example seems to show, however, that even the very weak form of downward inheritance suggested in McKinsey's qualification is rejected by both the dominance and orthodox accounts. Here, the group $\Gamma = \{\alpha, \beta\}$ does have an obligation to see to it that $A \wedge B$. And by failing to do his part, failing to see to it that A, the agent α would block the group from performing that action. Still, we cannot conclude that α is obligated not to fail to see to it that A; for in the example depicted, this is, in fact, equivalent to an obligation to see to it that A, and as we have seen, α has no such obligation on either account, and indeed, on the orthodox account, is obliged to see to it that $\neg A$.

settled true at m, since $Optimal_\alpha^m = \{K_1\}$ and K_1 guarantees the truth of A. And if we take $\Gamma = \{\alpha, \beta\}$, then $\Box([\alpha\ cstit: A] \supset [\Gamma\ cstit: A])$ is settled true as well, for as noted in Section 2.4, the present analysis of group action allows for free riders: whenever an individual sees to it that some proposition holds, any group containing that individual does so as well. But since $Optimal_\Gamma^m = \{K_1 \cap K_3, K_1 \cap K_4, K_2 \cap K_3\}$, and since one of these actions—namely, $K_2 \cap K_3$—does not guarantee the truth of A, the statement $\odot[\Gamma\ cstit: A]$ is settled false. The invalidity of the orthodox inference can be illustrated, again, by Figure 6.1, our swimming pool case. Here, as we have seen, $\oplus[\alpha\ cstit: \neg A]$ holds at m/h_1, and so, of course, where $\Gamma = \{\alpha, \beta\}$, the statement $\Box([\alpha\ cstit: \neg A] \supset [\Gamma\ cstit: \neg A])$ holds as well. But again, it is easy to see that $\oplus[\Gamma\ cstit: \neg A]$ fails at m/h_1, and indeed, we have $\oplus[\Gamma\ cstit: A]$ instead.

6.4 Rule utilitarianism

In this section, we step away from our primary concern with deontic logic and related act utilitarian theories to consider a particular formulation of rule utilitarianism, due to Richard Brandt [1963], according to which, very roughly, an action by an individual is classified as right whenever that action is one that the individual would perform in the best overall pattern of action. This style of rule utilitarianism has its roots in a proposal by the economist Roy Harrod [1936], originally put forth as an attempt to modify act utilitarianism in order to avoid some unfortunate consequences of that theory. Brandt, however, referred at least to his own interpretation of Harrod's proposal as a "specious" rule utilitarianism, because he felt that, rather than remedying any defects of ordinary act utilitarianism, this formulation turned out, instead, simply to agree with the act utilitarian theory.

Shortly after the publication of Brandt's paper, Gibbard [1965] and Sobel [1968] showed that this claim of agreement was mistaken by constructing a number of situations in which act utilitarianism and Brandt's rule utilitarianism classify different actions as right. The fact that these two theories led to such different results in the kind of situations described by Gibbard and Sobel suggested to many people that there might be a fundamental conflict between two ideas bound up in the general utilitarian principle of maximization—between the act utilitarian idea that an individual agent ought to do whatever leads to the best consequences in the situation in which he finds himself, and the rule utilitarian idea that an individual agent ought to play his proper role in the best overall pattern of action. And the sustained study of utilitarian theory carried out by Regan in [1980] was inspired, in part, by the project of reconciling the conflict between these two ideas.

The goal of the present discussion is not to advance the ethical debate in this area, but simply to illustrate the utility of the current framework by showing how naturally it allows for a formal explication of Brandt's rule utilitarianism, and then mapping out some of the relations between this theory and the two forms of act utilitarianism defined earlier. Still, by placing the matter in a context that distinguishes explicitly between the orthodox and dominance forms of act utilitarianism, this discussion may, in fact, have some bearing on the ethical issues. For most of the past work in the area—the work that has resulted in such a strong feeling of conflict between act and rule utilitarianism—has taken place entirely within the orthodox setting; but it turns out, as we will see, that the conflict between rule utilitarianism and the dominance theory of act utilitarianism is much less severe.

6.4.1   Formulating the theory

Brandt characterizes his rule utilitarianism loosely at first, as a theory according to which an act is right whenever it "conforms with that set of moral rules, general conformity with which would have best consequences," and then more precisely:

> An act is right if and only if it conforms with that set of general prescriptions for action such that, if everyone always did, from among all the things which he could do on a given occasion, what conformed with these prescriptions, then at least as much intrinsic good would be produced as by conformity with any other set of general prescriptions. [Brandt, 1963, p. 120]

In fact, the approach to be developed here is based, not exactly on Brandt's formulation, but on a formulation that results from his through two simplifications. First, Brandt's statement of the theory quantifies over times as well as agents; he speaks of moral rules as specifying what "everyone always" might do. But, as in much of the literature on this topic, we focus only on a single moment. Second, although Brandt speaks of sets of "moral rules," or "general prescriptions for action," we consider only the extensions of these rules. In general, such a rule extension could be thought of as a selection, for each agent and each moment, of some action from among those available to that agent at that moment; but since our attention is restricted to a single moment, it is enough to think of a rule extension as an assignment of actions to the various agents at the moment in question, a momentary pattern of action.[6]

---

[6] This notion of a rule extension at a moment agrees with what Regan describes as a "universal prescription for action," which, he says, can be thought of as a list containing "the names of all the agents in the moral universe," beside each of which "appears a prescription [for action] for that agent"—and indeed, when moral rules are thought of explicitly as involving only their extensions, Brandt's rule utilitarianism can be seen to

Now, one immediate problem confronting any attempt to provide a formal reconstruction of Brandt's theory—a problem first pointed out by Sobel [1968]—is that the theory is actually ill-defined. In the passage cited, Brandt characterizes an action by an agent as right whenever the agent would perform that action in the best overall pattern of action (whenever it conforms with "that set" of moral rules, or general prescriptions for action, leading to the best consequences), but as Sobel notes, there are situations in which no unique best pattern of action can be identified, since several different patterns might each lead to maximally ideal results. We have already seen such a case in Figure 5.6, the driving example. Here, there are two best patterns of action: $K_1 \cap K_4$, in which α swerves and β continues along the road, and $K_2 \cap K_3$, in which α continues along the road and β swerves. Evidently, Brandt's theory cannot apply exactly as formulated to this case: it is not possible to define an action by an agent as right whenever it is the action performed by that agent in the best overall pattern of action, since there are multiple best patterns.

There are two natural ways of reworking Brandt's rule utilitarianism to avoid this kind of problem. First, one might explicitly limit the applicability of the theory to situations in which there is a unique best pattern of action, or second, one might modify the theory so as to apply even in situations allowing multiple best patterns of action—classifying an action by an agent as right just in case it is the action performed by that agent in any one of these patterns.[7] We follow the second of these approaches here, primarily because the set of right actions characterized in this way holds some mild technical interest. But even though, on this second approach, the set of right actions is actually well defined in cases in which there is more than one best pattern, it is important to note that, in these cases, rule utilitarianism has very little to recommend it as a normative theory. There is no particular point in each member of a group of agents individually performing some action that he would perform in one or another of the best patterns. A

---

coincide with a theory that Regan describes as embodying the "co-ordinated optimization" principle, according to which an act is right whenever "it is prescribed . . . by that universal prescription for action, the universal satisfaction of which would produce the best possible consequences" [1980, p. 85]. The results of our discussion of Brandt's rule utilitarianism will thus carry over also to Regan's theory of coordinated optimization.

[7] Regan adopts the first of these approaches in the text of [1980], limiting the scope of his coordinated optimization theory to situations in which there is a unique best pattern of behavior [p. 85]; but in a footnote, he also describes a more complicated theory that allows for multiple best patterns of behavior [pp. 248–249]. Gibbard does not explicitly note the problem presented by multiple best patterns of action in his [1965], and initially simply quotes Brandt's formulation of the utilitarian theory, which presupposes uniqueness. However, he later [p. 215] speaks of the theory as one that characterizes an agent's action as right if it is in conformity with "a set" of best actions; and his discussion of a further example [pp. 218–219] makes it clear that he means to adopt the second of these two approaches, classifying an agent's action as right according to rule utilitarianism if it is an action performed by the agent in any best pattern.

best pattern can be achieved only if, by individually performing the actions belonging to some best pattern or another, the various members of the group somehow manage to perform the actions they would perform in the same best pattern; and setting aside the possibility of explicit coordination, that can be guaranteed only if there is a unique best pattern. Thus, although we advance a general definition, according to which rule utilitarianism is meaningful even in situations containing multiple best patterns of action, the theory should be viewed as applicable—possessing normative force— only when the best pattern is unique.

   An action available to an agent is to be defined as right according to rule utilitarianism, then, just in case it is an action that the agent would perform in some best pattern of action. In the present framework, it is natural to identify the set of best patterns of action available at a moment m with $Optimal^m_{Agent}$, the optimal patterns available to the entire group $Agent$. And it is easy to see also, whenever K is an action available to some individual and K' is a pattern of action available to the group $Agent$, that K is the action performed by the given individual in the group pattern K' just in case $K' \subseteq K$. The set of actions that an agent α might perform in some best pattern of action at the moment m—expressed here as $R\text{-}Optimal^m_\alpha$—can thus be characterized as follows.

Definition 6.16 ($R\text{-}Optimal^m_\alpha$) Where α is an agent and m a moment from a utilitarian stit frame,

$$R\text{-}Optimal^m_\alpha = \{ K \in Choice^m_\alpha : \text{there is a } K' \in Optimal^m_{Agent}. K' \subseteq K \}.$$

We can now define *rule utilitarianism*—our reconstruction of Brandt's theory—as the view that an action available to an agent α is *right* at an index m/h whenever that action belongs to $R\text{-}Optimal^m_\alpha$, and *wrong* at m/h otherwise; and we can say, as usual, that an agent *satisfies* rule utilitarianism at an index m/h whenever the action he performs at that index is classified there as right, and that he *violates* the theory otherwise.

   Like the dominance theories of individual and group act utilitarianism, the form of rule utilitarianism defined here leads to a classification of actions as right or wrong that is moment determinate: any action that is classified by rule utilitarianism as right at the index m/h must be classified as right also at the index m/h', for every history h' from H_m. Because of this, it may seem tempting to describe the theory presented here as a kind of dominance rule utilitarianism, in anticipation of a contrasting orthodox theory. This description would be misleading, however, since the dominance and orthodox points of view, which are distinct at the level of act utilitarianism, collapse at the level of rule utilitarianism into one. The reason for this is simple. Rule utilitarianism defines the right actions for an individual to perform in terms of the best patterns of action available to the entire group $Agent$, but as we have seen, and noted in Proposition 6.10, the dominance and orthodox characterizations of the best patterns of action available to the entire group *Agent* always coincide.

We can illustrate the theory of rule utilitarianism by returning to the Whiff and Poof example, Figure 5.4, now assuming, however, that the displayed agents α and β constitute the entire group of agents: $Agent = \{\alpha, \beta\}$. Under this assumption, there is a unique optimal pattern of action available to the entire group of agents: $Optimal^m_{Agent} = \{K_1 \cap K_3\}$. And so the set of right actions available to each of the two agents—the set of actions each would perform in some optimal pattern—is apparent: $R\text{-}Optimal^m_\alpha = \{K_1\}$ and $R\text{-}Optimal^m_\beta = \{K_3\}$. At the index m/h_2, then, where α performs the action K_1 and β performs the action K_3, each of the two agents satisfies rule utilitarianism, and an optimal pattern of action is achieved. At all other indices in this example, one or another of the two agents violates rule utilitarianism, and an optimal pattern of action is not achieved.

Simply in order to highlight the problems that would be involved if the current version of rule utilitarianism were applied to situations containing multiple optimal patterns, let us also consider the driving example from Figure 5.6, again under the assumption that $Agent = \{\alpha, \beta\}$. Here, as we have seen, there are two optimal patterns of action: $Optimal^m_{Agent} = \{K_1 \cap K_4, K_2 \cap K_3\}$. As a result, both of the actions available to both agents are classified as right by the rule utilitarian theory: $R\text{-}Optimal^m_\alpha = \{K_1, K_2\}$ and $R\text{-}Optimal^m_\beta = \{K_3, K_4\}$. Thus, at the index m/h_2, for example— where α performs the action K_1 and β performs the action K_3—each of these two agents could be said to satisfy rule utilitarianism; each performs a right action, and so neither could be faulted from a rule utilitarian point of view. But an optimal pattern of action would not be achieved.

6.4.2 Act and rule utilitarianism

Although Brandt had claimed that rule utilitarianism is actually equivalent to act utilitarianism (and is therefore specious), Gibbard and Sobel argue otherwise; and we are now in a position to verify their conclusion. Rule utilitarianism, as formulated here, differs from orthodox act utilitarianism: there are indices at which these two theories classify different sets of actions as right.

For illustration we return again to the Whiff and Poof case from Figure 5.4—which was originally introduced, after all, to establish exactly this point. Consider the index m/h_4, where neither of the two agents pushes his button. Here, we have $AU\text{-}right^{m/h_4}_\alpha = \{K_2\}$, so that, of the actions available to α, only K_2 is classified as right at m/h_4 according to orthodox act utilitarianism; but since $R\text{-}Optimal^m_\alpha = \{K_1\}$, it is the action K_1 that rule utilitarianism classifies as right. At the index m/h_4, then, where α performs the action K_2, this agent satisfies the orthodox theory of act utilitarianism, but violates rule utilitarianism. And it is easy to see, conversely, that α satisfies rule utilitarianism at the index m/h_1, where he performs the action K_1; but since $AU\text{-}right_\alpha^{m/h_1} = \{K_2\}$, he then violates orthodox act utilitarianism at that index.

This example shows that there are indices at which the theory of rule utilitarianism and the orthodox theory of act utilitarianism classify different sets of actions as right, and that it is possible to satisfy either theory without satisfying the other—but it also shows more. Earlier, in our Section 5.4 discussion of the contrast between dominance and orthodox act utilitarianism, we noted that, although distinct, these two theories are consistent at least in the weak sense of always, at any index, being jointly satisfiable. In the present case, however, as shown by the two indices m/h_1 and m/h_4 from the Whiff and Poof example, it is possible for the set of actions classified as right by rule utilitarianism to be, not just different, but actually disjoint from the set of actions classified as right by orthodox act utilitarianism. The clash between these two theories is thus very severe: there are situations in which they are not jointly satisfiable.

Let us now examine the relation of rule utilitarianism to the dominance theory of act utilitarianism. Since both of these theories offer moment determinate classifications of actions as right or wrong, it is sufficient to compare the sets of actions classified by each as right for an agent α at a moment m—that is, the sets $R\text{-}Optimal_\alpha^m$ and $Optimal_\alpha^m$.

Again, we can see at once from the Whiff and Poof case that these theories are distinct, and that, in particular, it is possible to satisfy dominance act utilitarianism without satisfying rule utilitarianism. Since $Optimal_\alpha^m = \{K_1, K_2\}$ but $R\text{-}Optimal_\alpha^m = \{K_1\}$, the agent α satisfies the dominance theory at the index m/h_4, for example, where he performs the action K_2, but he violates rule utilitarianism at this index. Moreover, if we allow ourselves to consider situations containing multiple optimal patterns of action, then Figure 5.5 shows that it is likewise possible to satisfy rule utilitarianism without satisfying dominance act utilitarianism. In this situation, as we have seen, the group $Agent$ has available three optimal patterns of action: $Optimal_{Agent}^m = \{K_1 \cap K_3, K_1 \cap K_4, K_2 \cap K_3\}$. In the first and second of these patterns, the individual α performs the action K_1, and in the third he performs the action K_2. Hence the set of actions classified as right by rule utilitarianism, those that α would perform in some optimal pattern or another, is $R\text{-}Optimal_\alpha^m = \{K_1, K_2\}$. But of course $Optimal_\alpha^m = \{K_1\}$, and so at the index m/h_4, for example, where α performs the action K_2, he satisfies rule utilitarianism but violates the dominance theory of act utilitarianism.

These examples show that there are moments at which rule utilitarianism and dominance act utilitarianism classify different sets of actions as right, that it is possible to satisfy the dominance theory without satisfying rule utilitarianism, and that, if we consider situations containing multiple best

patterns of action, it is possible also to satisfy rule utilitarianism without
satisfying the dominance theory. Still, while these examples do establish
a difference between rule utilitarianism and dominance act utilitarianism,
they do not demonstrate the kind of severe clash we saw between rule utilitarianism and the orthodox theory. In each of the two examples we have
considered, even though rule utilitarianism and the dominance account classify different sets of actions as right, these two sets of right actions overlap,
so that it is possible to satisfy both theories together. And indeed, this
represents the general case: as long as the theories of rule utilitarianism
and dominance act utilitarianism are individually satisfiable, they can be
satisfied jointly.

Proposition 6.17 Let m be a moment and α an agent from a finite choice
utilitarian stit frame in which the set *Agent* is finite. Then $R\text{-}Optimal_\alpha^m \cap Optimal_\alpha^m \neq \emptyset$

This result guarantees the consistency of rule utilitarianism and the dominance account even in situations allowing for multiple optimal patterns of
action. But as we have seen, rule utilitarianism is primarily applicable to
situations containing only a single best pattern, and if we limit our attention to these cases, we can derive a stronger connection between the two
theories. If there is only a single best pattern of action, then of course
each agent has available only a single action that he might perform in that
best pattern, only a single action that is classified by rule utilitarianism
as right. And in that case, since we are guaranteed some overlap between
the actions classified as right by rule utilitarianism and those classified as
right by the dominance theory, we then can conclude that the single action
that is classified as right by rule utilitarianism must be classified as right by
the dominance theory as well. Or, put another way: in those situations in
which rule utilitarianism is primarily applicable, where there is only one best
pattern of action, satisfying rule utilitarianism does in fact entail satisfying
dominance act utilitarianism.

Chapter 7

Strategic oughts

7.1 Strategies

The basic theory developed in Chapter 4, as well as the generalizations set out in Chapters 5 and 6, all focus only on single moments, specifying the normative concepts governing an agent at a moment entirely on the basis of the actions available at that moment alone, ignoring any actions that might be available later on. Of course, agents do not usually confine their attention to momentary actions; more often, they work out plans of action over intervals of time. And there are cases in which, by concentrating only on a moment, ignoring the later actions available to an agent, we are left with a distorted picture of the agent's real normative situation.

An example is provided by Figure 7.1, which depicts the options open to the agent α at the moment m_1, where the agent faces a choice between the actions K_1 and K_2, and then also at the later moment m_2, where he faces a choice between K_3 and K_4. The histories h_1 through h_4 carry the values indicated, and the statement A is true at the indices m_1/h_1, m_1/h_2, m_2/h_1, and m_2/h_2.

Now let us ask: what should the agent do at the moment m_1? Well, if we concentrate on this moment alone, the situation appears to be identical to that depicted in Figure 3.9, our initial gambling example: one choice results in a value of either 10 or 0; the other guarantees a value of 5. Neither of the actions K_1 or K_2 dominates the other, and so the theory as it stands cannot recommend either action over the other. Since both actions are optimal, the agent satisfies dominance act utilitarianism at m_1 by performing either one. And since one of these two optimal actions guarantees the truth of A while the other guarantees the truth of $\neg A$, both $\bigodot[\alpha \ cstit\colon A]$ and $\bigodot[\alpha \ cstit\colon \neg A]$ are settled false at m_1; we cannot say that α ought to see to it that A, or that α ought to see to it that $\neg A$.

From an intuitive standpoint, of course, this result is incorrect. The current situation is not like that of Figure 3.9, where the outcome of the

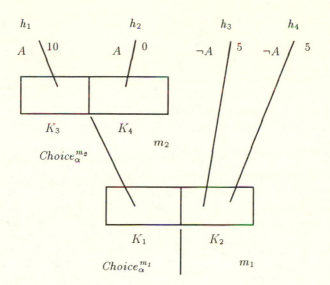

Figure 7.1: Oughts in time

gamble is beyond the agent's control. In the current case, it is as if the agent could first choose whether or not to gamble, by selecting either K_1 or K_2 at the moment m_1, and then later, if he decides to gamble, choose whether or not he is to win, by selecting either K_3 or K_4 at the moment m_2. By adopting the strategy of first choosing K_1 and then choosing K_3—deciding to gamble and then win—the agent can guarantee an outcome with a value of 10. And since K_1 is the action that α performs at m_1 in this strategy, the best available, it appears—from a more general perspective, which involves looking at later moments—that K_1 should be classified as a better action than K_2, and therefore, that α ought to see to it that A.

The goal of the current chapter is to accommodate the intuition suggested in this example by elaborating our general framework in a way that allows an agent's choices to be evaluated against the background of later possibilities. We begin in this section by studying a key technical concept—the notion of a strategy.

7.1.1 Basic ideas

The formal definition of a strategy for an agent is simple: it is nothing more than a partial function mapping each moment in the domain of the strategy into some action available to the agent at that moment.[1]

---

[1] The account of strategies developed here derives from that of Belnap [1994], which first introduced the concept into the present framework, and which offers a very general

Definition 7.1 (Strategies, Domains) Let α be an agent and *Tree* the set of moments from a stit frame. Then a *strategy* for α is a partial function σ on *Tree* such that $\sigma(m) \in Choice_\alpha^m$ for each moment m from $Dom(\sigma)$—the *domain* of σ, the subset of *Tree* on which σ is defined.

And the idea, of course, is that an agent carrying out a particular strategy σ will perform the action $\sigma(m)$ recommended by that strategy whenever he happens to arrive at a moment m belonging to $Dom(\sigma)$, a moment at which the strategy is defined.

In performing any single action, as we have seen, an agent constrains the future to lie within some definite set of futures, and the agent exercises a similar constraint in carrying out a strategy. We describe any history that might result from the faithful execution of a strategy as a history that is admitted by that strategy, where the notion is defined as follows.

Definition 7.2 (Admission) Let h be a history and σ a strategy for some agent from a stit frame. Then the strategy σ *admits* the history h just in case (1) $Dom(\sigma) \cap h \neq \emptyset$ and (2) for each $m \in Dom(\sigma) \cap h$ we have $h \in \sigma(m)$.

For a history to be admitted by a strategy, then, it must, first of all, pass through some moment at which the strategy is defined, and second, at every moment on the history at which the strategy is defined, the history must be consistent with the action recommended there by the strategy, a possible outcome of that action.

These ideas can be illustrated in the case of Figure 7.1 by considering the strategy $\sigma_1 = \{\langle m_2, K_3 \rangle\}$. This simple strategy is defined only on the moment m_2, and recommends the action K_3 there; that is, $Dom(\sigma_1) = \{m_2\}$ and $\sigma_1(m_2) = K_3$. Of the four histories displayed in the figure, only h_1 is admitted by σ_1. The history h_2 is not admitted because, although it passes through the domain of σ_1, there is a moment at which it is not consistent with the action recommended by that strategy: we have $m_2 \in Dom(\sigma_1) \cap h_2$, but $h_2 \notin \sigma_1(m_2)$. And the histories h_3 and h_4 are not admitted because they do not pass through the domain: $Dom(\sigma_1) \cap h_3 = Dom(\sigma_1) \cap h_4 = \emptyset$. As another example, we might consider the strategy $\sigma_2 = \{\langle m_1, K_2 \rangle, \langle m_2, K_4 \rangle\}$, which is defined on both of the depicted moments: $Dom(\sigma_2) = \{m_1, m_2\}$. This strategy admits the histories h_3 and h_4, since both of these histories intersect the domain of the strategy, and are consistent with the strategy at every point of intersection. But σ_2 does not admit the history h_2, for instance, because, although this history passes through the domain and is consistent with the strategy at the moment m_2, there is also another point of intersection, the moment m_1, at which h_2 is not consistent with the strategy.

and abstract treatment. Although the ideas underlying the definitions presented in this section are Belnap's, and much of his vocabulary is retained, the current account is considerably more specialized, adapting the concepts from his very general treatment for our own special purposes.

The histories admitted by a particular strategy σ are collected together into the set $Adh(\sigma)$, known as the admission set for σ.

Definition 7.3 (Admission set; $Adh(\sigma)$) Where σ is a strategy for some agent from a stit frame, the *admission set* for σ is

$$Adh(\sigma) = \{h : \sigma \text{ admits } h\}.$$

Thus, for example, where σ_1 and σ_2 are defined as above, we have $Adh(\sigma_1) = \{h_1\}$ and $Adh(\sigma_2) = \{h_3, h_4\}$.

7.1.2   Limiting the range

The range of strategies considered so far is very broad, and allows for strategies that might seem gappy or incoherent from an intuitive standpoint. For all the constraints so far imposed, I might adopt, for instance, the following strategy: to pick up a quart of milk this afternoon if I should find myself at the store; always to ask for another card whenever I find myself holding a seventeen point hand in blackjack; and to begin studying piano at age twelve, practicing every day thereafter. In order to rule out peculiar examples like this, we now explicitly limit the range of strategies under consideration to include only those exhibiting certain structural characteristics—resulting in a class of strategies with some claim to be considered as structurally ideal.

Thinking of an agent as positioned at some particular moment m in *Tree*, we begin by defining $Tree_m$ as the remainder of the tree of possibilities, from m on.

Definition 7.4 ($Tree_m$) Where m is a moment and *Tree* the set of moments from a stit frame,

$$Tree_m = \{m' : m \leq m'\}.$$

Once an agent has actually arrived at the moment m, there is a sense in which $Tree_m$ is all that the agent cares about—or at least, all that is still worth planning for. But even $Tree_m$ is a lot to care about: the entire future. Most real agents embrace comparatively robust plans only for a fragment of the future, ranging from hours to decades. We will refer to the region of the future for which an agent at a moment actively plans as a field of concern, or simply, a field.

Of course, in realistic cases, the boundaries of an agent's field of concern will be vague (our concern tapers off), and the field itself will generally have gaps in it: I may be committed to a definite plan for next Tuesday afternoon, for instance, even though Tuesday morning is entirely open. We idealize in our formal treatment, however, by supposing that the boundaries of a field are precise, and also that fields are downward closed, in the sense that any future moment lying prior to a moment contained in some field must also be contained in that field.

Definition 7.5 (Fields at a moment) Let m be a moment from a stit frame. Then a *field* at m is a nonempty subset M of $Tree_m$ subject to the condition of downward closure in $Tree_m$: for any moments m' and m'', if $m' \in M$ and $m'' \in Tree_m$ and $m'' \leq m'$, then $m'' \in M$.

A strategy in a field is then defined as a strategy whose domain does not extend beyond that field.

Definition 7.6 (Strategies in a field) Let α be an agent and M a field at some moment from a stit frame. Then σ is a *strategy for α in M* just in case σ is a strategy for α and $Dom(\sigma) \subseteq M$.

Since a field is supposed to represent the region of the future that is of active concern to an agent, and for which the agent actively plans, it is tempting to suppose that a structurally ideal strategy should exhaust the relevant field, specifying an action for each moment contained in the field. However, this seems to be too strong a requirement. Imagine, for example, that I am a relatively shortsighted agent with a field of concern consisting only of the next twenty-four hours of my life—the set of moments open to me as possibilities during that period. In fact, it is possible for me right now to drive to the airport and board a plane that will land in Denver at 3:00 this afternoon; and so there is a moment lying within my field of concern that has me, at 3:00 this afternoon, in the Denver airport. Nevertheless, it seems unreasonable to require even that a structurally ideal strategy for the next twenty-four hours should specify an action for me to perform if I happen to find myself in the Denver airport at 3:00 this afternoon, since I have no intention to go there.

Rather than requiring, then, that a structurally ideal strategy should exhaust the field of an agent's concern, recommending an action at each moment it contains, we will require instead only that the strategy should provide the information necessary in order to guide the agent through the field. An agent carrying out an ideal strategy in a field should never be left guessing: the strategy should start early enough in the field and not end too soon. Of course, it is easy enough to say what it means for a strategy to start early enough in a field: where M is a field at the moment m, the strategy σ starts early enough in M if it is defined right away, at the moment m—that is, if $m \in Dom(\sigma)$. And it is not difficult either to find a suitable sense in which a strategy can be said not to end too soon: although, as the Denver scenario shows, the strategy need not be defined at every moment in the field, it must at least be defined at every moment in the field that the agent might actually reach by executing that strategy.

Evidently, the moments that might actually be reached through the execution of a particular strategy σ are those moments lying on the histories belonging to $Adh(\sigma)$, the admission set for that strategy. We describe such moments as admitted by the strategy and group them together into the set $Adm(\sigma)$, as follows.

Definition 7.7 (Admitted moments; $Adm(\sigma)$) Where σ is a strategy for some agent from a stit frame, the set of *admitted moments* for σ is

$$Adm(\sigma) = \{m : m \in h \text{ for some } h \in Adh(\sigma)\}.$$

To say that a strategy must be defined on every moment in a field that the agent might reach by executing that strategy, then, is simply to say that it must be defined on the set of admitted moments from the field. This is ensured by the property of completeness.

Definition 7.8 (Completeness in a field) Let σ be a strategy for an agent in a field M. Then σ is *complete in M* just in case $Adm(\sigma) \cap M \subseteq Dom(\sigma)$.

And, for the sake of convenience, we assume also that the structurally ideal strategies should satisfy the property of irredundancy, a kind of converse to completeness.

Definition 7.9 (Irredundancy) Let σ be a strategy for an agent. Then σ is *irredundant* just in case $Dom(\sigma) \subseteq Adm(\sigma)$.

While completeness in a field tells us that a strategy is defined at every moment in the field that might be reached through the execution of that strategy, irredundancy tells us that the strategy is defined nowhere else: a strategy that is both complete in a field and irredundant is thus defined on all and only those moments from the field that might be reached through the execution of that strategy.

Throughout the remainder of the chapter, we will limit our attention to the class of structurally ideal strategies specified here—strategies for an agent in a field that are defined at the initial moment of that field, complete in the field, and irredundant. We collect together as $Strategy_{\alpha}^{M}$ the set of strategies for an agent α in the field M that are, in this sense, structurally ideal.

Definition 7.10 ($Strategy_{\alpha}^{M}$) Let α be an agent and m a moment from a stit frame, and let M be a field at m. Then $Strategy_{\alpha}^{M}$ is the set of strategies for α in M that are defined at m, complete in M, and irredundant.

The concept can be illustrated by returning to Figure 7.1. Suppose that we take the set $M = \{m_1, m_2\}$ as our field in this example. (We must assume that there are no moments lying between m_1 and m_2, so that this is a legitimate field, a downward closed subset of $Tree_{m_1}$.) Then $Strategy_{\alpha}^{M} = \{\sigma_3, \sigma_4, \sigma_5\}$, where $\sigma_3 = \{\langle m_1, K_1 \rangle, \langle m_2, K_3 \rangle\}$, $\sigma_4 = \{\langle m_1, K_1 \rangle, \langle m_2, K_4 \rangle\}$, and $\sigma_5 = \{\langle m_1, K_2 \rangle\}$.

7.2   Strategies and choices

7.2.1   Agency

It is best to think of $Strategy_\alpha^M$, the set of structurally ideal strategies available to the agent α in the field M, as a kind of generalization of $Choice_\alpha^m$, the set of actions available to the agent at the moment m. Just as $Choice_\alpha^m$ represents the options available to α at m, the set $Strategy_\alpha^M$ can be thought of as representing the options available to α throughout the entire field M—except that here the options are strategies, patterns of action over time, rather than individual actions themselves. And just as the agent, by performing some action K from $Choice_\alpha^m$, can guarantee that the history to be realized will lie within K, so the agent, by carrying out some strategy σ from $Strategy_\alpha^M$, can guarantee that the history to be realized will lie within $Adh(\sigma)$, the admission set for that strategy.

In fact, in the limiting case, where an agent's field of concern collapses to a single moment, the correspondence between actions and strategies is exact. The actions available to the agent α at the moment m coincide with the admission sets determined by the strategies available to α in the field $\{m\}$:

$$Choice_\alpha^m = \{Adh(\sigma) : \sigma \in Strategy_\alpha^{\{m\}}\}.$$

In the more general case, however, as the field of concern grows, the larger set of available strategies enables the agent to exercise a finer degree of control over possible outcomes, as the following result indicates.

Proposition 7.11 Let α be an agent and m a moment from a utilitarian stit frame, and let M and M' be two fields at m such that $M \subseteq M'$. Then (1) for each $\sigma' \in Strategy_\alpha^{M'}$ there is a $\sigma \in Strategy_\alpha^M$ such that $Adh(\sigma') \subseteq Adh(\sigma)$, and (2) for each $\sigma \in Strategy_\alpha^M$ there is a $\sigma' \in Strategy_\alpha^{M'}$ such that $Adh(\sigma') \subseteq Adh(\sigma)$.

The first part of this result tells us that it is always possible to find a strategy from the smaller field whose admission set includes that of any given strategy from the larger field; the second part tells us that it is always possible to find a strategy from the larger field whose admission set is included by that of any given strategy from the smaller field.

Because of the similarities between strategies and actions, it seems reasonable to suggest that a strategic analogue to our standard *cstit* operator might now be introduced—represented as *scstit*, perhaps, for "strategic Chellas stit." Just as the standard operator allows us to construct formulas of the form $[\alpha \; cstit : A]$, true at an index m/h whenever the action performed by α at that index guarantees the truth of A, one might expect that the strategic analogue to this operator should allow us to construct formulas of the form $[\alpha \; scstit : A]$, true at an index m/h whenever A is guaranteed by the strategy executed by α at that index.

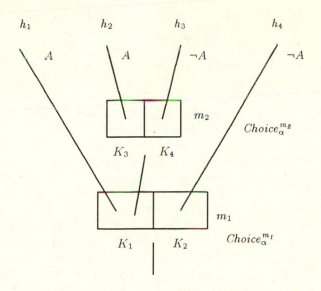

Figure 7.2: Is $[\alpha \; scstit: A]$ true at m_1/h_1?

Unfortunately, however, this suggestion leads to severe semantic difficulties. Since these difficulties are best illustrated through an example, we now turn to Figure 7.2, depicting a situation in which the agent α faces a choice at m_1 between K_1 and K_2, and then perhaps a later choice at m_2 between K_3 and K_4. The histories h_1 through h_4 are the possible outcomes at m_1, and the statement A is assumed to be true at the indices m_1/h_1, m_1/h_2, and m_2/h_2. Taking $M = \{m_1, m_2\}$ as our background field, the agent α then has available three strategies: $Strategy_\alpha^M = \{\sigma_1, \sigma_2, \sigma_3\}$, where $\sigma_1 = \{\langle m_1, K_1\rangle, \langle m_2, K_3\rangle\}$, $\sigma_2 = \{\langle m_1, K_1\rangle, \langle m_2, K_4\rangle\}$, and $\sigma_3 = \{\langle m_1, K_2\rangle\}$.[2]

Now let us ask: given the semantic account of the *scstit* operator suggested above, what value should be assigned to the formula $[\alpha \; scstit: A]$ at the index m_1/h_1? According to the proposed account, the formula should be true at this index just in case the truth of the statement A is guaranteed by the strategy that α is executing at this index—but what strategy is that? Evidently, the outcome h_1 is consistent both with the faithful execution of the strategy σ_1 and with the faithful execution of the strategy σ_2; that is, h_1 belongs to both the admission sets $Adh(\sigma_1)$ and $Adh(\sigma_2)$. But while the strategy σ_1 guarantees the truth of A, the strategy σ_2 does not. If the agent's performance of the action K_1 at the moment m_1 had led to the moment m_2, we could have then determined, through his choice

---

[2] The notational policy of this chapter is that the labeling of strategies begins fresh with each section. Thus, for example, the strategy σ_1 here differs from the strategy referred to as σ_1 in Section 7.1.

at that moment of K_3 or K_4, whether the agent was executing σ_1 or σ_2. But since, by hypothesis, the agent's performance of K_1 results instead in a future evolving along h_1, it seems that we simply do not have enough information to determine whether the agent is actually executing σ_1 or σ_2—and so, whether the strategy actually being executed by the agent guarantees the truth of A.

The problems involved in defining a strategic analogue to the *cstit* operator can be highlighted through a contrast with the momentary case. Here, as we recall, the set $Choice_\alpha^m$ of actions available to an agent α at a moment m is defined as a partition of H_m, the space of possible outcomes. Given an index m/h, we can therefore locate the unique action K from $Choice_\alpha^m$ that contains the history h—the unique action performed by α at this index— and then evaluate $[\alpha \; cstit: A]$ on the basis of whether or not K guarantees the truth of A. But it is different with strategies. Here, we find that, where M is a field at m, although the set $\{Adh(\sigma) : \sigma \in Strategy_\alpha^M\}$ of admission sets for the strategies available to the agent must cover the space H_m of possible outcomes, it will not, in general, partition this space. (In the present case, for example, we have $Adh(\sigma_1) = \{h_1, h_2\}$, $Adh(\sigma_2) = \{h_1, h_3\}$, and $Adh(\sigma_4) = \{h_4\}$, which fails to partition, as we have seen, since h_1 belongs to both $Adh(\sigma_1)$ and $Adh(\sigma_2)$.) Because the admission sets generated by an agent's strategies do not, in general, partition the space of outcomes, we cannot work backward from a history to a unique strategy that might lead to this history as its outcome. Although an index m/h provides us with enough information to identify the action performed by the agent, then, it does not provide enough information to identify the strategy being executed by the agent, and so, of course, it does not allow us to determine whether or not that strategy guarantees the truth of any particular statement.

It is not my intention here to resolve the issues involved in defining a strategic analogue to the *cstit* operator—indeed, I feel that a proper treatment of these issues might well push us beyond the borders of the current representational formalism.[3] Nevertheless, I would like simply to mention two ways in which these issues might be approached.

First, since we are generally unable to determine which particular strategy an agent is actually executing at an index, we might suppose that the truth of a strategic *cstit* statement should depend on the entire set of strategies that the agent might be executing. We could suppose, that is, that a statement of the form $[\alpha \; scstit: A]$ should be true at an index m/h whenever A is guaranteed by each of the strategies that the agent α might be executing at that index—or more exactly, where M is the background field,

---

[3]It might turn out, for example, that the only way to determine whether the agent α in Figure 7.2, having performed the action K_1 at the moment m_1 and now moving along the history h_1, is actually carrying out the strategy σ_1 or the strategy σ_2 is in terms of some psychological fact about the agent, which tells us what action he would have selected had he wound up, instead, at the moment m_2.

that $[\alpha \ scstit: A]$ should be true at m/h whenever $Adh(\sigma) \subseteq |A|_m$ for each $\sigma \in Strategy_\alpha^M$ such that $h \in Adh(\sigma)$. Such a proposal can be viewed as a kind of generalization of the evaluation rule for the standard $cstit$ operator, since, of course, a standard statement of the form $[\alpha \ cstit: A]$ is true at m/h just in case $K \subseteq |A|_m$ for each $K \in Choice_\alpha^m$ such that $h \in K$.

In order to put this first approach in perspective, it will be useful to return briefly to the problem originally confronting Prior in formulating the semantics for future tense statements in branching time, and discussed here in Section 2.1. In this case, as we recall, it seemed difficult to evaluate a future tense statement FA on the basis of the information provided by a moment alone, since A might hold true in the future along some histories through that moment, but not along others. Now, one approach to this problem—not the "Ockhamist" approach adopted in this book, but another, which Prior describes as "Peircian"—is to suppose that the evaluation of the statement FA at a moment m might depend on the entire set of histories through m, that FA should be true at m just in case A holds at some point in the future along each history through m. Our first approach to the strategic $cstit$ problem is like that. Since an m/h index alone does not provide us with the information necessary to determine the strategy under execution by an agent, we suppose that $[\alpha \ scstit: A]$ holds there just in case A is guaranteed by each of the various strategies consistent with that index.

A second approach to the strategic $cstit$ problem is more similar to the Ockhamist approach to the future tense problem that is adopted in this book. In the previous case, since a moment m alone did not provide sufficient information for the evaluation of future tense statements, this approach recommended that these statements should be evaluated instead at indices consisting of m/h pairs, where $h \in H_m$. And in the same way, since even these m/h pairs do not seem to provide the information necessary for the evaluation of strategic $cstit$ statements, we might now consider supplementing the indices of evaluation even further. We might suppose, for example, that formulas are to be evaluated at triples of the form $m/h/J$, where $h \in J$ and $J \subseteq H_m$. Just as the h-component of an index provided the extra information necessary for evaluating future tense statements, the new J-component would allow us to evaluate strategic $cstit$ statements as well: given a background field M, a statement of the form $[\alpha \ scstit: A]$ could then be defined as true at a triple $m/h/J$ just in case there is some $\sigma \in Strategy_\alpha^M$ such that $J = Adh(\sigma)$ and $J \subseteq |A|_m$. And again, it could be argued that this evaluation rule generalizes that for the standard $cstit$ operator, since a standard statement of the form $[\alpha \ cstit: A]$ can likewise be defined as true at an index $m/h/J$ whenever there is some $K \in Choice_\alpha^m$ such that $J = K$ and $J \subseteq |A|_m$, with the proviso that, in this special case, the J-component of the index is determined from the h-component according to the formula $J = Choice_\alpha^m(h)$.

As indicated, although I believe that both of these two approaches suggest reasonable directions of investigation, I do not want to recommend either as a solution to the strategic *cstit* problem. I mention them simply to illustrate some ways in which the problem might be addressed in the current setting.

7.2.2   Ability

In our treatment of momentary action, after introducing the *cstit* operator to represent agency in Section 2.2, we then combined this operator with ordinary historical possibility in Section 2.3, allowing for the construction of statements of the form $\Diamond[\alpha \ cstit\colon A]$, taken to represent the idea that the agent α has the ability to see to it that A by performing an available action. Even though the task of introducing a strategic analogue to the standard *cstit* operator leads to conceptual difficulties that we have not resolved, it turns out that we can simply bypass these difficulties in the treatment of strategic ability through the introduction of a fused operator $\Diamond[\ldots \ scstit\colon \ldots]$, allowing for the construction of statements of the form

$$\Diamond[\alpha \ scstit\colon A],$$

taken to mean that α has the ability to guarantee the truth of A by carrying out an available strategy.

Of course, the strategies available to an agent depend on the background field of concern, and so the evaluation of these strategic ability statements must again be relativized to a more complicated index—supplemented, this time, with an indication of the background field. Let us define an *extended index* as a triple of the form $m/h/M$, where m/h is an ordinary index and M is a field at m. We can then say that the statement $\Diamond[\alpha \ scstit\colon A]$ holds at such an index whenever the agent α has available a strategy in the field M whose execution guarantees the truth of A.

Definition 7.12 (Evaluation rule: $\Diamond[\alpha \ scstit\colon A]$) Where α is an agent and $m/h/M$ is an extended index from a stit model $\mathcal{M}$,

- $\mathcal{M}, m/h/M \models \Diamond[\alpha \ scstit\colon A]$ if and only if there is a strategy $\sigma \in Strategy_\alpha^M$ such that $Adh(\sigma) \subseteq |A|_m^{\mathcal{M}}$.

And it is important to observe that, according to this rule, the truth or falsity of a strategic ability statement is independent of the h-component of the index at which it is evaluated. This observation can be made precise by first extending the ideas of settledness and determination from moments to fields, as follows: where M is a field at the moment m, a statement is *settled true (settled false)* in the field M just in case it is true (false) at $m/h'/M$ for each history h' from H_m; and a statement is *determinate* in the field M

just in case it is either settled true or settled false in M. We can then note that strategic ability statements are determinate in any field.

The strategic ability operator can be illustrated through Figure 7.2. Taking $M = \{m_1, m_2\}$ as our background field, it is, as we have seen, difficult to say whether the statement $[\alpha \; scstit : A]$ should be regarded as true or false at $m/h_1/M$; as the agent α moves along h_1, we cannot tell whether he is carrying out a strategy that guarantees the truth of A or not. But there is no question that α has the ability to carry out a strategy in the field M that guarantees the truth of A; that strategy is simply $\sigma_1 = \{\langle m_1, K_1 \rangle, \langle m_2, K_3 \rangle\}$, defined earlier. Since $Adh(\sigma_1) \subseteq |A|_{m_1}$, it follows from our evaluation rule that $\Diamond[\alpha \; scstit : A]$ is true at the extended index $m_1/h_1/M$, and so, of course, settled true in the field M.

The current notion of strategic ability generalizes the previous momentary idea, in the sense that $\Diamond[\alpha \; cstit : A]$ holds at the ordinary index m/h whenever $\Diamond[\alpha \; scstit : A]$ holds at the corresponding extended index $m/h/\{m\}$. But the more general strategic analysis allows us also to consider two issues that might be described as *inflation* and *deflation*: are the abilities attributed to an agent preserved as the background field is inflated or deflated in size? Of course, deflation fails, as is apparent already from Figure 7.2. Here, as we have seen, the statement $\Diamond[\alpha \; scstit : A]$ is settled true in the field M, defined above; but taking $M' = \{m_1\}$, so that $M' \subseteq M$, we have $\Diamond[\alpha \; scstit : A]$ settled false in the field M'. Abilities are preserved under inflation, however. For where M and M' are fields at m, suppose $M \subseteq M'$, and that $\Diamond[\alpha \; scstit : A]$ is settled true in the smaller field M—that is, that $Adh(\sigma) \subseteq |A|_m$ for some strategy σ from $Strategy_\alpha^M$. It then follows from Proposition 7.11 that $Adh(\sigma') \subseteq Adh(\sigma)$ for some strategy σ' from $Strategy_\alpha^{M'}$. Hence, $Adh(\sigma') \subseteq |A|_m$ as well, and so $\Diamond[\alpha \; scstit : A]$ must be settled true also in the larger field M'.

In its treatment of inflation and deflation the current analysis of strategic ability seems to accord with intuition: whatever I can do in a month I can do in a year (by doing it in a month, and then doing something else for the rest of the year), but there are things I can do in a year that I cannot do in a month.

7.3 Strategic dominance and optimality

7.3.1 Dominance

The goal of this section is to extend the notions of dominance and optimality defined in Chapter 4 for momentary actions to the current strategic setting. We begin, however, by setting out an important restriction on the scope of our discussion.

As we recall, our earlier treatment of dominance relations among actions required a notion of states, thought of as the most specific causally independent propositions confronting an agent at a moment, and defined, according to our preliminary analysis, as those patterns of actions simultaneously available to all other agents. This analysis was meant to provide a helpful approximation, but as we saw in Section 4.4, there are a number of ways in which it misleads. In particular, while it seems best to view some, but not all, later actions by other agents as causally independent of a given agent's present actions, the preliminary analysis neglects this distinction by grouping all later actions together as not causally independent.

Previously, when considering only momentary actions, it seemed reasonable to set this problem aside as a minor distortion. But in the strategic setting, where an agent's actions throughout a field might be interspersed with the actions of others, some of which may be and others of which may not be independent of the agent's earlier actions in that very field, the distortion resulting from a misleading analysis of causal independence would be much more severe. Rather than extending the current account in a way that may be radically incorrect, therefore, we now limit the scope of our discussion to a setting in which our treatment of causal independence is more accurate. Although many later actions by others are causally independent of an agent's present actions, it does seem natural to suppose, at least as an idealization, that each of an agent's own later actions should lie under the causal influence of his present choices. Our preliminary analysis, which groups all later actions together as not causally independent, is not so terribly misleading, then, when there is only a single agent involved, so that all later actions are actions by that very agent. We therefore explicitly restrict our attention to these single agent situations throughout the remainder of the chapter.

Definition 7.13 (Single agent stit frames/models) A *single agent stit frame* is a stit frame in which the set *Agent* contains only one individual. A *single agent stit model* is a model based on a single agent stit frame.

Taking α as the agent from a single agent stit frame, it is easy to see that $State_\alpha^m = \{H_m\}$ for any moment m, so that the states drop out of the picture, and, as noted in Section 4.1, the dominance orderings on the actions available to α at a moment coincide with the propositional orderings defined over those actions in Definition 4.1. Since the strategies available to an agent determine propositions, through their admission sets, it is now natural to define the dominance relations among strategies simply by lifting the preference orderings from the admission sets they determine to the strategies themselves.

Definition 7.14 (Strategic dominance; $\preceq$, $\prec$) Let α be the agent and m a moment from a single agent utilitarian stit frame, and where M is a field at m, let σ and σ' be members of $Strategy_\alpha^M$. Then $\sigma \preceq \sigma'$ (σ' *weakly* *dominates* σ) if and only if $Adh(\sigma) \leq Adh(\sigma')$; and $\sigma \prec \sigma'$ (σ' *strongly dominates* σ) if and only if $\sigma \preceq \sigma'$ and it is not the case that $\sigma' \preceq \sigma$.

And it can then be shown that the ordering properties established in Proposition 4.7 for dominance relations among individual actions can be extended to the dominance relations defined here among strategies, since the analogous properties are already established in Proposition 4.3 for preference relations among propositions.

7.3.2   Optimality

Once the dominance relations among strategies have been mapped out, it is a simple matter to define the set of optimal strategies available to the agent α in a field M—that is, $Optimal_\alpha^M$—as the set of strategies available to α in M that are not strongly dominated.

Definition 7.15 (*$Optimal_\alpha^M$*) Where α is the agent and m a moment from a single agent utilitarian stit frame, and where M is a field at m,

$$Optimal_\alpha^M = \{\sigma \in Strategy_\alpha^M : \text{ there is no } \sigma' \in Strategy_\alpha^M . \sigma \prec \sigma'\}.$$

And of course, when we limit our attention to single agent frames, this definition of the optimal strategies can be seen to generalize our earlier treatment of optimal actions, in the sense that the admission sets determined by the optimal strategies available to α in the field $\{m\}$ coincide with the optimal actions available at the moment m:

$$Optimal_\alpha^m = \{Adh(\sigma) : \sigma \in Optimal_\alpha^{\{m\}}\}.$$

We noted earlier that the existence of optimal actions was guaranteed by the finite choice condition, but even in a finite choice framework, it is still possible for an agent's field to present him with infinitely many strategies, each dominated by another. Such a situation is depicted in Figure 7.3. Given $M = \{m_1, m_2, m_3 \ldots\}$ as a field at the moment m_1, it is clear that $Strategy_\alpha^M = \{\sigma_1, \sigma_2, \sigma_3, \ldots, \sigma_\omega\}$, where $\sigma_1 = \{\langle m_1, K_1^1 \rangle\}$, $\sigma_2 = \{\langle m_1, K_2^1 \rangle, \langle m_2, K_1^2 \rangle\}$, and in general $\sigma_i = \{\langle m_j, K_2^j \rangle : j < i\} \cup \{\langle m_i, K_1^i \rangle\}$, and where $\sigma_\omega = \{\langle m_i, K_2^i \rangle : 1 \leq i\}$. With regard to the displayed tree of choices, each σ_i is the strategy of choosing the right cell until the moment m_i and choosing the left cell there; σ_ω is the strategy of choosing the right cell forever. Let us assume that $H_m = \{h_1, h_2, h_3, \ldots, h_\omega\}$, with each history h_i branching off to the left at the moment m_i and carrying a value of i, and with the history h_ω proceeding all the way along the right-hand spine of the choice tree, passing through each cell K_2^i, and carrying a value of 0. We therefore have $Adh(\sigma_i) = \{h_i\}$ for each i, and $Adh(\sigma_\omega) = \{h_\omega\}$; and from this we can conclude that the strategy σ_ω is dominated by the strategy σ_1,

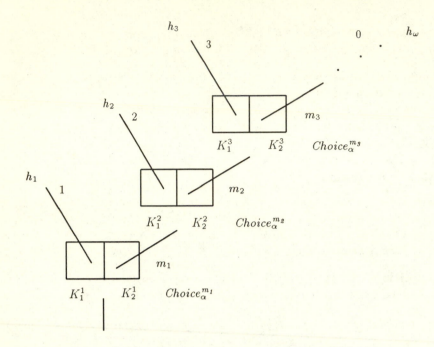

Figure 7.3: No optimal strategy

and also that each strategy σ_i is dominated by the strategy σ_{i+1}, so that the set of optimal strategies available to the agent α in the field M is empty.

In order to guarantee, then, that the set of optimal strategies available to an agent in a field is nonempty, it is necessary to impose stronger restrictions than the finite choice condition—and it suffices to impose a condition of finite branching.

Definition 7.16 (Finite branch stit frames/models) A *finite branch stit frame* is a stit frame in which the set H_m is finite, for each moment m. A *finite branch stit model* is a model based on a finite branch stit frame.

Of course, the finite branch condition implies the finite choice condition, since any moment at which an agent is faced with an infinite number of choices would also have to be a moment through which there passed an infinite number of histories, at least one for each choice confronting the agent. But the finite branch condition also yields the consequence that the number of strategies confronting an agent in any field must itself be finite. For where M is a field at the moment m, the number of nonvacuous choice points throughout the field M cannot be greater than the number of histories passing through m, since each nonvacuous choice point corresponds to a branch between at least two histories, both of which must pass through m. And since the number of strategies available to the agent in the field M

cannot be greater than the number of nonvacuous choice points in that field multiplied by the greatest number of choices available at any such choice point, and both of these numbers must be finite, the number of available strategies must be finite as well.

Because the finite branch condition guarantees that the number of strategies available to an agent in a field is finite, it allows us to reach the desired results—both that the set of optimal strategies confronting an agent in a field is nonempty, and that each nonoptimal strategy is dominated by an optimal strategy.

Proposition 7.17 Let α be the agent and M a field from a finite branch single agent utilitarian stit frame. Then $Optimal_\alpha^M \neq \emptyset$.

Proposition 7.18 Let α be the agent and M a field from a finite branch single agent utilitarian stit frame. Then for each strategy $\sigma \in Strategy_\alpha^M - Optimal_\alpha^M$ there is a strategy $\sigma' \in Optimal_\alpha^M$ such that $\sigma \prec \sigma'$.

But the finite branch condition is really very strong. Although useful as a simplifying assumption for the depiction of certain scenarios, this condition is surely unreasonable as a postulate concerning the structure of real historical possibility. It would be nice to know of weaker and more plausible conditions that might also suffice to guarantee the existence of optimal strategies in nontrivial fields.

7.4 A strategic ought operator

7.4.1 The definition

The treatment of strategic oughts presented here follows the standard procedure first set out in Chapter 4—indeed, the whole point of our discussion is to show how this procedure generalizes to the strategic setting.[4] We begin by introducing a strategic ought operator allowing for the construction of statements of the form

$$\odot[\alpha \; scstit\colon A].$$

Like our strategic ability formulas, such a strategic ought statement is to be evaluated at an extended index of the form $m/h/M$, and carries the intuitive meaning that the agent α ought to guarantee the truth of A as a result of his actions throughout the field M.

As usual, the official evaluation rule for strategic oughts is formulated for the general case, applying even when the set of optimal strategies available to an agent in a field is empty.

---

[4]Since we have simplified in this strategic setting by ignoring the states confronting an agent, we generalize only the dominance ought operator set out earlier, entirely neglecting any corresponding orthodox account as dependent on a prior treatment of states.

Definition 7.19 (Evaluation rule: $\bigodot[\alpha\ scstit\colon A]$) Where α is the agent and $m/h/M$ an extended index from a single agent utilitarian stit model $\mathcal{M}$,

- $\mathcal{M}, m/h/M \models \bigodot[\alpha\ scstit\colon A]$ if and only if, for each strategy $\sigma \in Strategy_\alpha^M$ such that $Adh(\sigma) \not\subseteq |A|_m^{\mathcal{M}}$, there is a strategy $\sigma' \in Strategy_\alpha^M$ such that (1) $\sigma \prec \sigma'$, and (2) $Adh(\sigma') \subseteq |A|_m^{\mathcal{M}}$, and (3) $Adh(\sigma'') \subseteq |A|_m^{\mathcal{M}}$ for each strategy $\sigma'' \in Strategy_\alpha^M$ such that $\sigma' \preceq \sigma''$.

But again, this evaluation rule can be simplified if we limit our attention to finite branch models, where optimal strategies are guaranteed to exist; for here, it can be shown that α ought to see to it that A in the strategic sense just in case guaranteeing the truth of this statement is a necessary condition for carrying out an optimal strategy.

Proposition 7.20 Let α be the agent and $m/h/M$ an extended index from a finite branch single agent utilitarian stit model $\mathcal{M}$. Then $\mathcal{M}, m/h/M \models \bigodot[\alpha\ scstit\colon A]$ if and only if $Adh(\sigma) \subseteq |A|_m^{\mathcal{M}}$ for each $\sigma \in Optimal_\alpha^M$.

Returning to Figure 7.1 for illustration, and taking $M = \{m_1, m_2\}$ as our field, it is clear that $Optimal_\alpha^M = \{\sigma_1\}$, where $\sigma_1 = \{\langle m_1, K_1\rangle, \langle m_2, K_3\rangle\}$. Evidently, $Adh(\sigma_1) = \{h_1\}$, and of course $|A|_{m_1} = \{h_1, h_2\}$, so that, since $Adh(\sigma_1) \subseteq |A|_{m_1}$, we can conclude that $\bigodot[\alpha\ scstit\colon A]$ is settled true in the field M.

7.4.2 Logical points

Like the momentary ought operator, our strategic ought is normal, validating the principles $RE_\alpha^\sigma \bigodot$, $N_\alpha^\sigma \bigodot$, $M_\alpha^\sigma \bigodot$, and $C_\alpha^\sigma \bigodot$ (analogues of $RE_\alpha \bigodot$, $N_\alpha \bigodot$, $M_\alpha \bigodot$, and $C_\alpha \bigodot$, but with *scstit* for *cstit*). The operator also validates the principle

$$D_\alpha^\sigma \bigodot. \qquad \bigodot[\alpha\ scstit\colon A] \supset \Diamond[\alpha\ scstit\colon A],$$

the appropriate form of the characteristic deontic formula, linking strategic oughts with strategic ability. And as with strategic ability, strategic ought formulas are determinate in any field, always either settled true or settled false.

Of course, the strategic ought operator defined here generalizes the earlier momentary concept, in the sense that an ought statement $\bigodot[\alpha\ cstit\colon A]$ holds at the ordinary index m/h just in case the strategic ought statement $\bigodot[\alpha\ scstit\colon A]$ holds at the corresponding extended index $m/h/\{m\}$. And again, the strategic setting also provides an environment within which we can consider the issues of inflation and deflation: how are an agent's oughts affected as the background field varies in size?

As with strategic ability, deflation fails for strategic oughts; the oughts attributed to agents in larger fields need not be preserved in smaller fields.

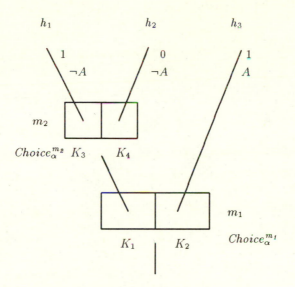

Figure 7.4: Failure of inflation

Given the validity of the characteristic deontic formula $D_\alpha^\sigma \odot$, this failure of deflation for strategic oughts follows from the corresponding failure for strategic ability, and a concrete counterexample can be found in Figure 7.1. Here, taking $M = \{m_1, m_2\}$ and $M' = \{m_1\}$, so that $M' \subseteq M$, we have $\odot[\alpha \ scstit : A]$ settled true in the field M but settled false in the field M'. Somewhat more surprisingly, the inflation property, which holds for strategic ability, also fails for strategic oughts; the oughts attributed to agents in smaller fields need not be preserved in larger fields. This failure is illustrated in Figure 7.4, where we take $M = \{m_1\}$ and $M' = \{m_1, m_2\}$, so that $M \subseteq M'$. Here, we have $Optimal_\alpha^M = \{\sigma_2\}$, with $\sigma_2 = \{\langle m_1, K_2 \rangle\}$; and since $Adh(\sigma_2) \subseteq |A|_{m_1}$, the statement $\odot[\alpha \ scstit : A]$ is settled true in M. But $Optimal_\alpha^{M'} = \{\sigma_2, \sigma_3\}$, with $\sigma_3 = \{\langle m_1, K_1 \rangle, \langle m_2, K_3 \rangle\}$; and since $Adh(\sigma_3) \not\subseteq |A|_{m_1}$, the statement $\odot[\alpha \ scstit : A]$ is now settled false in M'.

In fact, inflation poses even more severe problems, for it turns out that different ways of inflating a field might lead, not only to different oughts, but to oughts that are actually inconsistent. This possibility is illustrated in Figure 7.5, where we take $M = \{m_1\}$, $M' = \{m_1, m_2\}$, and $M'' = \{m_1, m_3\}$, so that both $M \subseteq M'$ and $M \subseteq M''$. Here, it is easy to see that $Optimal_\alpha^{M'} = \{\sigma_4\}$ and $Optimal_\alpha^{M''} = \{\sigma_5\}$, with $\sigma_4 = \{\langle m_1, K_1 \rangle, \langle m_2, K_3 \rangle\}$, and $\sigma_5 = \{\langle m_1, K_2 \rangle, \langle m_3, K_5 \rangle\}$. But since $Adh(\sigma_4) \subseteq |A|_{m_1}$ and $Adh(\sigma_5) \subseteq |\neg A|_{m_1}$, we have $\odot[\alpha \ scstit : A]$ settled true in the field M' but $\odot[\alpha \ scstit : \neg A]$ settled true in the field M''.

Nevertheless, in spite of the fact that different ways of inflating a given

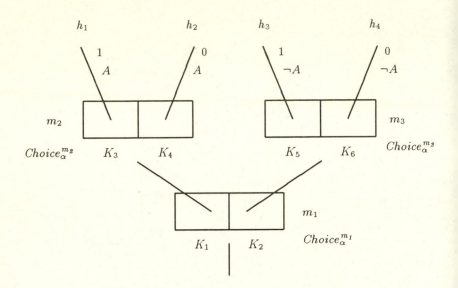

Figure 7.5: Inconsistent strategic oughts

field can lead to inconsistent strategic oughts, we know at least that the oughts generated by larger and smaller fields must be consistent, a result worth recording explicitly.

Proposition 7.21 Let α be the agent and $m/h/M$ and $m/h/M'$ two extended indices from a single agent utilitarian stit model, with $M \subseteq M'$. Then it is impossible to have both $\mathcal{M}, m/h/M \models \odot[\alpha \ scstit : A]$ and $\mathcal{M}, m/h/M' \models \odot[\alpha \ scstit: \neg A]$.

And since, as we have seen, the theory of strategic oughts developed here generalizes the earlier account of momentary oughts, it follows as a corollary that an agent's momentary oughts at any given moment must be consistent with the strategic oughts generated by any field at that moment.

7.4.3   Actualism and possibilism

In this final section, we turn briefly to a distinction between two views—sometimes known as *actualism* and *possibilism*—concerning the way in which an agent's future choices might be thought to impact his current oughts. Very roughly, actualism is the view that an agent's current actions are to be evaluated against the background of the actions that he is actually going to perform in the future; possibilism is the view that an agent's current actions are to be evaluated against the background of the actions that he might perform in the future, the available future actions. The past two decades have seen the growth of a considerable literature advocating one or another of these views, and it is not my aim here to attempt to resolve the issue.[5] My modest goal is simply to explore some ways in which the contrast between these two positions can be cast within the current framework.

It is best to approach the issue through a concrete example. Of course, the literature in the area is full of examples, but the following case, due to Jackson and Pargetter, is typical:

> Professor Procrastinate receives an invitation to review a book. He is the best person to do the review, has the time, and so on. The best thing that can happen is that he says yes, and then writes the review when the book arrives. However, suppose it is further the case that were Procrastinate to say yes, he would not in fact get around to writing the review. Not because of incapacity or outside interference or anything like that, but because he would keep on putting the task off. (This has been known to happen.) Thus, although the best that can happen is for Procrastinate to say yes and then write, and he *can* do exactly this, what *would* in fact happen were he to say yes is that he would not write the review. Moreover, we may suppose, this latter is the worst that can happen. [Jackson and Pargetter, 1986, p. 235]

In terms of this example, Jackson and Pargetter then describe the conflicting conclusions suggested by actualism and possibilism in this way:

> According to Possibilism, the fact that Procrastinate would not write the review were he to say yes is irrelevant. What matters is simply what is possible for Procrastinate. He can say yes and then write; that is best; that requires *inter alia* that he say yes; therefore, he ought to say yes. According to Actualism, the fact that Procrastinate would not actually write the review were he to say yes is crucial. It means that to say yes would be in fact to realize the worst. Therefore, Procrastinate ought to say no. [Jackson and Pargetter, 1986, p. 235]

Let us begin by depicting the situation through a stit model, as in Figure 7.6. Here, m_1 is the moment at which Procrastinate, represented as the agent α, chooses whether or not to accept the invitation: K_1 represents the choice of accepting, K_2 the choice of declining. If Procrastinate accepts the invitation, he then faces at m_2 the later choice of writing the review or not. Although it ignores the psychology of real procrastination, we will suppose

---

[5] The problem of relating present oughts to future choices was originally presented in a trio of papers: Goldman [1976], Sobel [1976], and Thomason [1981a]. Further discussion can be found, for example, in Bergström [1977], Carlson [1995], Feldman [1986], Goldman [1978], Greenspan [1978], Humberstone [1983], Jackson [1985], Jackson [1988], Jackson and Pargetter [1986], McKinsey [1979], and Zimmerman [1990].

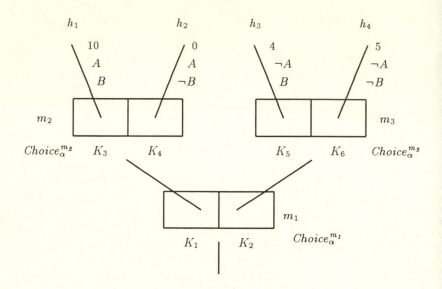

Figure 7.6: Procrastinate's choices

for convenience that this choice is momentary: K_3 represents the choice of writing the review, K_4 another choice that results in the review's not being written. And, also for convenience, we will suppose that Procrastinate faces at m_3 a similar choice whether or not to write the review (an option that is still open, after all, even if he declines the invitation): K_5 represents the choice of writing, K_6 the choice of not writing. The history h_1, in which Procrastinate accepts the invitation and then writes the review, carries the greatest value of 10; the history h_2, in which he accepts the invitation and then neglects the task, the least value of 0; the history h_4, in which Procrastinate declines, so that a less competent authority reviews the book, carries an intermediate value of 5; and the peculiar history h_3, in which Procrastinate declines the invitation but then reviews the book anyway, carries a slightly lower value of 4, since it wastes Procrastinate's time, apart from doing no one else any good. The statement A represents the proposition that Procrastinate accepts the invitation; the statement B represents the proposition that Procrastinate will write the review.

When the situation is depicted in this way, one very natural analysis of the case moves through the theory of strategic oughts, with $M = \{m_1, m_2, m_3\}$ selected as the background field. It is then clear that $Optimal_\alpha^M = \{\sigma_6\}$, with $\sigma_6 = \{\langle m_1, K_1 \rangle, \langle m_2, K_3 \rangle\}$. And since $Adh(\sigma_6) \subseteq |A|_{m_1}$, the strategic ought statement $\odot[\alpha \; scstit: A]$ is settled true in the field M. This straightforward application of the current theory, then, supports the possibilist intuition: Procrastinate ought to accept the invitation because this is the action determined by the best available strategy—first accepting the invitation, and then writing the review.

Now, how do we arrive at an analysis that supports the actualist intuition? Well, one might first suggest narrowing the background field to the set $M' = \{m_1\}$—an idea that is equivalent, of course, to a shift from the strategic to the momentary theory of oughts. In that case, since $Optimal_\alpha^{m_1} = \{K_1, K_2\}$ and $K_2 \not\subseteq |A|_{m_1}$, we would have $\odot[\alpha \ cstit: A]$ settled false at the moment m_1, contrary to the possibilist conclusion that Procrastinate ought to accept the invitation. Still, although it avoids the possibilist conclusion, this analysis does not yet allow us to accommodate the actualist intuition that Procrastinate ought to decline the invitation, since we also have $K_1 \not\subseteq |\neg A|_{m_1}$, so that $\odot[\alpha \ cstit: \neg A]$ is likewise settled false at m_1. By shifting to the momentary theory, it is as if we choose to view Procrastinate, in deciding whether to accept the invitation, as gambling on his own later choice: perhaps he will write the review, perhaps not. But from the actualist perspective, the situation is not to be viewed as a gamble; an important background assumption—and the reason that Procrastinate should decline the invitation—is that he will not, in fact, write the review.

Of course, this background assumption is not represented in Figure 7.6, which holds no bias in favor of either of Procrastinate's future choices; and in the current framework, it seems that the most natural way of incorporating the additional information is by moving to the theory of conditional oughts, from Chapter 5. Rather than asking about the oughts governing Procrastinate at the moment m_1 from Figure 7.6, then, we now ask about the oughts governing Procrastinate at this moment given the additional assumption that he will not actually write the review—given the assumption, that is, that the statement $\neg B$ is true. Here, it is easy to see that $Optimal_\alpha^{m_1}/|\neg B|_{m_1} = \{K_2\}$. And since $K_2 \subseteq |\neg A|_{m_1}$, we have $\odot([\alpha \ cstit: \neg A] / \neg B)$ settled true at m_1. This conditional analysis thus supports the actualist intuition: Procrastinate ought to decline the invitation, given that he will not write the review. And it is interesting to note that, as presented here, actualism and possibilism are not really conflicting views at all: there is nothing wrong with saying that the strategic ought $\odot[\alpha \ scstit: A]$ is settled true in the field M, defined above, while the conditional ought $\odot([\alpha \ cstit: \neg A] / \neg B)$ is settled true at the moment m_1.[6]

Our interpretation casts the actualist judgment as a conditional ought. But then, what are we to make of the apparently unconditional judgments found in the writings of many actualists, such as Jackson and Pargetter's claim, above: "Procrastinate ought to say no." From the current perspective, it is perhaps best to read judgments like these as conditional oughts

---

[6]A conditional analysis of the actualist position was first suggested by Greenspan [1978], who also emphasized the consistency, on this analysis, between actualism and possibilism.

in which the statement of the antecedent conditions has been suppressed: Procrastinate ought to say no (given that he will not write the review). But it is also possible to express the actualist judgment as an absolute ought through an appeal to the orthodox deontic operator defined in Section 5.4.

Suppose, as suggested once before, toward the end of Section 4.4, that we suspend Definition 4.4 in favor of the stipulative treatment of the states confronting an agent suggested in Section 4.1; and imagine that we were to stipulate, in Figure 7.6, that $State_\alpha^{m_1} = \{|B|_{m_1}, |\neg B|_{m_1}\}$. The intuitive content of this stipulation, of course, is that Procrastinate's later decision whether or not to write the review is causally independent of his current choice whether or not to accept the invitation. Now pick some history in which he will not, in fact, write the review—say, h_4. In that case, Definition 5.15 would yield $AU\text{-}right_\alpha^{m_1/h_4} = \{K_2\}$, and then, since $K_2 \subseteq |A|_{m_1}$, we could conclude from Proposition 5.18 that the statement $\bigoplus[\alpha \ cstit: \neg A]$ is true at the index m_1/h_4. The idea underlying this chain of reasoning is that the best choice available to Procrastinate in the state in which he finds himself at the index m_1/h_4, the state in which he will not write the review, is to decline the invitation, so that this is what he ought to do. This orthodox analysis does manage to generate the actualist judgment as an absolute ought, but only at the cost of a peculiar treatment of states. It forces us to imagine that, in evaluating his current choices, an agent might legitimately view those propositions whose truth or falsity can be guaranteed by his own later actions as causally independent states of the world, like the weather, or the independent choices of other agents. And it is exactly this feature of actualism—that it allows the agent to reason about his very own later choices as if they were the actions of someone else entirely—that its critics find so objectionable.[7]

---

[7]For objections along these lines, see Humberstone [1983] and especially Thomason [1981b].

Appendix A

Proofs of validities and propositions

A.1 Validities

Validity A.1 *The statement $C\bigcirc$ is valid in the class of general deontic stit models in which the underlying space of values is subject to a linear ordering.*

Proof Where $\mathcal{M}$ is a general deontic stit model with a linear ordering of values, suppose $\mathcal{M}, m/h \models \bigcirc A \wedge \bigcirc B$. We know from the evaluation rule that there exist histories $h_1, h_2 \in H_m$ such that

(∗) $\mathcal{M}, m/h_1 \models A$, and $\mathcal{M}, m/h'' \models A$ for all histories $h'' \in H_m$ such that $Value_m(h_1) \leq Value_m(h'')$,

and

(∗∗) $\mathcal{M}, m/h_2 \models B$, and $\mathcal{M}, m/h'' \models B$ for all histories $h'' \in H_m$ such that $Value_m(h_2) \leq Value_m(h'')$.

In order to show that $\mathcal{M}, m/h \models \bigcirc(A \wedge B)$, we must show that there is some history $h' \in H_m$ such that (1) $\mathcal{M}, m/h' \models A \wedge B$, and (2) $\mathcal{M}, m/h'' \models A \wedge B$ for all histories $h'' \in H_m$ such that $Value_m(h') \leq Value_m(h'')$. Since the underlying space of values is subject to a linear ordering, we have either $Value_m(h_1) \leq Value_m(h_2)$ or $Value_m(h_2) \leq Value_m(h_1)$. We can thus reason by cases.

Suppose $Value_m(h_1) \leq Value_m(h_2)$. In this case, we identify h' with h_2. Then (∗∗) tells us that $\mathcal{M}, m/h' \models B$, and we can conclude from (∗), since $Value_m(h_1) \leq Value_m(h')$, that $\mathcal{M}, m/h' \models A$. Thus we have (1) $\mathcal{M}, m/h' \models A \wedge B$. Now consider a history $h'' \in H_m$ such that $Value_m(h') \leq Value_m(h'')$. From (∗∗), we know that $\mathcal{M}, m/h'' \models B$. And since $Value_m(h_1) \leq Value_m(h')$, we can conclude that $Value_m(h_1) \leq Value_m(h'')$; and so (∗) tells us also that $\mathcal{M}, m/h'' \models A$. Therefore, $\mathcal{M}, m/h'' \models A \wedge B$; and so we have established that (2) $\mathcal{M}, m/h'' \models A \wedge B$ for all histories $h'' \in H_m$ such that $Value_m(h') \leq Value_m(h'')$.

The argument is symmetric in the case in which $Value_m(h_2) \leq Value_m(h_1)$.

∎

Validity A.2 *The statement* $C \odot$ *is valid in the class of utilitarian stit models.*

Proof Where m/h is an index in a utilitarian stit model $\mathcal{M}$, suppose $\mathcal{M}, m/h \models \odot[\alpha \; cstit: A] \wedge \odot[\alpha \; cstit: B]$. Then we know that both

> (∗) for each action $K \in Choice_\alpha^m$ such that $K \not\subseteq |A|_m^{\mathcal{M}}$, there is an action $K' \in Choice_\alpha^m$ such that $K \prec K'$, and $K' \subseteq |A|_m^{\mathcal{M}}$, and $K'' \subseteq |A|_m^{\mathcal{M}}$ for each action $K'' \in Choice_\alpha^m$ such that $K' \preceq K''$,

and

> (∗∗) for each action $K \in Choice_\alpha^m$ such that $K \not\subseteq |B|_m^{\mathcal{M}}$, there is an action $K' \in Choice_\alpha^m$ such that $K \prec K'$, and $K' \subseteq |B|_m^{\mathcal{M}}$, and $K'' \subseteq |B|_m^{\mathcal{M}}$ for each action $K'' \in Choice_\alpha^m$ such that $K' \preceq K''$.

In order to show that $\mathcal{M}, m/h \models \odot[\alpha \; cstit: A \wedge B]$, we must establish that, for each action $K \in Choice_\alpha^m$ such that $K \not\subseteq |A \wedge B|_m^{\mathcal{M}}$, we have:

> (∗ ∗ ∗) there is an action $K' \in Choice_\alpha^m$ such that $K \prec K'$, and $K' \subseteq |A \wedge B|_m^{\mathcal{M}}$, and $K'' \subseteq |A \wedge B|_m^{\mathcal{M}}$ for each action $K'' \in Choice_\alpha^m$ such that $K' \preceq K''$.

Consider, then, an arbitrary action $K \in Choice_\alpha^m$ such that $K \not\subseteq |A \wedge B|_m^{\mathcal{M}}$. From this it follows that either $K \not\subseteq |A|_m^{\mathcal{M}}$ or $K \not\subseteq |B|_m^{\mathcal{M}}$, and so we reason by cases.

Case I: $K \not\subseteq |A|_m^{\mathcal{M}}$. Then (∗) tells us that there is an action $K_1 \in Choice_\alpha^m$ such that (1) $K \prec K_1$, and (2) $K_1 \subseteq |A|_m^{\mathcal{M}}$, and (3) $K'' \subseteq |A|_m^{\mathcal{M}}$ for each action $K'' \in Choice_\alpha^m$ such that $K_1 \preceq K''$. Now as a matter of logic, we know that either

> (A) both $K_1 \subseteq |B|_m^{\mathcal{M}}$, and $K'' \subseteq |B|_m^{\mathcal{M}}$ for each $K'' \in Choice_\alpha^m$ such that $K_1 \preceq K''$,

or

> (B) either $K_1 \not\subseteq |B|_m^{\mathcal{M}}$, or $K'' \not\subseteq |B|_m^{\mathcal{M}}$ for some $K'' \in Choice_\alpha^m$ such that $K_1 \preceq K''$;

and so we reason by subcases.

Case I.A: Both (4) $K_1 \subseteq |B|_m^{\mathcal{M}}$, and (5) $K'' \subseteq |B|_m^{\mathcal{M}}$ for each $K'' \in Choice_\alpha^m$ such that $K_1 \preceq K''$. From (2) and (4) we then have (6) $K_1 \subseteq |A \wedge B|_m^{\mathcal{M}}$. And from (3) and (5) we have (7) $K'' \subseteq |A \wedge B|_m^{\mathcal{M}}$ for each $K'' \in Choice_\alpha^m$ such that $K_1 \preceq K''$. In this case, then, (∗ ∗ ∗) follows from (1), (6), and (7).

Case I.B: Either (8) $K_1 \not\subseteq |B|_m^{\mathcal{M}}$, or (9) $K'' \not\subseteq |B|_m^{\mathcal{M}}$ for some $K'' \in Choice_\alpha^m$ such that $K_1 \preceq K''$. We treat the two disjuncts of this case separately, through further subcases.

Case I.B.1: (8) $K_1 \not\subseteq |B|_m^{\mathcal{M}}$. Then $(**)$ tells us that there is a K_2 such that (10) $K_1 \prec K_2$, and (11) $K_2 \subseteq |B|_m^{\mathcal{M}}$, and (12) $K'' \subseteq |B|_m^{\mathcal{M}}$ for each action $K'' \in Choice_\alpha^m$ such that $K_2 \preceq K''$. From (1) and (10) we then have (13) $K \prec K_2$ by Proposition 4.7. From (3) and (10) we have (14) $K_2 \subseteq |A|_m^{\mathcal{M}}$. And from (11) and (14) we have (15) $K_2 \subseteq |A \wedge B|_m^{\mathcal{M}}$. Finally, consider a $K'' \in Choice_\alpha^m$ such that (16) $K_2 \preceq K''$. From (12) and (16) we have (17) $K'' \subseteq |B|_m^{\mathcal{M}}$. From (10) and (16) we have (18) $K_1 \preceq K$ by Proposition 4.7, and so (19) $K'' \subseteq |A|_m^{\mathcal{M}}$ from (3) and (18). Hence, we have $K'' \subseteq |A \wedge B|_m^{\mathcal{M}}$ from (17) and (19), and so we can conclude that (20) $K'' \subseteq |A \wedge B|_m^{\mathcal{M}}$ for each action $K'' \in Choice_\alpha^m$ such that $K_2 \preceq K''$. In this case, therefore, $(***)$ follows from (13), (15), and (20).

Case I.B.2: (9) $K'' \not\subseteq |B|_m^{\mathcal{M}}$ for some $K'' \in Choice_\alpha^m$ such that $K_1 \preceq K''$. Here, we let K_3 be a particular action from $Choice_\alpha^m$ such that (21) $K_1 \preceq K_3$ and (22) $K_3 \not\subseteq |B|_m^{\mathcal{M}}$. From (22) and $(**)$ we know that there is another action $K_4 \in Choice_\alpha^m$ such that (23) $K_3 \prec K_4$, and (24) $K_4 \subseteq |B|_m^{\mathcal{M}}$, and (25) $K'' \subseteq |B|_m^{\mathcal{M}}$ for each $K'' \in Choice_\alpha^m$ such that $K_4 \preceq K''$. From (1), (21), and (23), we know by Proposition 4.7 that (26) $K \prec K_4$. From (21) and (23), we know, again by Proposition 4.7, that $K_1 \preceq K_4$; and together with (3) this yields $K_4 \subseteq |A|_m^{\mathcal{M}}$, which combines with (24) to yield (27) $K_4 \subseteq |A \wedge B|_m^{\mathcal{M}}$. Finally, consider a $K'' \in Choice_\alpha^m$ such that (28) $K_4 \preceq K''$. From (25) and (28) we have (29) $K_4 \subseteq |B|_m^{\mathcal{M}}$. From (21), (26), and (28), we have (30) $K_1 \preceq K''$ by Proposition 4.7, and so (31) $K'' \subseteq |A|_m^{\mathcal{M}}$ from (3) and (30). Hence we have $K'' \subseteq |A \wedge B|_m^{\mathcal{M}}$ from (29) and (31), and so we can conclude that (32) $K'' \subseteq |A \wedge B|_m^{\mathcal{M}}$ for each action $K'' \in Choice_\alpha^m$ such that $K_4 \preceq K''$. In this case, then, $(***)$ follows from (26), (27), and (32).

The fact that $(***)$ therefore holds in each subcase of Case I.B, and so in each subcase of Case I.

Case II: $K \not\subseteq |B|_m^{\mathcal{M}}$. An argument analogous to that of Case I allows us to establish $(***)$ in this case as well.

The fact that $(***)$ therefore holds in both of the main subcases, and so the proof is complete. ∎

Validity A.3 *The statement* $D_\alpha^* \odot \bigcirc$ *is valid in the class of utilitarian stit models.*

Proof Suppose the contrary, that there is an index m/h in a utilitarian stit model $\mathcal{M}$ such that (1) $\mathcal{M}, m/h \models \odot[\alpha \ cstit: A]$ and (2) $\mathcal{M}, m/h \models \bigcirc[\alpha \ cstit: \neg A]$. From (2) we know by the evaluation rule for $\bigcirc$ that there is an $h_1 \in H_m$ such that (3) $\mathcal{M}, m/h_1 \models [\alpha \ cstit: \neg A]$ and (4) $\mathcal{M}, m/h'' \models [\alpha \ cstit: \neg A]$ for each $h'' \in H_m$ such that $Value(h_1) \leq Value(h'')$. Of course,

$Choice_\alpha^m(h_1) \not\subseteq |A|_m^{\mathcal{M}}$, and so (1) together with the $\odot$ evaluation rule tells us that there is a $K' \in Choice_\alpha^m$ such that (5) $Choice_\alpha^m(h_1) \prec K'$ and (6) $K' \subseteq |A|_m^{\mathcal{M}}$. From (5), it follows, of course, that (7) $Choice_\alpha^m(h_1) \preceq K'$. From (7) we have (8) for each $S \in State_\alpha^m$, $Choice_\alpha^m(h_1) \cap S \leq K' \cap S$; and then from (8) we have (9) for each $S \in State_\alpha^m$, $Value(h) \leq Value(h')$ for each $h \in Choice_\alpha^m(h_1) \cap S$ and $h' \in K' \cap S$.

Now pick some history $h_2 \in K' \cap State_\alpha^m(h_1)$. Then since $h_1 \in Choice_\alpha^m(h_1)$ $\cap State_\alpha^m(h_1)$ and $h_2 \in K' \cap State_\alpha^m(h_1)$, we know from (9) that (10) $Value(h_1) \leq Value(h_2)$. We can then conclude from (4) and (10) that $\mathcal{M}, m/h_2 \models [\alpha\ cstit: \neg A]$, so that (11) $Choice_\alpha^m(h_2) \subseteq |\neg A|_m^{\mathcal{M}}$. But since $h_2 \in K'$, we know that $Choice_\alpha^m(h_2) = K'$, so that (11) contradicts (6). ∎

Lemma A.4 *Let α be an agent and m a moment from a utilitarian stit frame, and let K and K' be members of $Choice_\alpha^m$, and X a proposition at m. Then $K \preceq_X K'$ if $K \preceq K'$.*

Proof Straightforward. ∎

Lemma A.5 *Let α be an agent and m a moment from a utilitarian stit frame, and where X is a proposition at m, let K and K' be members of $Choice_\alpha^m$ such that $K, K' \subseteq X$. Then (1) $K \preceq_X K'$ if and only if $K \preceq K'$, and (2) $K \prec_X K'$ if and only if $K \prec K'$.*

Proof Right to left of part (1) follows from Lemma A.4. For left to right of part (1), suppose $K \preceq_X K'$—that is, that $(*)$ $K \cap S \cap X \leq K' \cap S \cap X$ for all $S \in State_\alpha^m$. Now consider an arbitrary S from $State_\alpha^m$ and arbitrary h and h' such that $h \in K \cap S$ and $h' \in K' \cap S$. Since $K, K' \subseteq X$, it follows that $h \in K \cap S \cap X$ and $h' \in K' \cap S \cap X$, and so we know from $(*)$ that $Value(h) \leq Value(h')$. Therefore, we have $K \cap S \leq K' \cap S$ for all $S \in State_\alpha^m$, or simply $K \preceq K'$, completing the proof of part (1). Part (2) then follows from part (1), since strong dominance (both absolute and conditional) is defined through weak dominance. ∎

Lemma A.6 *Let α be an agent and m a moment from a finite choice utilitarian stit frame. Then if $K \subseteq |B|_m^{\mathcal{M}}$ for each action $K \in Optimal_\alpha^m$, it follows that $Optimal_\alpha^m \subseteq Optimal_\alpha^m/|B|_m^{\mathcal{M}}$.*

Proof Assuming that $(*)$ $K \subseteq |B|_m^{\mathcal{M}}$ for each action $K \in Optimal_\alpha^m$, suppose the conclusion fails—that there is some K such that (1) $K \in Optimal_\alpha^m$ and (2) $K \notin Optimal_\alpha^m/|B|_m^{\mathcal{M}}$. From $(*)$ and (1), we know that (3) $K \subseteq |B|_m^{\mathcal{M}}$, so that $K \in Choice_\alpha^m/|B|_m^{\mathcal{M}}$. Therefore, we can conclude from (2) that there is a K' such that (4) $K \prec_{|B|_m^{\mathcal{M}}} K'$.

Now, we know that (5) $K' \notin Optimal_\alpha^m$. For if $K' \in Optimal_\alpha^m$, we would then have $K' \subseteq |B|_m^{\mathcal{M}}$ from $(*)$; and so Lemma A.5 would allow us to conclude from (3) and (4) that $K \prec K'$, contrary to (1). From (5), then, we can conclude from Proposition 4.11 that there must be a K'' such that (6) $K'' \in Optimal_\alpha^m$ and $K' \prec K''$, so that, of course, (7) $K' \preceq K''$. From (7) we have (8) $K' \preceq_{|B|_m^\mathcal{M}} K''$ from Lemma A.4. From (4) and (8) we then have (9) $K \prec_{|B|_m^\mathcal{M}} K''$ from Proposition 4.7. From (∗) and (6) we know that (10) $K'' \subseteq |B|_m^\mathcal{M}$. Therefore, Lemma A.5 allows us to conclude from (3), (9), and (10) that $K \prec K''$, which contradicts (1). ∎

Validity A.7 *The statement* $(\odot([\alpha \ cstit: \ A] \ / \ B) \wedge \odot[\alpha \ cstit: \ B]) \supset \odot[\alpha \ cstit: A]$ *is valid in the class of utilitarian stit models.*

Proof (sketch) We verify the result only for finite choice models, so that we can appeal to the evaluation rule for ought and conditional oughts suggested in Propositions 4.13 and 5.9. The proof relies on the previous Lemma A.6, and so on Lemmas A.4 and A.5. (The infinite case, which also relies on Lemmas A.4 and A.5, is more complicated, but involves no new ideas.) Assuming, then, that both $\odot([\alpha \ cstit: A] \ / \ B)$ and $\odot[\alpha \ cstit: B]$ hold at an index m/h of a finite choice model $\mathcal{M}$, we know from Propositions 4.13 and 5.9 that (1) $K \subseteq |A|_m^\mathcal{M}$ for each $K \in Optimal_\alpha^m/|B|_m^\mathcal{M}$, and (2) $K \subseteq |B|_m^\mathcal{M}$ for each $K \in Optimal_\alpha^m$. In order to show that $\odot[\alpha \ cstit: A]$ holds at m/h, we must establish that (3) $K \subseteq |A|_m^\mathcal{M}$ for each $K \in Optimal_\alpha^m$. So consider a $K \in Optimal_\alpha^m$. From (2), Lemma A.6 tells us that $Optimal_\alpha^m \subseteq Optimal_\alpha^m/|B|_m^\mathcal{M}$. Hence $K \in Optimal_\alpha^m/|B|_m^\mathcal{M}$, and so we can conclude from (1) that $K \subseteq |A|_m^\mathcal{M}$, which verifies (3). ∎

A.2 Propositions

Proposition 4.2 *Let X and Y be propositions at some moment from a utilitarian stit frame. Then $X < Y$ if and only if (1) $Value(h) \leq Value(h')$ for each $h \in X$ and each $h' \in Y$, and (2) $Value(h) < Value(h')$ for some $h \in X$ and some $h' \in Y$.*

Proof Straightforward. ∎

Proposition 4.3 *Let X and Y be propositions at some moment from a utilitarian stit frame. Then:*

1. *If $X < Y$, then $X \leq Y$.*

2. *If $X \leq Y$ and $Y \leq Z$, then $X \leq Z$.*

3. *If $X \leq Y$ and $Y < Z$, then $X < Z$.*

4. *If $X < Y$ and $Y \leq Z$, then $X < Z$.*

5. *If $X < Y$ and $Y < Z$, then $X < Z$.*

6. *If $X < Y$, then it is not the case that $Y < X$.*

7. *It is not the case that $X < X$.*

Proof Straightforward. ∎

Proposition 4.6 *Let α be an agent and m a moment from a utilitarian stit frame, and let K and K' be members of $Choice_\alpha^m$. Then $K \prec K'$ if and only if (1) $K \cap S \leq K' \cap S$ for each state $S \in State_\alpha^m$, and (2) $K \cap S < K' \cap S$ for some state $S \in State_\alpha^m$.*

Proof Left to right. Assuming $K \prec K'$, we must establish (1) $K \cap S \leq K' \cap S$ for each state $S \in State_\alpha^m$, and (2) $K \cap S < K' \cap S$ for some $S \in State_\alpha^m$. From our assumption, it follows that (3) $K \preceq K'$ and (4) it is not the case that $K' \preceq K$. From (3) we have (1) directly; and from (1) it follows that (5) for each $S \in State_\alpha^m$, $Value(h) \leq Value(h')$ for each $h \in K \cap S$ and each $h' \in K \cap S$. From (4) we have (6) for some $S \in State_\alpha^m$, $Value(h) < Value(h')$ for some $h \in K \cap S$ and some $h' \in K' \cap S$. We therefore select a particular state $S' \in State_\alpha^m$ such that (7) $Value(h) < Value(h')$ for some $h \in K \cap S'$ and some $h' \in K' \cap S'$. From (5), of course, we have (8) $Value(h) \leq Value(h')$ for each $h \in K \cap S'$ and each $h' \in K \cap S'$. And by Proposition 4.2, we know that (7) and (8) yield (9) $K \cap S' < K' \cap S'$, from which we have (2). The proof from right to left is similar. ∎

Proposition 4.7 *Let α be an agent and m a moment from a utilitarian stit frame, and let K, K', and K'' be members of $Choice_\alpha^m$. Then:*

1. *If $K \prec K'$, then $K \preceq K'$.*

2. *If $K \preceq K'$ and $K' \preceq K''$, then $K \preceq K''$.*

3. *If $K \preceq K'$ and $K' \prec K''$, then $K \prec K''$.*

4. *If $K \prec K'$ and $K' \preceq K''$, then $K \prec K''$.*

5. *If $K \prec K'$ and $K' \prec K''$, then $K \prec K''$.*

6. *If $K \prec K'$, then it is not the case that $K' \prec K$.*

7. *It is not the case that $K \prec K$.*

Proof We prove Clause 2 only, by way of illustration. Suppose, then, that $K \preceq K'$ and $K' \prec K''$. From $K \preceq K'$, we have (1) $K \cap S \leq K' \cap S$

for each $S \in State_\alpha^m$. And from $K \prec K''$, we know by Proposition 4.6 that (2) $K' \cap S \leq K'' \cap S$ for each $S \in State_\alpha^m$, and (3) $K' \cap S < K'' \cap S$ for some $S \in State_\alpha^m$. Proposition 4.3 tells us that (1) and (2) yield (4) $K \cap S \leq K'' \cap S$ for each $S \in State_\alpha^m$. Now, by (3), we select a particular state $S' \in State_\alpha^m$ such that (5) $K' \cap S' < K'' \cap S'$. By (1), of course, we know that (6) $K \cap S' \leq K' \cap S'$; Proposition 4.3 tells us that (5) and (6) yield (7) $K \cap S' < K'' \cap S'$, which gives us (8) $K \cap S < K'' \cap S$ for some $S \in State_\alpha^m$. Proposition 4.6 then tells us that (4) and (8) imply that $K \prec K''$. ∎

Proposition 4.10 *Let α be an agent and m a moment from a finite choice utilitarian stit frame. Then $Optimal_\alpha^m \neq \emptyset$.*

Proof Pick an action $K \in Choice_\alpha^m$. Either $K \in Optimal_\alpha^m$ or, by Proposition 4.11, there is an action $K' \in Optimal_\alpha^m$ such that $K \prec K'$. In either case, $Optimal_\alpha^m \neq \emptyset$. ∎

Proposition 4.11 *Let α be an agent and m a moment from a finite choice utilitarian stit frame. Then for each action $K \in Choice_\alpha^m - Optimal_\alpha^m$, there is an action $K' \in Optimal_\alpha^m$ such that $K \prec K'$.*

Proof Since $K \in Choice_\alpha^m - Optimal_\alpha^m$, there must be some $K_1 \in Choice_\alpha^m$ such that $K \prec K_1$. Now either K_1 is itself optimal or not. If so, then K_1 can be identified as K'. If not, there must be an action $K_2 \in Choice_\alpha^m$ such that $K_1 \prec K_2$, and if K_2 is not optimal, yet another action $K_3 \in Choice_\alpha^m$ such that $K_2 \prec K_3$, and so on. This procedure, evidently, must either terminate in an optimal action or else yield an infinite sequence of nonoptimal actions $K \prec K_1 \prec K_2 \prec K_3 \ldots$, each drawn from $Choice_\alpha^m$, and each dominated by its successor. In the latter case, however, since the $\prec$ relation is transitive and irreflexive by Proposition 4.7, each action in the sequence would have to be distinct; but that is impossible if $Choice_\alpha^m$ is finite. Hence, the procedure must terminate in an optimal action, which we can identify as K'; and we can conclude by the transitivity of $\prec$ that $K \prec K'$. ∎

Lemma A.8 *Let α be an agent and m a moment from a utilitarian stit frame. Then for any actions $K, K' \in Choice_\alpha^m$, if $K \in Optimal_\alpha^m$ and $K \preceq K'$, then $K' \in Optimal_\alpha^m$.*

Proof Assuming that $K \in Optimal_\alpha^m$ and $K \preceq K'$, suppose $K' \notin Optimal_\alpha^m$. Then there is an action $K'' \in Choice_\alpha^m$ such that $K' \prec K''$. But if $K \preceq K'$ and $K' \prec K''$, we know from Proposition 4.7 that $K \prec K''$, contrary to the assumption that $K \in Optimal_\alpha^m$. ∎

Proposition 4.13 *Let α be an agent and m/h an index from a finite choice utilitarian stit model $\mathcal{M}$. Then $\mathcal{M}, m/h \models \bigodot[\alpha \; cstit: A]$ if and only if $K \subseteq |A|_m^{\mathcal{M}}$ for each $K \in Optimal_\alpha^m$.*

Proof Left to right. Assume $\mathcal{M}, m/h \models \bigodot[\alpha \; cstit: A]$, so that: $(*)$ for each action $K \in Choice_\alpha^m$ such that $K \nsubseteq |A|_m^{\mathcal{M}}$, there is an action $K' \in Choice_\alpha^m$ such that (1) $K \prec K'$, and (2) $K' \subseteq |A|_m^{\mathcal{M}}$, and (3) $K'' \subseteq |A|_m^{\mathcal{M}}$ for each action $K'' \in Choice_\alpha^m$ such that $K' \preceq K''$. Now suppose there is an action $K \in Optimal_\alpha^m$ such that $K \nsubseteq |A|_m^{\mathcal{M}}$. Then by clause (1) of $(*)$ there is another action K' such that $K \prec K'$, which contradicts the supposition that $K \in Optimal_\alpha^m$. Therefore, we must have $K \subseteq |A|_m^{\mathcal{M}}$ for each $K \in Optimal_\alpha^m$.

Right to left. Assume that $K \subseteq |A|_m^{\mathcal{M}}$ for each $K \in Optimal_\alpha^m$. To show that $\mathcal{M}, m/h \models \bigodot[\alpha \; cstit: A]$, we must establish $(*)$ above; so pick a particular action $K \in Choice_\alpha^m$ such that $K \nsubseteq |A|_m^{\mathcal{M}}$ (if there are no such actions, $(*)$ is vacuously true). We know from our assumption, then, that $K \notin Optimal_\alpha^m$, and so by Proposition 4.11, there is an action $K' \in Optimal_\alpha^m$ such that (1) $K \prec K'$. From our assumption again, since $K' \in Optimal_\alpha^m$, we therefore have (2) $K' \subseteq |A|_m^{\mathcal{M}}$. Finally, consider an action $K'' \in Choice_\alpha^m$ such that $K' \preceq K''$. Since $K' \in Optimal_\alpha^m$, it then follows from Lemma A.8 that $K'' \in Optimal_\alpha^m$ as well; and so our assumption, yet again, yields $K'' \subseteq |A|_m^{\mathcal{M}}$, which verifies (3). ∎

Proposition 4.18 *Let α be an agent and m a moment from a stit model $\mathcal{M}$. Then the proposition $|B|_m^{\mathcal{M}}$ expressed by the statement B at the moment m is causally independent of the actions available to α at m if and only if, for each action $K \in Choice_\alpha^m$, the statement $B \supset (A_\alpha^K \; \square{\rightarrow} B)$ is settled true at m.*

Proof Left to right. Assume that $|B|_m^{\mathcal{M}}$ is independent of the actions available to α at m—that is, that $|B|_m^{\mathcal{M}} = \bigcup_{S \in \mathcal{S}}$ for some $\mathcal{S} \subseteq State_\alpha^m$. Note that, since $State_\alpha^m$ is a partition of H_m, this implies that $(*)$ $S \subseteq |B|_m^{\mathcal{M}}$ whenever $S \cap |B|_m^{\mathcal{M}} \neq \emptyset$, for any $S \in State_\alpha^m$. Now, for an action $K \in Choice_\alpha^m$, to show that the statement $B \supset (A_\alpha^K \; \square{\rightarrow} B)$ is settled true at m, we must establish that $\mathcal{M}, m/h \models B$ implies $\mathcal{M}, m/h \models (A_\alpha^K \; \square{\rightarrow} B)$ for each $h \in H_m$. So pick an arbitrary $h \in H_m$, and suppose $\mathcal{M}, m/h \models B$. To show that $\mathcal{M}, m/h \models (A_\alpha^K \; \square{\rightarrow} B)$, we need only show that $f_m(h, K) \subseteq |B|_m^{\mathcal{M}}$— that is, that $State_\alpha^m(h) \cap K \subseteq |B|_m^{\mathcal{M}}$. But of course, $State_\alpha^m(h) \cap K \subseteq State_\alpha^m(h)$; and since $\mathcal{M}, m/h \models B$ by assumption, we have $State_\alpha^m(h) \cap |B|_m^{\mathcal{M}} \neq \emptyset$, so that $State_\alpha^m(h) \subseteq |B|_m^{\mathcal{M}}$, by $(*)$. Therefore, $State_\alpha^m(h) \cap K \subseteq |B|_m^{\mathcal{M}}$.

Right to left. We argue by contraposition. Assume, then, that $|B|_m^{\mathcal{M}}$ is not independent of the actions available to α at m—that is, that there is no

$S \subseteq State_\alpha^m$ for which $|B|_m^{\mathcal{M}} = \bigcup_{S \in \mathcal{S}}$. Since $State_\alpha^m$ is a partition of H_m, this implies that there is some $S \in State_\alpha^m$ such that both $S \cap |B|_m^{\mathcal{M}} \neq \emptyset$ and $S \cap |\neg B|_m^{\mathcal{M}} \neq \emptyset$; so pick $h \in S \cap |B|_m^{\mathcal{M}}$ and $h' \in S \cap |\neg B|_m^{\mathcal{M}}$. Then of course $\mathcal{M}, m/h \models B$. But where $K = Choice_\alpha^m(h')$, we have $f_m(h, K) \not\subseteq |B|_m^{\mathcal{M}}$, since $h' \in f_m(h, K)$ but $h' \notin |B|_m^{\mathcal{M}}$. Therefore $\mathcal{M}, m/h \not\models A_\alpha^K \square\!\!\rightarrow B$, from which we can conclude that there is some $K \in Choice_\alpha^m$ for which $B \supset (A_\alpha^K \square\!\!\rightarrow B)$ is not settled true at m. ∎

Proposition 5.3 *Let α be an agent and m a moment from a utilitarian stit frame, and let K and K' be members of $Choice_\alpha^m$, and X a proposition at m. Then $K \prec_X K'$ if and only if (1) $K \cap X \cap S \leq K' \cap X \cap S$ for each state $S \in State_\alpha^m$, and (2) $K \cap X \cap S < K' \cap X \cap S$ for some state $S \in State_\alpha^m$.*

Proof Similar to proof of Proposition 4.6. ∎

Proposition 5.4 *Let α be an agent and m a moment from a utilitarian stit frame, and let K, K', and K'' be members of $Choice_\alpha^m$, and X be a proposition at m. Then:*

1. *If $K \prec_X K'$, then $K \preceq_X K'$.*

2. *If $K \preceq_X K'$ and $K' \preceq_X K''$, then $K \preceq_X K''$.*

3. *If $K \preceq_X K'$ and $K' \prec_X K''$, then $K \prec_X K''$.*

4. *If $K \prec_X K'$ and $K' \preceq_X K''$, then $K \prec_X K''$.*

5. *If $K \prec_X K'$ and $K' \prec_X K''$, then $K \prec_X K''$.*

6. *If $K \prec_X K'$ then it is not the case that $K' \prec_X K$.*

7. *It is not the case that $K \prec_X K$.*

Proof Similar to proof of Proposition 4.7. ∎

Proposition 5.6 *Let α be an agent and m a moment from a finite choice utilitarian stit frame, and let X be a consistent proposition at m. Then $Optimal_\alpha^m / X \neq \emptyset$.*

Proof Similar to proof of Proposition 4.10. ∎

Proposition 5.7 *Let α be an agent and m a moment from a finite choice utilitarian stit frame, and let X be a proposition at m. Then for each action*

$K \in Choice_\alpha^m/X - Optimal_\alpha^m/X$, *there is an action* $K' \in Optimal_\alpha^m/X$ *such that* $K \prec_X K'$.

Proof Similar to proof of Proposition 4.11. ∎

Proposition 5.9 *Let* α *be an agent and* m/h *an index from a finite choice utilitarian stit model* $\mathcal{M}$. *Then* $\mathcal{M}, m/h \models \odot([\alpha$ *cstit*: $A] / B)$ *if and only if* $K \subseteq |A|_m^{\mathcal{M}}$ *for each* $K \in Optimal_\alpha^m/|B|_m^{\mathcal{M}}$.

Proof Similar to proof of Proposition 4.13. ∎

Proposition 5.11 *Let* α *be an agent and* m *a moment from a utilitarian stit frame; let* K *and* K' *be members of* $Choice_\alpha^m$; *and let* $\{X_1, \ldots, X_n\}$ *be a partition of* H_m *that is independent of the actions available to* α *at* m. *Then* $K \preceq K'$ *if and only if* $K \preceq_X K'$ *for each* $X \in \{X_1, \ldots, X_n\}$.

Proof Left to right. From the assumption that $K \preceq K'$, we know that (1) $K \cap S \leq K' \cap S$ for each $S \in State_\alpha^m$. And then in order to establish the conclusion that $K \preceq_X K'$ for each $X \in \{X_1, \ldots, X_n\}$, it suffices to show that, for each $X \in \{X_1, \ldots, X_n\}$ and each $S \in State_\alpha^m$, we have (2) $K \cap X \cap S \leq K' \cap X \cap S$. So pick an arbitrary $X \in \{X_1, \ldots, X_n\}$ and an arbitrary $S \in State_\alpha^m$. Because X is independent of the actions available to α at m, we know that either (3) $S \cap X = \emptyset$ or (4) $S \subseteq X$. If (3), then $K \cap X \cap S = K' \cap X \cap S = \emptyset$; so (2) follows from the fact that $\emptyset \leq \emptyset$. If (4), then $K \cap X \cap S = K \cap S$ and $K' \cap X \cap S = K' \cap S$; so (2) follows from (1).

Right to left. From the assumption that $K \preceq_X K'$ for each $X \in \{X_1, \ldots, X_n\}$, we have (5) $K \cap X \cap S \leq K' \cap X \cap S$ for each $X \in \{X_1, \ldots, X_n\}$ and each $S \in State_\alpha^m$. And then in order to establish the conclusion that $K \preceq K'$, it suffices to show that, for each $S \in State_\alpha^m$, we have (6) $K \cap S \leq K' \cap S$. So pick an arbitrary $S \in State_\alpha^m$. Since the set $\{X_1, \ldots, X_n\}$ is a partition of H_m independent of the actions available to α at m, there must be some $X \in \{X_1, \ldots, X_n\}$ such that $S \subseteq X$. But because $S \subseteq X$, we know that $K \cap X \cap S = K \cap S$ and $K' \cap X \cap S = K' \cap S$; and so (6) follows from (5). ∎

Proposition 5.12 *Let* α *be an agent and* m *a moment from a utilitarian stit frame; let* K *and* K' *be members of* $Choice_\alpha^m$; *and let* $\{X_1, \ldots, X_n\}$ *be a partition of* H_m *that is independent of the actions available to* α *at* m. *Then* $K \prec K'$ *if and only if (1)* $K \preceq_X K'$ *for each* $X \in \{X_1, \ldots, X_n\}$, *and (2)* $K \prec_X K'$ *for some* $X \in \{X_1, \ldots, X_n\}$.

Proof Left to right. Assuming $K \prec K'$, we must establish (1) $K \preceq_X K'$ for each $X \in \{X_1, \ldots, X_n\}$, and (2) $K \prec_X K'$ for some $X \in \{X_1, \ldots, X_n\}$.

From our assumption, it follows that (3) $K \preceq K'$ and (4) it is not the case that $K' \preceq K$. From (3), Proposition 5.11 yields (1) directly; and then from (4), Proposition 5.11 allows us to conclude that there is some particular $X' \in \{X_1, \ldots, X_n\}$ such that (5) it is not the case that $K' \preceq_{X'} K$. From (1) of course we have (6) $K \preceq_{X'} K'$. By combining (5) and (6), we then know that $K \prec_{X'} K'$, which leads us at once to (2). The proof from right to left is similar. ∎

Lemma A.9 *Let α be an agent and m a moment from a utilitarian stit frame, and let $\{X_1, \ldots, X_n\}$ be a partition of H_m that is independent of the actions available to α at m. Then $Optimal_\alpha^m / X_1 \cap \ldots \cap Optimal_\alpha^m / X_n \subseteq Optimal_\alpha^m$.*

Proof For some $K \in Choice_\alpha^m$, assume $K \in Optimal_\alpha^m / X_1 \cap \ldots \cap Optimal_\alpha^m / X_n$, but suppose $K \notin Optimal_\alpha^m$. Then there is a $K' \in Choice_\alpha^m$ such that $K \prec K'$. From part (2) of Proposition 5.12, we therefore have $K \prec_X K'$ for some $X \in \{X_1, \ldots, X_n\}$, so that $K \notin Optimal_\alpha^m / X$, contrary to assumption. ∎

Proposition 5.14 *Let α be an agent and m/h an index from a utilitarian stit model $\mathcal{M}$, and let $\{B_1, \ldots, B_n\}$ represent a partition of H_m that is independent of the actions available to α at m. Then if $\mathcal{M}, m/h \models \bigodot([\alpha \ cstit: A_\alpha^K] \, / \, B_i)$ for each $1 \leq i \leq n$, it follows that $\mathcal{M}, m/h \models \bigodot[\alpha \ cstit: A_\alpha^K]$.*

Proof (sketch) We verify the result only for finite choice models, so that we can appeal to the evaluation rule for ought and conditional oughts suggested in Propositions 4.13 and 5.9. (The infinite case involves no new ideas, but is more complicated.) Note that K is the only action that can guarantee the truth of the statement A_α^K; that is, (∗) $K_i \subseteq |A_\alpha^K|_m^\mathcal{M}$ if and only if $K_i = K$.

Assume, then, that $\mathcal{M}, m/h \models \bigodot([\alpha \ cstit: A_\alpha^K] \, / \, B_i)$ for each $1 \leq i \leq n$. From Proposition 5.9 together with (∗), we can conclude that (1) $Optimal_\alpha^m / |B_i|_m^\mathcal{M} = \{K\}$ for each $1 \leq i \leq n$. Therefore, Lemma A.9 tells us that (2) $K \in Optimal_\alpha^m$. Now consider some $K' \in Choice_\alpha^m$ such that $K' \neq K$. From (1) we have $K' \notin Optimal_\alpha^m / |B_i|_m^\mathcal{M}$ for each $1 \leq i \leq n$. Together with (1), then, Proposition 5.7 allows us to conclude that $K' \prec_{|B_i|_m^\mathcal{M}} K$ for each $1 \leq i \leq n$, and so Proposition 5.12 tells us that $K' \prec K$. We thus know that (3) $K' \notin Optimal_\alpha^m$ whenever $K' \neq K$. It follows from (2) and (3) that $Optimal_\alpha^m = \{K\}$, and so Proposition 4.13 together with (∗) tells us that $\mathcal{M}, m/h \models \bigodot[\alpha \ cstit: A]$. ∎

Lemma A.10 *Let α be an agent and m a moment from a utilitarian stit frame, and let X be a proposition at m. Then for any actions $K, K' \in Choice_\alpha^m/X$, if $K \in Optimal_\alpha^m/X$ and $K \preceq_X K'$, then $K' \in Optimal_\alpha^m/X$.*

Proof Similar to proof of Lemma A.8. ∎

Proposition 5.16 *Let α be an agent and m a moment from a finite choice utilitarian stit frame. Then $AU\text{-}right_\alpha^{m/h} \cap Optimal_\alpha^m \neq \emptyset$ for each $h \in H_m$.*

Proof Pick some action $K \in AU\text{-}right_\alpha^{m/h}$—that is, a K such that (1) $K \in Optimal_\alpha^m/State_\alpha^m(h)$. (Since the proposition $State_\alpha^m(h)$ is consistent, there must be such a K by Proposition 5.6.) If $K \in Optimal_\alpha^m$, we are done; so suppose $K \notin Optimal_\alpha^m$. Then by Proposition 4.11, there is an action K' such that (2) $K' \in Optimal_\alpha^m$ and (3) $K \prec K'$. From (3), we know that $K \preceq_S K'$ for each $S \in State_\alpha^m$, and in particular, that (4) $K \preceq_{State_\alpha^m(h)} K'$. From (1) and (4), Lemma A.10 then tells us that $K' \in Optimal_\alpha^m/State_\alpha^m(h)$—that is, that (5) $K' \in AU\text{-}right_\alpha^{m/h}$. And (5) combines with (2) to yield the result. ∎

Proposition 5.18 *Let α be an agent and m/h an index from a finite choice utilitarian stit model $\mathcal{M}$. Then $\mathcal{M}, m/h \models \bigoplus[\alpha \; cstit \colon A]$ if and only if $K \subseteq |A|_m^{\mathcal{M}}$ for each $K \in AU\text{-}right_\alpha^{m/h}$.*

Proof Similar to proof of Proposition 4.13. ∎

Proposition 6.4 *Let Γ be a finite group of agents and m a moment from a finite choice utilitarian stit frame. Then $Optimal_\Gamma^m \neq \emptyset$.*

Proof Similar to proof of Proposition 4.10. ∎

Proposition 6.5 *Let Γ be a finite group of agents and m a moment from a finite choice utilitarian stit frame. Then for each action $K \in Choice_\Gamma^m - Optimal_\Gamma^m$, there is an action $K' \in Optimal_\Gamma^m$ such that $K \prec K'$.*

Proof Similar to proof of Proposition 4.11. ∎

Proposition 6.10 *Let $Agent$ be the set of agents and m/h an index from a utilitarian stit frame. Then $AU\text{-}right_{Agent}^{m/h} = Optimal_{Agent}^m$.*

Proof Presented in text. ∎

Proposition 6.11 *Let Γ be a group of agents and m/h an index from a utilitarian stit frame. Then whenever $Choice_\Gamma^m(h) \in AU\text{-}right_\Gamma^{m/h}$, we have $Choice_\alpha^m(h) \in AU\text{-}right_\alpha^{m/h}$ for each $\alpha \in \Gamma$.*

Proof Note to begin with that, for any $\alpha \in \Gamma$,

$$(*) \quad State_\alpha^m(h) = Choice_{Agent-\{\alpha\}}^m(h)$$
$$= Choice_{\Gamma-\{\alpha\}}^m(h) \cap Choice_{Agent-\Gamma}^m(h)$$
$$= Choice_{\Gamma-\{\alpha\}}^m(h) \cap State_\Gamma^m(h).$$

The first line of this equality follows from the definition of $State_\alpha^m$; the second line follows from the general fact that $Choice_{\Gamma \cup \Gamma'}^m(h) = Choice_\Gamma^m(h) \cap Choice_{\Gamma'}^m(h)$ for any groups Γ and Γ'; and the third line follows from the definition of $State_\Gamma^m$.

In order to establish the main result, we now argue by contraposition: assuming that (1) $Choice_\alpha^m(h) \notin AU\text{-}right_\alpha^{m/h}$ for some $\alpha \in \Gamma$, we show (2) $Choice_\Gamma^m(h) \notin AU\text{-}right_\Gamma^{m/h}$. Having fixed α, let us identify $K = Choice_\alpha^m(h)$, so that (1) tells us that $K \notin Optimal_\alpha^m/State_\alpha^m(h)$, from which we can conclude that there is an action $K' \in Choice_\alpha^m/State_\alpha^m(h)$ such that (3) $K \prec_{State_\alpha^m(h)} K'$. But since $State_\alpha^m$ is a partition of H_m, the definition of conditional dominance then tells us that (3) is equivalent to

$$(4) \quad [K \cap State_\alpha^m(h)] < [K' \cap State_\alpha^m(h)].$$

Now it is easy to see that (5) $Choice_\Gamma^m(h) = K \cap Choice_{\Gamma-\{\alpha\}}^m(h)$—that is, the action performed by the group Γ at the index m/h is identical with the action performed by the group $\Gamma-\{\alpha\}$ together with K, the action performed at this index by α. And we can see likewise that $K' \cap Choice_{\Gamma-\{\alpha\}}^m(h)$ represents another action from $Choice_\Gamma^m$—the action in which each member of Γ except for α performs the same action he did at m/h, but α performs the action K' instead. In order to establish (2), then, it is sufficient to show (6) $K \cap Choice_{\Gamma-\{\alpha\}}^m(h) \prec_{State_\Gamma^m(h)} K' \cap Choice_{\Gamma-\{\alpha\}}^m(h)$—that the group action $K \cap Choice_{\Gamma-\{\alpha\}}^m(h)(= Choice_\Gamma^m(h))$ is dominated by the group action in which α performs K' and all other members of Γ act as at m/h. And since $State_\Gamma^m$, again, is a partition of H_m, the definition of conditional group dominance tells us that (6) is equivalent to

$$(7) \quad [K \cap Choice_{\Gamma-\{\alpha\}}^m(h) \cap State_\Gamma^m(h)] < [K' \cap Choice_{\Gamma-\{\alpha\}}^m(h) \cap State_\Gamma^m(h)].$$

But since we know from $(*)$ that $State_\alpha^m(h) = Choice_{\Gamma-\{\alpha\}}^m(h) \cap State_\Gamma^m(h)$, (7) follows immediately from (4). ∎

Proposition 6.14 *Let Γ be a finite group of agents and m/h an index from a finite choice utilitarian stit model $\mathcal{M}$. Then $\mathcal{M}, m/h \models \bigcirc[\Gamma \; cstit: A]$ if and only if $K \subseteq |A|_m^{\mathcal{M}}$ for each $K \in Optimal_\Gamma^m$.*

Proof Similar to proof of Proposition 4.13. ∎

Proposition 6.15 *Let Γ be a finite group of agents and m/h an index from a finite choice utilitarian stit model $\mathcal{M}$. Then $\mathcal{M}, m/h \models \bigoplus [\Gamma \; cstit: A]$ if and only if $K \subseteq |A|_m^{\mathcal{M}}$ for each $K \in A U\text{-}right_\Gamma^{m/h}$.*

Proof Similar to proof of Proposition 4.13. ∎

Lemma A.11 *Let Agent be the set of agents and m a moment from a utilitarian stit frame. Then for any actions $K, K' \in Choice_{Agent}^m$, if $K \in Optimal_{Agent}^m$ and $K \leq K'$, then $K' \in Optimal_{Agent}^m$.*

Proof Note first that $State_{Agent}^m = \{H_m\}$, so that $K \preceq K'$ just in case $K \leq K'$, for $K, K' \in Choice_{Agent}^m$. The proof is then similar to the proof of Lemma A.8, but appealing to Proposition 4.3 rather than Proposition 4.7. ∎

Proposition 6.17 *Let m be a moment and α an agent from a finite choice utilitarian stit frame in which the set Agent is finite. Then $R\text{-}Optimal_\alpha^m \cap Optimal_\alpha^m \neq \emptyset$*

Proof Where *Agent* is the set of agents from the frame, pick some action K such that (1) $K \in Optimal_{Agent}^m$ (there must be such a K by Proposition 6.4). Evidently, (2) $K = K_1 \cap K_2$, where (3) $K_1 \in Choice_{Agent-\{\alpha\}}^m$ and $K_2 \in Choice_\alpha^m$. Therefore, (4) $K_2 \in R\text{-}Optimal_\alpha^m$. If $K_2 \in Optimal_\alpha^m$, we are done; so suppose $K \notin Optimal_\alpha^m$. Then by Proposition 4.11, there is an action K_3 such that (5) $K_3 \in Optimal_\alpha^m$ and (6) $K_2 \prec K_3$. From (6), we know that (7) $K_2 \cap S \leq K_3 \cap S$ for each $S \in State_\alpha^m$; and so, since (3) tells us that $K_1 \in State_\alpha^m$, (7) tells us in particular that (8) $K_2 \cap K_1 \leq K_3 \cap K_1$. Evidently, $K_3 \cap K_1 \in Choice_{Agent}^m$, and so Lemma A.11 allows us to conclude from (1), (2), and (8) that $K_3 \cap K_1 \in Optimal_{Agent}^m$. Therefore, (9) $K_3 \in R\text{-}Optimal_\alpha^m$, and so the result follows from (9) and (5). ∎

Proposition 7.11 *Let α be an agent and m a moment from a utilitarian stit frame, and let M and M' be two fields at m such that $M \subseteq M'$. Then (1) for each $\sigma' \in Strategy_\alpha^{M'}$ there is a $\sigma \in Strategy_\alpha^M$ such that $Adh(\sigma') \subseteq Adh(\sigma)$, and (2) for each $\sigma \in Strategy_\alpha^M$ there is a $\sigma' \in Strategy_\alpha^{M'}$ such that $Adh(\sigma') \subseteq Adh(\sigma)$.*

Proof (sketch) We sketch the proof only for the first part of this result. Suppose, then, that $\sigma' \in Strategy_\alpha^{M'}$, and define $\sigma = \sigma'|M$ (that is, define σ as the restriction of σ' to the field M). Where m is the shared initial moment of the fields M and M', it is easy to see that $m \in Dom(\sigma)$. In order to show that $\sigma \in Strategy_\alpha^M$, therefore, we need only establish that σ is complete in M and irredundant.

It is evident from the definition of σ that (1) $Dom(\sigma) = Dom(\sigma') \cap M$, and we note without proof that (2) $Adm(\sigma) = Adm(\sigma') \cap M$ (the full argument for this fact requires ordinal induction for the infinite case). Now suppose σ were not complete in M—that is, that there were a moment $m' \in M$ such that $m' \in Adm(\sigma)$ but $m' \notin Dom(\sigma)$. Since $m' \in M$, we could then conclude from (2) that $m' \notin Adm(\sigma')$ and from (1) that $m' \notin Dom(\sigma')$, so that σ' would also have to be incomplete in M', contrary to the assumption that $\sigma' \in Strategy_\alpha^{M'}$. A similar argument shows that σ must be irredundant, since σ' is. Hence, $\sigma \in Strategy_\alpha^M$.

It remains only to show that $Adh(\sigma') \subseteq Adh(\sigma)$, by showing that (3) $h \in Adh(\sigma')$ implies (4) $h \in Adh(\sigma)$. From (3) we have (5) $Dom(\sigma') \cap h \neq \emptyset$ and (6) $h \in \sigma'(m)$ for each $m' \in Dom(\sigma') \cap h$. From (5) we can conclude that $h \in H_m$, which tells us that (7) $Dom(\sigma) \cap h \neq \emptyset$ as well. Now consider a particular moment $m' \in Dom(\sigma) \cap h$. Since $Dom(\sigma) \subseteq Dom(\sigma')$, we know also that $m' \in Dom(\sigma') \cap h$, and so (6) tells us $h \in \sigma'(m')$. But since $m' \in Dom(\sigma) \subseteq M$, we have $\sigma(m') = \sigma'(m')$ by the definition of σ, so that $h \in \sigma(m')$. We thus have (8) $h \in \sigma(m')$ for each $m' \in Dom(\sigma) \cap h$ as well; and of course, (7) and (8) yield (4).

The second part of the result can be verified by adapting the strategy extension techniques from Belnap [1994] (see especially the proof there of Lemma 25) to show that a strategy $\sigma \in Strategy_\alpha^M$ can be extended to a strategy $\sigma' \in Strategy_\alpha^{M'}$, and proceeding as in the previous paragraph to show that $Adh(\sigma') \subseteq Adh(\sigma)$. ∎

Proposition 7.17 *Let α be the agent and M a field from a finite-branch single-agent utilitarian stit frame. Then $Optimal_\alpha^M \neq \emptyset$.*

Proof Similar to proof of Proposition 4.10. ∎

Proposition 7.18 *Let α be the agent and M a field from a finite-branch single-agent utilitarian stit frame. Then for each strategy $\sigma \in Strategy_\alpha^M -$ $Optimal_\alpha^M$ there is a strategy $\sigma' \in Optimal_\alpha^M$ such that $\sigma \prec \sigma'$.*

Proof Similar to proof of Proposition 4.11. ∎

Proposition 7.20 *Let α be the agent and M a field from a finite-branch single-agent utilitarian stit model $\mathcal{M}$. Then $\mathcal{M}, m/h/M \models \odot[\alpha \ scstit: A]$ if and only if $Adh(\sigma) \subseteq |A|_m^{\mathcal{M}}$ for each $\sigma \in Optimal_\alpha^M$.*

Proof Similar to proof of Proposition 4.13. ∎

Proposition 7.21 *Let α be the agent and $m/h/M$ and $m/h/M'$ two extended indices from a single-agent utilitarian stit model $\mathcal{M}$, with $M \subseteq M'$. Then it is impossible to have both $\mathcal{M}, m/h/M \models \odot[\alpha\ scstit : A]$ and $\mathcal{M}, m/h/M' \models \odot[\alpha\ scstit: \neg A]$.*

Proof Suppose the contrary, that (1) $\mathcal{M}, m/h/M \models \odot[\alpha\ scstit : A]$ and (2) $\mathcal{M}, m/h/M' \models \odot[\alpha\ scstit : \neg A]$. From (2) we know that there is a strategy $\sigma_1 \in Strategy_\alpha^{M'}$ such that (3) $Adh(\sigma_1) \subseteq |\neg A|_m^{\mathcal{M}}$ and (4) $Adh(\sigma') \subseteq |A|_m^{\mathcal{M}}$ for each strategy $\sigma' \in Strategy_\alpha^{M'}$ such that $\sigma_1 \preceq \sigma'$. From the first part of Proposition 7.11, we know that there is a strategy $\sigma_2 \in Strategy_\alpha^M$ such that (5) $Adh(\sigma_1) \subseteq Adh(\sigma_2)$, which together with (3) allows us to conclude that $Adh(\sigma_2) \not\subseteq |A|_m^{\mathcal{M}}$. Therefore, we know from (1) that there is a strategy $\sigma_3 \in Strategy_\alpha^M$ such that (6) $\sigma_2 \prec \sigma_3$ and (7) $\sigma_3 \subseteq |A|_m^{\mathcal{M}}$. From the second part of Proposition 7.11, we now know that there is a strategy $\sigma_4 \in Strategy_\alpha^{M'}$ such that (8) $Adh(\sigma_4) \subseteq Adh(\sigma_3)$, which together with (7) allows us to conclude that (9) $Adh(\sigma_4) \not\subseteq |\neg A|_m^{\mathcal{M}}$. From (5), (6), and (8), however, it is easy to see that (10) $\sigma_1 \preceq \sigma_4$. And then, from (4) and (10), we can conclude that (11) $Adh(\sigma_4) \subseteq |\neg A|_m^{\mathcal{M}}$, which contradicts (9). ∎

Bibliography

[Anderson, 1956] Alan Anderson. The formal analysis of normative systems. Technical Report No. 2, Contract No. SAR/Nonr-609 (16), Office of Naval Research, Group Psychology Branch, 1956. Reprinted in Nicholas Rescher, editor, *The Logic of Decision and Action*, pages 147–213, University of Pittsburgh Press, 1967.

[Anderson, 1962] Alan Anderson. Logic, norms, and roles. *Ratio*, 4:32–49, 1962.

[Åqvist, 1969] Lennart Åqvist. Improved formulations of act-utilitarianism. *Nous*, 3:299–323, 1969.

[Åqvist, 1984] Lennart Åqvist. Deontic logic. In Dov Gabbay and Franz Guethner, editors, *Handbook of Philosophical Logic, Volume II: Extensions of Classical Logic*, pages 605–714. D. Reidel Publishing Company, 1984.

[Åqvist and Hoepelman, 1981] Lennart Åqvist and Japp Hoepelman. Some theorems about a tree system of deontic tense logic. In Risto Hilpinen, editor, *New Studies in Deontic Logic*, pages 187–221. D. Reidel Publishing Company, 1981.

[Bartha, 1993] Paul Bartha. Conditional obligation, deontic paradoxes, and the logic of agency. *Annals of Mathematics and Artificial Intelligence*, 9:1–23, 1993.

[Belnap, 1991a] Nuel Belnap. Backwards and forwards in the modal logic of agency. *Philosophy and Phenomenological Research*, 51:8–37, 1991.

[Belnap, 1991b] Nuel Belnap. Before refraining: concepts for agency. *Erkenntnis*, 34:137–169, 1991.

[Belnap, 1994] Nuel Belnap. An austere theory of strategies. Manuscript, Philosophy Department, University of Pittsburgh, 1994.

[Belnap and Perloff, 1988] Nuel Belnap and Michael Perloff. Seeing to it that: a canonical form for agentives. *Theoria*, 54:175–199, 1988.

[Belnap and Perloff, 1993] Nuel Belnap and Michael Perloff. In the realm of agents. *Annals of Mathematics and Artificial Intelligence*, 9:25–48, 1993.

[Belnap, Perloff, and Xu, 2001] Nuel Belnap, Michael Perloff, and Ming Xu. *Facing the Future*. Oxford University Press, 2001.

[Bergström, 1966] Lars Bergström. *The Alternatives and Consequences of Actions*, volume 4 of *Stockholm Studies in Philosophy*. Almqvist and Wiksell, 1966.

[Bergström, 1971] Lars Bergström. Utilitarianism and alternative actions. *Nous*, 5:237–252, 1971.

[Bergström, 1977] Lars Bergström. Utilitarianism and future mistakes. *Theoria*, 43:84–102, 1977.

[Brandt, 1963] Richard Brandt. Toward a credible form of utilitarianism. In Hector-Neri Castañeda and George Nakhnikian, editors, *Morality and the Language of Conduct*, pages 107–144. Wayne State University Press, 1963.

[Brown, 1988] Mark Brown. On the logic of ability. *Journal of Philosophical Logic*, 17:1–26, 1988.

[Carlson, 1995] Erik Carlson. *Consequentialism Reconsidered*, volume 20 of *Theory and Decision Library, Series A: Philosophy and Methodology of the Social Sciences*. Kluwer Academic Publishers, 1995.

[Castañeda, 1968] Hector-Neri Castañeda. A problem for utilitarianism. *Analysis*, 28:141–142, 1968.

[Castañeda, 1969] Hector-Neri Castañeda. Ought, value, and utilitarianism. *American Philosophical Quarterly*, 8:157–175, 1969.

[Chellas, 1969] Brian Chellas. *The Logical Form of Imperatives*. PhD thesis, Philosophy Department, Stanford University, 1969.

[Chellas, 1980] Brian Chellas. *Modal Logic: An Introduction*. Cambridge University Press, 1980.

[Chellas, 1992] Brian Chellas. Time and modality in the logic of agency. *Studia Logica*, 51:485–517, 1992.

[Chisholm, 1963] Roderick Chisholm. Supererogation and offence: a conceptual scheme for ethics. *Ratio*, 5:1–14, 1963.

[Chisholm, 1964] Roderick Chisholm. The ethics of requirement. *American Philosophical Quarterly*, 1:147–153, 1964.

[Chisholm, 1967] Roderick Chisholm. He could have done otherwise. *Journal of Philosophy*, 64:409–417, 1967.

[Conee, 1983] Earl Conee. Review of Regan [Regan, 1980]. *Journal of Philosophy*, 80:415–424, 1983.

[Eells, 1982] Ellery Eells. *Rational Decision and Causality*. Cambridge University Press, 1982.

[Ellsberg, 1961] Daniel Ellsberg. Risk, ambiguity, and the Savage axioms. *Quarterly Journal of Economics*, 75:643–669, 1961.

[Feinberg, 1968] Joel Feinberg. Collective responsibility. *Journal of Philosophy*, 65:674–688, 1968.

[Feldman, 1986] Fred Feldman. *Doing the Best We Can: An Essay in Informal Deontic Logic*. D. Reidel Publishing Company, 1986.

[Føllesdal and Hilpinen, 1971] Dagfinn Føllesdal and Risto Hilpinen. Deontic logic: an introduction. In Risto Hilpinen, editor, *Deontic Logic: Introductory and Systematic Readings*, pages 1–35. D. Reidel Publishing Company, 1971.

[Frankfurt, 1969] Harry Frankfurt. Alternate possibilities and moral responsibility. *Journal of Philosophy*, 66:828–839, 1969.

[García, 1986] Jorge García. The *tunsollen*, the *seinsollen*, and the *soseinsollen*. *American Philosophical Quarterly*, 23:267–276, 1986.

[Gärdenfors and Sahlin, 1988] Peter Gärdenfors and Nils-Eric Sahlin, editors. *Decision, Probability, and Utility: Selected Readings*. Cambridge University Press, 1988.

[Geach, 1982] Peter Geach. Whatever happened to deontic logic? *Philosophia*, 11:1–12, 1982.

[Gibbard, 1965] Allan Gibbard. Rule-utilitarianism: merely an illusory alternative? *Australasian Journal of Philosophy*, 43:211–220, 1965.

[Gibbard and Harper, 1978] Allan Gibbard and William L. Harper. Counterfactuals and two kinds of expected utility. In C. A. Hooker, J. J. Leach, and E. F. McClennen, editors, *Foundations and Applications of Decision Theory*, volume 13 of *Western Ontario Series in Philosophy of Science*, pages 125–162. D. Reidel Publishing Compamy, 1978.

[Goldman, 1976] Holly Goldman. Dated rightness and moral imperfection. *The Philosophical Review*, 85:449–487, 1976.

[Goldman, 1978] Holly Goldman. Doing the best one can. In A. I. Goldman and J. Kim, editors, *Values and Morals*, pages 185–214. D. Reidel Publishing Compamy, 1978.

[Greenspan, 1975] Patricia Greenspan. Conditional oughts and hypothetical imperatives. *Journal of Philosophy*, 72:259–276, 1975.

[Greenspan, 1978] Patricia Greenspan. Oughts and determinism: a response to Goldman. *Philosophical Review*, pages 77–83, 1978.

[Hansson, 1971] Bengt Hansson. An analysis of some deontic logics. In Risto Hilpinen, editor, *Deontic Logic: Introductory and Systematic Readings*, pages 121–147. D. Reidel Publishing Company, 1971.

[Harman, 1983] Gilbert Harman. Human flourishing, ethics, and liberty. *Philosophy and Public Affairs*, 12:307–322, 1983.

[Harman, 1986] Gilbert Harman. *Change in View: Principles of Reasoning*. The MIT Press, 1986.

[Harrod, 1936] Roy Harrod. Utilitarianism revised. *Mind*, 55:137–156, 1936.

[Held, 1970] Virginia Held. Can a random collection of individuals be morally responsible? *Journal of Philosophy*, 67:471–481, 1970.

[Hilpinen, 1974] Risto Hilpinen. On the semantics of personal directives. In *Semantics and Communication*, pages 162–179. North-Holland Publishing Company, 1974.

[Hilpinen, 1997] Risto Hilpinen. On action and agency. In Eva Ejerhed and Sten Lindström, editors, *Logic, Action, and Cognition*, pages 3–27. Kluwer Academic Publishers, 1997.

[Horty, 1989] John Horty. An alternative stit operator. Manuscript, Philosophy Department, University of Maryland, 1989.

[Horty, 1996] John Horty. Agency and obligation. *Synthese*, 108:269–307, 1996.

[Horty and Belnap, 1995] John Horty and Nuel Belnap. The deliberative stit: a study of action, omission, ability, and obligation. *Journal of Philosophical Logic*, 24:583–644, 1995. Reprinted in *The Philosopher's Annual, Volume 18–1995*, Ridgeview Publishing Company, 1997.

[Humberstone, 1971] I. L. Humberstone. Two sorts of 'ought's. *Analysis*, 32:8–11, 1971.

[Humberstone, 1983] I. L. Humberstone. The background of circumstances. *Pacific Philosophical Quarterly*, 64:19–34, 1983.

[Jackson, 1985] Frank Jackson. On the semantics and logic of obligation. *Mind*, 94:177–195, 1985.

[Jackson, 1988] Frank Jackson. Understanding the logic of obligation. In *Proceedings of the Aristotelian Society, Supplementary Volume 62*. Harrison and Sons, 1988.

[Jackson and Pargetter, 1986] Frank Jackson and Robert Pargetter. Oughts, options, and actualism. *Philosophical Review*, 99:233–255, 1986.

[Jeffrey, 1965] Richard Jeffrey. *The Logic of Decision*. Mc-Graw-Hill Book Company, 1965.

[Kanger, 1957] Stig Kanger. New foundations for ethical theory. Privately Distributed, 1957. Reprinted in Risto Hilpinen, editor, *Deontic Logic: Introductory and Systematic Readings*, pages 36–58, D. Reidel Publishing Company, 1971.

[Kanger, 1972] Stig Kanger. Law and logic. *Theoria*, 38:105–132, 1972.

[Kanger and Kanger, 1966] Stig Kanger and Helle Kanger. Rights and parliamentarism. *Theoria*, 32:85–115, 1966.

[Kaplan, 1989] David Kaplan. Demonstratives: an essay on the semantics, logic, metaphysics, and epistemology of demonstratives and other indexicals. In Joseph Almog, John Perry, and Howard Wettstein, editors, *Themes from Kaplan*, pages 481–563. Oxford University Press, 1989.

[Kenny, 1975] Anthony Kenny. *Will, Freedom, and Power*. Basil Blackwell, 1975.

[Kenny, 1976] Anthony Kenny. Human abilities and dynamic modalities. In Juha Manninen and Raimo Tuomela, editors, *Essays on Explanation and Understanding: Studies in the Foundations of Humanities and Social Sciences*, pages 209–232. D. Reidel Publishing Company, 1976.

[Kenny, 1979] Anthony Kenny. *Aristotle's Theory of the Will*. Yale University Press, 1979.

[Lewis, 1973] David Lewis. *Counterfactuals*. Oxford University Press, 1973.

[Lewis, 1974] David Lewis. Semantic analyses for dyadic deontic logic. In Søren Stenlund, editor, *Logical Theory and Semantic Analysis*, pages 1–14. D. Reidel Publishing Company, 1974.

[Lewis, 1981] David Lewis. Causal decision theory. *Australasian Journal of Philosophy*, 59:5–30, 1981.

[Luce and Raiffa, 1957] R. Duncan Luce and Howard Raiffa. *Games and Decisions*. John Wiley and Sons, 1957.

[McKinsey, 1979] Michael McKinsey. Levels of obligation. *Philosophical Studies*, 35:385–395, 1979.

[McKinsey, 1981] Michael McKinsey. Obligations to the starving. *Nous*, 15:309–323, 1981.

[Montague, 1968] Richard Montague. Pragmatics. In R. Klibansky, editor, *Contemporary Philosophy: A Survey*. Florence, 1968.

[Moore, 1912] G. E. Moore. *Ethics*. Oxford University Press, 1912.

[Nagel, 1976] Thomas Nagel. Moral luck. In *Proceedings of the Aristotelian Society, Supplementary Volume 50*. Harrison and Sons, 1976.

[Parfit, 1984] Derek Parfit. *Reasons and Persons*. Oxford University Press, 1984.

[Pollock, 1984] John Pollock. How do you maximize expectation value? *Nous*, 17:409–421, 1984.

[Postow, 1977] B. C. Postow. Generalized act utilitarianism. *Analysis*, 37:49–52, 1977.

[Prawitz, 1968] Dag Prawitz. A discussion note on utilitarianism. *Theoria*, 34:76–84, 1968.

[Prawitz, 1970] Dag Prawitz. The alternatives to an action. *Theoria*, 36:116–126, 1970.

[Prior, 1955] Arthur Prior. *Formal Logic*. Oxford University Press, 1955. Second edition, 1962.

[Prior, 1956] Arthur Prior. The consequences of actions. In *Proceedings of the Aristotelian Society, Supplementary Volume 30*. Harrison and Sons, 1956.

[Prior, 1967] Arthur Prior. *Past, Present, and Future*. Oxford University Press, 1967.

[Rabinowicz, 1989] Wlodzimierz Rabinowicz. Act-utilitarian prisoner's dilemmas. *Theoria*, 55:1–44, 1989.

[Ramsey, 1931] Frank Ramsey. Truth and probability. In R. B. Braithwaite, editor, *The Foundations of Mathematics and Other Logical Essays*, pages 156–191. Routledge and Kegan Paul, 1931. Originally published in 1926.

[Regan, 1980] Donald Regan. *Utilitarianism and Co-operation*. Clarendon Press, 1980.

[Savage, 1951] Leonard Savage. The theory of statistical decision. *Journal of the American Statistics Association*, 46:55–67, 1951.

[Savage, 1954] Leonard Savage. *The Foundations of Statistics*. John Wiley and Sons, 1954. Second revised edition published by Dover Publications, 1972.

[Scott, 1967] Dana Scott. A logic of commands. Manuscript, Philosophy Department, Stanford University, 1967.

[Segerberg, 1992] Krister Segerberg. Getting started: beginnings in the logic of action. *Studia Logica*, 51, 1992.

[Skyrms, 1980] Brian Skyrms. *Causal Necessity*. Yale University Press, 1980.

[Slote, 1989] Michael Slote. *Beyond Optimizing: A Study of Rational Choice.* Harvard University Press, 1989.

[Sobel, 1968] J. Howard Sobel. Rule-utilitarianism. *Australasian Journal of Philosophy,* 46:146–165, 1968.

[Sobel, 1971] J. Howard Sobel. Value, alternatives, and utilitarianism. *Nous,* 4:373–384, 1971.

[Sobel, 1976] J. Howard Sobel. Utilitarianism and past and future mistakes. *Nous,* 10:195–219, 1976.

[Stalnaker, 1975] Robert Stalnaker. Indicative conditionals. *Philosophia,* 5:269–286, 1975.

[Statman, 1993] Daniel Statman, editor. *Moral Luck.* State University of New York Press, 1993.

[Tännsjö, 1989] Torbjörn Tännsjö. The morality of collective actions. *The Philosophical Quarterly,* 39:221–228, 1989.

[Thomason, 1970] Richmond Thomason. Indeterminist time and truth-value gaps. *Theoria,* 36:264–281, 1970.

[Thomason, 1981a] Richmond Thomason. Deontic logic and the role of freedom in moral deliberation. In Risto Hilpinen, editor, *New Studies in Deontic Logic,* pages 177–186. D. Reidel Publishing Company, 1981.

[Thomason, 1981b] Richmond Thomason. Deontic logic as founded on tense logic. In Risto Hilpinen, editor, *New Studies in Deontic Logic,* pages 165–176. D. Reidel Publishing Company, 1981.

[Thomason, 1984] Richmond Thomason. Combinations of tense and modality. In Dov Gabbay and Franz Guethner, editors, *Handbook of Philosophical Logic, Volume II: Extensions of Classical Logic,* pages 135–165. D. Reidel Publishing Company, 1984.

[Thomason and Horty, 1996] Richmond Thomason and John Horty. Nondeterminism and dominance: foundations of planning and qualitative decision theory. In *Proceedings of the Sixth International Conference on Theoretical Aspects of Rationality and Knowledge (TARK-96),* pages 229–250. Morgan Kaufmann Publishers, 1996.

[van Fraassen, 1972] Bas van Fraassen. The logic of conditional obligation. *The Journal of Philosophical Logic,* 72:417–438, 1972.

[van Fraassen, 1973] Bas van Fraassen. Values and the heart's command. *The Journal of Philosophy,* 70:5–19, 1973.

[van Inwagen, 1978] Peter van Inwagen. Ability and responsibility. *Philosophical Review,* 87:201–224, 1978.

[von Kutschera, 1986] Franz von Kutschera. Bewirken. *Erkenntnis,* 24:253–281, 1986.

[von Wright, 1951] G. H. von Wright. Deontic logic. *Mind,* 60:1–15, 1951.

[von Wright, 1963] G. H. von Wright. *Norm and Action: A Logical Enquiry.* Routledge and Kegan Paul, 1963.

[von Wright, 1968] G. H. von Wright. *An Essay in Deontic Logic and the General Theory of Action*. North-Holland Publishing Company, 1968.

[von Wright, 1976] G. H. von Wright. Replies. In Juha Manninen and Raimo Tuomela, editors, *Essays on Explanation and Understanding: Studies in the Foundations of Humanities and Social Sciences*, pages 371–413. D. Reidel Publishing Company, 1976.

[von Wright, 1981] G. H. von Wright. On the logic of norms and actions. In Risto Hilpinen, editor, *New Studies in Deontic Logic*, pages 3–35. D. Reidel Publishing Company, 1981.

[von Wright, 1983] G. H. von Wright. Norms, truth, and logic. In G. H. von Wright, editor, *Practical Reason: Philosophical Papers, Volume 1*, pages 130–209. Cornell University Press, 1983.

[Wansing, 1998] Heinrich Wansing. Nested deontic modalities: another view of parking on highways. *Erkenntnis*, 49:185–199, 1998.

[Williams, 1976] Bernard Williams. Moral luck. In *Proceedings of the Aristotelian Society, Supplementary Volume 50*, pages 115–135. Harrison and Son, 1976.

[Xu, 1994a] Ming Xu. Decidability of deliberative stit theories with multiple agents. In Dov Gabbay and Jans Ohlbach, editors, *Proceedings of the First International Conference on Temporal Logic (ICTL '94)*. Springer-Verlag, 1994.

[Xu, 1994b] Ming Xu. Decidability of stit theory with a single agent and refref equivalence. *Studia Logica*, 53:259–298, 1994.

[Xu, 1994c] Ming Xu. Doing and refraining from refraining. *Journal of Philosophical Logic*, 23:621–632, 1994.

[Xu, 1995] Ming Xu. Busy choice sequences, refraining formulas, and modalities. *Studia Logica*, 54:267–301, 1995.

[Xu, 1998] Ming Xu. Axioms for deliberative stit. *Journal of Philosophical Logic*, 27:505–552, 1998.

[Zimmerman, 1990] Michael Zimmerman. Where did I go wrong? *Philosophical Studies*, 59:55–77, 1990.

Index